Breaking Free

A facilitator's guide to participatory action research practice

Breaking Free

A facilitator's guide to participatory action research practice

Timothy Pyrch

ISBN 978-1-105-55194-9

For Jeanneo "best friend and best researcher"

Contents

Acknowledgments

Students who have taken courses at the University of Calgary's Faculty of Social Work are significant contributors to this book. Their creative efforts are documented throughout and attest to the passionate commitment to be found in the classroom to all forms of justice. This commitment reflects the energy needed to counter global agendas, aimed at reducing democracy to the margins of the human condition, serving unbridled capitalism. To this end, we join the movement inspired by activists and scholars from the Global South, to democratize knowledge-making processes through trans-disciplinary inquiry. I am grateful to my mentor, the late Professor Orlando Fals Borda, a pioneer of Participatory Action Research as an academic discipline and as a way of life. Special thanks to Stasha Huntingford and Thomas Griffith for thoughtful advice and formatting brilliance.

Preface

Breaking Free describes the act of freeing up conditions to prepare citizens to contribute actively to research carried out on their behalf. It is a practical guide to facilitating self-directing educational processes into participatory action research (PAR), enabling interested people to contribute what they can as active participants in research projects. As such, it is designed primarily for these participants rather than the academic researcher in order to introduce them to authentic contributions they can make as activists in matters relating to their personal well being and research-based interests. At the same time, *Breaking Free* could guide academic researchers towards helpful practices, enriching their search for meaningful ways to make their work more inclusive. As an adult educator committed to facilitating conditions for learning about PAR as a knowledge-making process, I am particularly interested in what constitutes knowledge and who creates it. There is an international interdisciplinary literature of PAR philosophy, history, theory, and practice commencing in the 1960s. This literature is introduced in *Breaking Free* in a manner facilitating the systematic learning of educational processes to bring PAR to life in formal academic settings, non-formal community settings, and informal settings of human commitment to social justice. Our purpose – me and my readers - is to experience the practice of PAR, present this experience in multi-media forms, and reflect critically on the meaning of this experience while blending these three purposes into a useful guide for students, teachers, and all members of the commonwealth. Our hands-on, practical yet disciplined approach to facilitating PAR will prepare readers to craft their own individual guide as they prepare for the PAR lifestyle. We are focusing on learning about PAR and how we can fit into it rather than directly engaging in PAR. This is in keeping with the democratic imperative of PAR by opening it up for popular engagement no matter our individual position in society. This opens up the world of knowledge-making to people long silenced by forces intent on controlling knowledge for the educated elite. PAR broadens participation in the world of research by treating people as subjects and actors in the academic process rather than objects of systematic inquiry. It invites people to contribute as they can and be acknowledged for their contributions. Acknowledging our knowledge enables a place for all of us in our democratic aspirations.

We can learn. We have knowledge. We have the capacity to contribute to the academic world. Our learning involves knowledge-making. Learning is life-long. Knowledge-making is a dynamic social process blending individual and collective work. It implies action learning rather than the passive behaviour of narrow schooling. These truths are the core values of my approach to facilitating adult education. These truths have been hidden by humankind's rush to turn our values into commodities to serve the interests of the few at the expense of the many. Learning itself has been locked into institutions of schooling. The rigid structure of schooling holds us back from true knowledge acquisition. We lose sight of the fact that most learning takes place in everyday life and routine work outside those institutions. We have been conditioned otherwise and miss learning opportunities regularly appearing all around us. We aren't keen to look for these chances, and they simply pass us by. In this guide, I argue that we must recover these learning opportunities and greet the enormous challenges of the twenty-first century with confidence in our own knowledge-making abilities, opportunities, and responsibilities. The time is right for change. Recognising our revolutionary times in terms of what constitutes knowledge-making and how it functions in expansive communication technologies, I am proposing to employ these technologies in this guide. Recognizing our revolutionary times in terms of emerging global expressions of people's power facilitated by these technologies, we need to learn afresh, innovative method to facilitate active citizenship in our democracy.

I invite readers to join with me and the many story tellers to be found in this guide in dialogue as we reflect upon and explore knowledge-making experiences, ideas, and possibilities. I suggest we are story tellers in the way of British philosopher Alasdair

MacIntyre (1984), who returned to Aristotle's virtues as the base of western morality, values housed within our stories. One of the most influential philosophers of our time, MacIntyre reintroduces us to the moral foundations of our society that includes the subjectivity of knowledge and its dissemination through narrative shared in our local communities. The guide is a space where hopes and dreams of life-long learning become attainable, where diversity of perspective contributes to deepening appreciation and understanding of difference within and across cultures. Within this space, differences are not simply tolerated but welcomed with open arms. To welcome is to open, respect, and authentically engage *with* one another. At the same time, we need to be aware of the powerful concept of "repressive tolerance" outlined in the work of German/American philosopher Herbert Marcuse. Our adult education colleagues counter the notion of repressive tolerance with experiences of "liberating tolerance" (Brookfield & Holst, 2011). Liberating tolerance implies opening up latent human strengths rather than the repressive implications of being merely "tolerated". There are endless possibilities and potential when we gather together in community with open hearts and minds. I have named this space *Breaking Free*.

Breaking Free is a practical, historical, and philosophical introduction to the liberatory adult education tradition reflected in PAR. The guide illuminates some of the processes and practices of like-minded souls who individually and collectively seek a more inclusive and fair world. Beyond our diversity of discipline, individual roles, and experiences, we stand on common ground, unified in our shared hope and commitment to liberatory education. Liberatory processes and practices are respectful of democratic and trans-disciplinary traditions in our timeless search for stability, peace, and social justice. These processes and practices draw from a dynamic balance, engaging direct social action with philosophical musing and are neither defined nor limited by gender, age, culture, religion, race, tradition, physical/mental ability, profession, job, or geographical location. They are boundless, and they are undeniable. Additionally, these processes and practices acknowledge forms of life energy beyond humankind to include and respect all forms of energies in a holistic interplay and symbiotic relationship with the natural environment.

Liberatory adult educational processes also have a practical side in that learning how to engage in knowledge-making processes enhances our ability to improve our work-based responsibilities in an efficient and effective manner. This is in keeping with Aristotle's practical wisdom he called "*phronēsis*". PAR itself is judged by practical results. Applying our learnings to everyday life guided by *Breaking Free* prepares us to healthily balance both work and play. This balancing is dynamic and creates new energies through their mutual exchange; new opportunities for improved performance in all aspects of adulthood throughout life.

Voices composing this guide are drawn from an international body of literature, local communities, and classrooms of adult learners. They span cultures, time, and continents. I maintain that our formal educational systems are hugely inefficient and lose sight of the most sustainable part of our learning journey—our own learning and the learning of others—most of which is indigenous to local spaces, including our classrooms. Local knowledge-making privileges learning processes within classrooms, course assignments, case studies, and graduate theses and dissertations. Much of this knowledge remains unrecorded in a systematic way and is therefore lost to the world. Our lifelong learning journey is as much about recovery as it is about discovery.

A history of resistance to the domination of public life by narrow interpretations of knowledge and knowledge-making, as privileges of the educated elite, casts a critical spotlight on rigid notions and practices of knowledge and power. At the same time, there is evidence of a growing willingness within this elite to break free of what American political scientist James Scott (1998) calls "imperial science." He makes a case against a hegemonic planning mentality that ignores local knowledge and know-how. Scott's position recognizes the knowledge within and around us. I position this local knowledge as a key concept in the liberatory education movement, at least since the 1920s, when a distinct adult education literature commenced with very close ties to emerging social justice work in Canada and the United States. Notions of 'start where the learner is' are significantly more than a practical instructional strategy as they honour the knowledge within learners, no matter their circumstances. Starting where the learner *is* recognizes and values indigenous or local wisdom within local communities. From this respectful point of departure, we can commence a lifelong learning journey with confidence and a sense of solidarity.

In solidarity we work together to co-create conditions for a renewed effort to facilitate lifelong learning. We will encounter many obstacles along the way representing the seemingly inescapable flow of the status quo. This includes gatekeepers of the powerful "positivist" tradition in the social sciences. These gatekeepers seek to maintain control of knowledge based on a narrow view of science and evidence as measurable, predictable, and controllable. In *Breaking Free* we might ask, "control by whom and for what reasons; who benefits and how?" I pose many questions about the concept of knowledge. What constitutes knowledge? How is knowledge created? Whose knowledge has value? Who is it for? Knowledge for what? Canadian adult educator dian marino (1997) contributed to this critical discourse and wrote, "We need also to generate alternative knowledge and images, making new visions out of the mud of our current interpretations" (p. 118). I embrace this focus and propose many questions about the concept of freedom. What is it to be free? How is this expressed over time? What is it to be free to acknowledge the knowledge we all have? Why is this difficult? Why is it hopeful? What do we hope for? Who fears the validation of this type of knowledge? Who welcomes it?

Our—I refer to readers and me together to show solidarity—preliminary reflections are also guided by the assumption that liberatory traditions in the adult education movement are situated within a broader and deeper resistance movement to our confinement to a mechanical world-view. This deleterious world-view fragments and isolates nature and humanity into commodities in the service and interests of unbridled capitalism, placing humanity and nature on the chopping block in favour of boundless economic growth. It cannot sustain itself. It must be resisted. In fact, resistance is a fundamental part of our practice. marino (1997) reminded us that "one of our roles as teachers ought to be to help people gather up their long personal histories, and sometimes social histories, of resistance and transformation so they aren't so fragmented and incoherent" (p. 130). I—taking personal responsibility when is seems appropriate for me to do so—am grateful to those who have generously shared their stories in support of this work and invite you, the reader, to critically reflect on the exhibits, narratives, and perspectives which follow. I invite you to engage with me in dialogue, as we seek to co-create spaces for inclusive community. I refer to a community rooted in hope, unbounded compassion, and inspired by endless possibility. I maintain that, despite globalization, centralization, and professionalism, there is profound power and possibility for individual and collective transformation when small-scale experiences are explored, interpreted, and validated, to secure the knowledge-making potential embedded within each and every one of us. PAR provides the discipline for this evolution. As global economies collapse and oppressive frameworks are exposed, we turn nearby to what we know best—our own lifelong learning experiences and actions gathering along the way.

Design elements in *Breaking Free* support a spiral learning process and include philosophical musings, exhibits and lessons learned, reflections, invitations to dialogue, and other activity suggestions. Narratives and perspectives of adult educators and adult learners (educator as learner and learner as educator) reside at the heart of these design elements.

As they show my field of study, I privilege the stories and reflections of graduate and undergraduate students in the Faculty of Social Work at the University of Calgary throughout. As you move through this document, you will see that these stories and reflections comprise the bulk of its contents, but they are not the story of *Breaking Free*. *Breaking Free* is a story in itself. American scholar of religion James Carse (1986) tells us that "if we cannot tell a story about what happened to us, nothing happened to us" (p. 167). Being unwilling to accept that nothing happened to me, I am obliged to become a storyteller. Trusting that you, the reader, are also unwilling to accept that nothing has happened to you, you are likewise obliged to become a storyteller. After all, we do count for something. We have stories to tell and people who will listen. The great American oral historian and journalist Studs Terkel summed up almost a century of living in one sentence: "If I did one thing I'm proud of, it's to make people feel that together, they count" (p. 7). Collectively we all have it within our power to make the people we work with know that they count! The stories contained within this guide illustrate this power and are drawn from both past and present with an eye to the future.

My primary focus is liberatory learning within an adult education context most clearly emerging within the PAR movement. I interpret *Exhibits* to be a representation of a particular theme or topic. Exhibits are both text and visual based to embrace the creative element, not unlike those we might view at a museum, gallery, or exhibition. Exhibits provide an additional lens in support of understanding and exploring particular traditions, perspectives, and practices. As some of the exhibits are lengthy, scholarly practice would have me paraphrase in order to interpret rather than simply present. Selecting the exhibits is interpretative in itself. My intention is to respect exhibit contents and leave readers to do the interpreting. For me, this is in keeping with Freirean pedagogy as it is with the Maltese adult educator Peter Mayo. Writing about the democratic possibility of museums, the Freirean practitioner Mayo (2004) argues that the museum visitor is never

> ...a passive recipient. Neither should one assume, in a rather patronizing manner, that the visitor requires the challenge of a critical museum educator to engage in a critical reading of the texts on display... What is being called for is the development of the museum and other centres as democratic public spaces that allow possibilities for different meanings to be exchanged, appropriated and negotiated. This can hopefully enable the visitor to be a subject in a process of co-investigation involving the museum educator and the visitor mediated by the exhibit. In such a context, knowledge would not be static but dynamic resulting from the dialogue, surrounding the object of co-investigation, engaged in by both museum educator and visitor. (p. 133)

I invite you to see yourself as this visitor. Throughout the guide, *lessons learned* refer to insights gained by the reader/visitor pondering an exhibit and finding deeper meaning. I encourage you to reflect on the exhibits presented and to add your own lessons learned. At this point, I would like to respectfully acknowledge curriculum designers at Deakin University in Australia for creating a wealth of exhibits in their work, processes that I try to model herein (Chambers, 1982). Additionally, Australian social change activist Katrina Shields (1991) crafted an empowerment guide for social action with humour and clarity that models the best in communication technology. I am indebted to her work as well.

Stories and other forms of narrative contribute to the rich dialogue woven throughout the guide. Collectively, we draw from imagery, stories, and experiences of the past to illuminate current experiences and narratives yet to be written. Part One, titled *Introduction: Breaking free* is my introduction to this complex, life-long journey. Part Two, titled *Breaking free of narrow individualism*, focuses on the power of collective inquiry and action. We move beyond a narrow view of our individual self in isolation and move into individual in community through this action. Part Three, titled *Breaking free of silence*, reintroduces us to the strength of our own voice as we replace the culture of fear with a culture of hope and joy by listening to our individual and collective power. Part Four, titled *Breaking free of apathy*, moves our growing confidence in our own individual and collective voice into activities supporting a renewed commitment to living actively in our Canadian, and increasingly global, society. Part Five, titled *Breaking free of imperial science*, celebrates committed leadership to a lifelong, ageless pursuit of knowledge-making through trans-disciplinary democratic processes. Part Six, titled *Re-connecting work and learning*, aims at removing the fragmentation created by the unnatural separation of work and learning in the past. Part Seven, titled *Beginnings: the infinite game* reflects on new beginnings to make the pursuit of social justice timeless and disciplined. We are seeking "a vision of life as play and possibility" (Carse, 1986), learning the skills required to play finite and infinite games. Your own individual guide might contain a different sequence of parts or might include other parts reflecting your own understanding and meaning. Remind yourself that the guide is for the betterment of yourself; only you can create your perfect guide. You are invited to engage freely with yourself while blending in the experiences of others we meet along the way.

In rediscovering our indigenous strength, we are in tune with Canadian philosopher John Ralston Saul's (2008) notion of Canada as "a fair country" where equilibrium has been a sustaining quality ever since Europeans blended with Aboriginal peoples, starting in the sixteenth century. My concept of breaking free guided by adult education practices fits in well to this notion of equilibrium, fits well into Saul's notion of Canada as a society that wishes to be inclusive and balanced. In order to be fair and inclusive, we need to break free of narrow individualism, silence, apathy, and imperial science. As we are breaking free of these inhibitors to our fundamental human needs, we begin reconnecting work and learning to their mutual well being. We do this knowing our journey is life-long, interconnecting, and thoroughly committed to action. *Breaking Free* is designed to challenge adult learners wherever they might be learning, whether in classrooms or in settings where, in fact, most learning takes place—in the university of life and the college of the streets. Additionally, *Breaking Free* offers practical contemporary examples of Canadians learning fairness and inclusivity together, thereby extending and supporting Saul's discourse with real life narratives. It is encouraging for us to see contemporary adult educators joining us in this arduous quest. Anglo-American professors of adult education Stephen Brookfield and John Holst (2011) conclude their rediscovery of socialism as a guiding beacon for our movement. "Fairness and inclusion and the common stewardship of material resources cannot happen when individuals and communities only look inward than outward" (p. 216). This guide may be just the thing to engage humankind fairly and inclusively in a respectful and supportive place, stressing the importance of looking outward for solidarity and knowledge-acquisition.

By way of design, I place *Lessons* in a variety of containers (circles, boxes, cylinders), highlighting ideas I have found useful in liberatory adult education. You are encouraged to add your own lessons as they come to you. In this way, you might fashion your own guide—a variation on our theme. Brazilian educator Paulo Freire (1994) said we should always re-write the books we read, meaning we interpret what we read and present it in our unique way. "Success" will be your own version of this guide for your practice as a citizen committed to social justice. At all times, be aware of how you are forming and presenting your ideas. How we present our experiences is a way of knowing in itself (Heron, 1992). Our presentations are organic, take on limitless shapes and

forms, and will vary from learner to learner, from context to context, from time to time. Tacit knowledge lies within these presentational forms (Seeley & Reason, 2008); in other words, that knowledge which is understood but unstated—opaque rather than transparent—is housed here. I present my own PAR lessons in open circles, inviting energies in and out as our learning evolves. Our resistance is protected from hegemonies bent on controlling our lives and our understanding. We are free to create and recover our own interpretations of our learning and knowledge-making. Everyone with whom we work is entitled to the same opportunity, the same respect. Everyone is welcome to share their stories wherein lies their expressive knowledge. "Expressive knowledge is generated by the researcher adopting a receptive rather than a proactive stance, allowing an element of the world—in this case adult education practice—to present itself for contemplation, then attempting to construct a text which accounts for that experience in its wholeness" (Willis, 2008, p. 50). This construction is most rewarding and productive when done collectively with fellow workers, students, and the broader community, whether local, national, or global. Moreover, opening our expressive selves to the performing arts enriches this constructing. "Expression inhabits our bodies, and expression is a medium that is not accessible only to the expresser; it is connected in relationship to all those who have the ability to express" (Unrau, 2008, p. 10). I invite you, the reader, to contribute in ways that are most meaningful to you in your own lived experience. Let the dance of dialogue begin.

Glossary of terms. This is an introductory note inviting you to add more to this list in the language of your choice. These words are intended to help you understand some of the language within the guide rather than impose definitions. By their nature, definitions exclude as much as they include. Please reserve judgement on meaning until you travel through this guide to its ending. You might choose to skip this glossary entirely at this point and make up your own mind about appropriate language and meaning.

Aboriginal peoples have blood ties with the original people inhabiting the land. These original peoples are the primary sources of indigenous energies.

Adult education is a field of study and practice of processes aiming to make learning efficient and effective beyond the socializing imperative of public schooling. Originally, it arose from inadequacies in state systems of formal education requiring the attention of reformers. As it evolved, adult education grew richer in meaning and deeper in societal critique. It is currently reviving its facilitative powers to make global social movements, in addition to their unique mission, knowledge-making opportunities open to all people and respectful of diversity.

Commonwealth refers to the well-being, privileges, and responsibilities of a collective grouping of humankind. This is practical in the sense of the material, social, and spiritual elements of life. This is ideal in the sense of our imaging a longed for age of peace, social justice, and equity.

Hegemony can be interpreted as persuasion from the dominant class and consent by the subordinate class. Hegemony functions to obscure power relations and to development of a common-sense that accepts structural class inequality as an accidental by-product of the larger political system.

Indigenous energies are those natural forces, animate and inanimate, comprising the essence of localities. These energies include Aboriginal peoples and, in addition, newcomers inhabiting localities in the past, present, and future.

Liberatory education encompasses a movement focusing on creating conditions necessary for dialogue and critique in direct relationship with social action. It incorporates terms like adult, continuing, and popular education, terms that refer to educational provisions outside the mainstream public and private educational systems. Core values include:

- Direct experience provides the foundation for human learning.
- Everything we need is near at hand.
- We commit ourselves to social change.
- Knowledge-making is a democratic collective relationship of equals.
- Acting knowledgably is empowering.
- Clarity of language and purpose.
- Disciplined, thoughtful hope.
- Liberatory processes are holistic, intertwined and mutually interdependent.

Liberatory tradition refers to age-old human strivings for freedom from all forms of oppression. In its modern meaning, it is used to represent the radical side of social work and adult education which is committed to direct and regular actions enabling and promoting social justice. Fundamental in this tradition is the notion of people speaking for themselves—the strength and richness of people's individual knowledge.

Participatory action research (PAR) is a trans-disciplinary approach to knowledge-making enabling us to take control of our lives by combining formal and informal knowledge and using that new knowledge to transform our realities. It is a holistic research perspective incorporating elements of education, action, and social investigation. It differs from other research perspectives in its commitment to fundamental social change, aiming to break down the hegemonies binding us. PAR provides people with knowledge-making opportunities within research projects affecting their lives, joining "experts" and "common" people in mutually disciplined inquiry into issues of social justice. It is a contemporary expression of the liberatory education movement. Core values include:

- The PAR process is organic.
- PAR encompasses spirituality.
- PAR seeks coherence.
- PAR is about empowerment.
- PAR translates knowledge into action and action into knowledge.
- PAR is inclusive of all forms of knowledge.
- A sense of community is an integral part of PAR.
- PAR is practical.
- PAR is based on trust.
- PAR builds self-awareness.
- PAR demands time.
- PAR is hopeful

Participatory video shares similarities to Photovoice but with moving images. It is a collaborative research method where communities use visual media to film and explore their lived realities and share their stories in the wider community to spark more discussion and create societal and attitudinal changes.

People's knowledge (*la sagesse populaire* in French) is common sense intelligence drawing from one's lived experiences (*vivencias* in Spanish) and usually shared in narrative form. I see three kinds of knowledge: official knowledge represents the state, expert knowledge represents the professions, and people's knowledge represents us. How might these concepts be expressed in Cree and Blackfoot? Indeed, how can any of these terms in the glossary be translated into your language?

Photovoice is a democratic research method whereby people are given cameras and asked to photograph their realities. The photographs are used to focus collective analysis of social conditions too difficult to describe only with words. A photovoice is worth a thousand voices.

Popular education (*educación popular* in Spanish) is rooted in the real interests and struggles of ordinary people. It is overtly political and critical of the status quo. It is committed to progressive social and political change in the interests of a fairer and more egalitarian society. Its approach to knowledge-making and learning is compatible with social justice work.

Stage Left, a Calgary founded and based organization, is internationally recognized for work in advancing the global disability culture movement and through performance-based social justice work. "We use the arts to provide accessible tools through which to foster a sense of creative expression and personal empowerment. The Stage Left model offers increased opportunity for self-advocacy, creative exploration, and direct representation of personal concerns and social justice issues. Stage Left, then, practices a solid balance between artistry and activism, enabling both personal and social awareness and transformation "www.stage-left.org".

Trans-disciplinary inquiry is an approach to research reconnecting the spiritual with the rational in an effort to facilitate relationship amongst all knowledge-making traditions. The approach is holistic in the sense that all forms of life, past, present and future are connected in a dance of infinite rhythm.

Keep in mind that our definitions are imperfect and are included in the beginning of the guide to facilitate initial inquiry. I invite readers to select appropriate terms for their individual guide.

Part One

Introduction: *Breaking Free*

The Ganma metaphor of the Yolngu of Arnhemland in the Northern Territory of Australia describes a transformation when a river of water from the sea (Western knowledge) and a river of water from the land (Aboriginal knowledge) mutually engulf each other upon flowing into a common lagoon and become one rich body of water. In coming together, the streams of water mix across the interface of the two currents, and foam is created at the surface so that the process of Ganma is marked by lines of foam. A new kind of knowledge is thereby created and resides within the foam (Marika, Ngurruwutthun & White, 1992). To avoid any suggestion of commodification—foam as a product—this knowledge (foam) becomes part of a dynamic relationship with the rivers themselves wherein knowledge-making is continuous, unbounded, and free flowing. This relationship resembles Peter Mayo's example of the museum educator and a visitor mediated by an exhibit. The water mark within this paragraph appears throughout this guide on pages where the Ganma process appears. The Yolgnu have given me permission to use this image in this fashion.

I first learned about Ganma at the third World PAR Congress, held at the University of Calgary in 1989. The metaphor is appearing more and more in print as a result of on-going dialogue between researchers in Arnhemland and Australian Universities initiated by Deakin University in Geelong, Victoria. The concept of Ganma figures prominently in the Deakin University publication *Singing The Land, Signing The Land* (Watson & Chambers, 1989), providing an excellent introduction to Yolngu knowledge. University of Melbourne mathematician Helen Watson-Verran, co-author of the book while acknowledging she was speaking on behalf of the Yolngu community at Yirrkala, has been working at Yirrkala creating a Ganma Maths course since 1986 (Watson-Verran, 1992). Ganma is described orally in the videotape[1] we produced after the Congress wherein one of the Australian team of four "whitefellas" and two Yolngu women cautioned that Ganma represented "common" knowledge and was easily shared. It did not represent deep and abstract knowledge, which is sacred and not shareable outside the Yolngu world. The point was clear. Only a certain amount of an ancient knowledge tradition was to be shared at the conference and the Aborigines were fully in control of that tradition. What I remember most about the team of six was the wonderful friendship and regard they had for each other without any hint that one wanted to take over the other, that one was superior to the other. The Yolngu remain Aboriginal Australians, and the "whitefellas"—or *Balanda* as non-Aborigines are known to the Yolngu—remain true to themselves, individuals. By being close but apart, they shared deeply without losing their integrity, just like the rivers of Ganma.

This simple and complex respectful sharing is pictured in the following story by a Yolngu educator:

> Here are two "Yalu" (nest) and they are very different from each other but have some things in common. Between the Yalu there are rivers, mountains and all kinds of things that stop the miny'tji from seeing each other and they are worried about not seeing each other.
>
> So they start planning and working out ways so that they can communicate/translate and be partners in sharing, doing, talking and doing things better for both "Yalu" and help them in growing and developing the miny'tji and Yalu from both sides.
>
> To do this they sat down with their miny'tji and made plans to improve their relationship and when they have made their plans they send out messengers to deliver their plans and meet some place in between. They meet in the middle and showed each other their plans, made

---

1 http://wcmprod2.ucalgary.ca/studentpar/guide/part03/freedom_within_margins

> changes, added more and put their plan so that there was some similarity with their plans.
>
> This was a new start, a start to a new journey; they started doing things together, sharing culture, skill, ideas and languages. This is like Yolngu (yalu) and Balanda (yalu). We Yolngu teachers are getting rom from the Balanda (yalu) and taking them back to the miny'tji we come from. The Balanda is also doing the same from their yalu, but this doesn't mean that the Yolngu becomes Balanda and the Balanda becomes Yolngu, but they stay in their own djalkiri and yalu. We only can change skills, ideas and ways of doing things but not ourselves, we stay the way we were, are and will be: Yolngu stays Yolngu and Balanda stays Balanda (G. Ngurruwutthun cited in White, 1991, p. 97-8).

This is PAR. Yolngu and Balanda are engaging in free and respectful association—participating in an authentic way. They are engaging in research by collecting information, making their plans and revising them to their mutual satisfaction. Then they take action by starting on a journey together. Throughout, they are being directed by Ganma—the world view that is guiding them—the model driving their science. *Breaking Free* is being directed by Ganma—our world view—the methodology driving our inquiry.

Aboriginal Australians successfully attracted PAR support globally after the 1989 Calgary Congress, in particular recruiting to their cause Colombian scholar/activist Orlando Fals Borda. After attending the World Congress in Brisbane in 1992, Fals Borda, having been adopted by Yolgnu during the Calgary Congress, took the opportunity to visit his family in Yirrkala. He wrote to me a few weeks after returning home to Colombia and summed up his experience in one sentence. "I went to Yirrkala where I stayed with Leon White and family, visited the region, went hunting with my brethren, and **swimming with the crocodiles** (emphasis added)—they respected me as

they are my totem". I marvelled at these words since they seemed so different from his usual scholarly discourse. Perhaps for us both—I too had been adopted by Yolgnu into the shark clan—Yirrkala is a place where we find the courage to celebrate our connections with other forms of knowledge and understanding. Being submerged in a totally different culture while reflecting on life's meaning might place us in touch with these other forms of wisdom, and we are able to become more deeply in touch with ourselves as a result. I write this to remind myself that my own brief visit to Yirrkala—the source of Ganma and the home of my aboriginal family—remains an overwhelmingly meaningful experience for me as I travel the PAR journey.

Our challenge

People everywhere are breaking free of controlling paradigms while recovering "satisfiers" of the fundamental human need for freedom so we all might live dignified and peaceful lives. I say recover rather than discover as "it is the voices and visionaries of the past that need to be revisited and reclaimed" (Kawalilak, 2006). Historically conscious adult educators see how valuable our memory is, how important it is to know where we are coming from, and how rich our knowledge-making traditions are. According to Chilean economist Manfred Max Neef (1991), satisfiers of the fundamental human need for freedom include being passionate, having equal rights, acting with commitment, and interacting with soul mates, past and future. We are breaking free of "destroyers" of freedom—such as obedience—and "inhibiting" satisfiers of freedom—such as unlimited permissiveness. Grass-roots people are breaking free of capitalism's "global project," (Esteva & Prakash, 1998) most recently in Egypt and in other parts of the Arab world. Stephen Brookfield and John Holst (2011) are breaking free of neoliberal capitalist domination of the world to revive concepts of economic democracy and democratic socialism. Their book is published by a mainstream American publisher, perhaps indicating a new tone in the US. Scholars from many academic disciplines are breaking free of the domination of knowledge-making by a single world-view. We are searching through eddies and peripheries outside the controlling intentions of the mainstream. In order to engage in these world-wide trends, adult educators must break free of forces aiming to reduce our work to instrumental support of the commodification of life and the controlling intentions of the nation state, the professions, and institutions. In this we join the movement of movements, the revolution articulated at the first World Social Forum in Porto Alegre, Brazil, in January 2002 (Fisher & Ponniah, 2003). We do this in keeping with a strong commitment to the international trans-disciplinary world, especially emerging Aboriginal voices. At the same time, we do this in our local communities, knowing full well this sort of action is occurring in communities everywhere—a global resistance to "destroyers" and "inhibitors" of freedom. As a consequence, these processes are moving us beyond mere "resistance" to become more "resilient" liberatory education practitioners of the PAR way of life.

What do I mean by commodification of life, and what has it got to do with our resistance? I maintain that our work is devalued by a preoccupation with economic growth as capitalism insists on constant material production at any cost. There are political consequences.

> Today, commodities proliferate while meaningful democratic options shrink. Frivolous consumer choices multiply, but a sense of political impotence sets in about our capacity to confront effectively mounting social and environmental problems: global South poverty, global warming, and deteriorating essential public services. (Soron & Laxer, 2006, p. 16)

Our essential values are deeply compromised. Italian sociologist Silvia Gherardi (2003) cautioned: "When knowledge is reduced to mere instrumentality, what is lost is knowledge as a desire that takes us far from the realm of necessity, structuring and cognition as expressions of mental activity, and brings us closer to pleasure, play and aesthetic knowledge" (p. 17). We lose contact with our spiritual self. We become fragmented, confused by powerful forces. How can we make sense out of the current state of economic uncertainty without our spiritual center?

As we moved beyond the painful opening years of the twenty-first century, Indian physicist and activist Vandana Shiva (2002) posed some critical questions regarding the radical choices that challenge us daily.

> Why are we as a species destroying the very basis of our survival and existence? Why has insecurity been the result of every attempt to build security? How can we as members of the Earth community reinvent security to ensure the survival of all species and the future of diverse cultures? How do we turn from the ruins of the culture of

> death and destruction, to the culture that sustains and celebrates life? We can do it by **breaking free** (emphasis added) of the mental prison of separation and exclusion and see the world in its interconnectedness and non-separability, allowing new alternatives to emerge. (p. 30)

She posed tough and important questions immediately following 9/11, but her ruminations are manageable within that part of our liberatory movement always searching for release from controlling forces of all kinds. In these times of shifting paradigms, we critically reflect on and contribute to the discourse on alternate perspectives and knowledge acquisition traditions and on the deeper questions posed by Shiva in her writing about the *Earth Democracy Paradigm.*

There are many other world-views in the frightening yet liberating twenty-first century. We interpret life and the universe in our own way and present our learnings as metaphor. I have been searching for appropriate metaphors while trying to understand social justice, our place in it, and how to share this understanding with learners we are privileged to meet along the way. The notion of "breaking free" suggests to me a continuous process of identifying controlling forces, understanding them, and in so doing, transforming these forces into liberatory moments. We accomplish this together as we learn and act in a spirit of mutuality and respect. For me, social justice is about "breaking free" in the sense imagined by Shiva. Breaking free of what? To do what, how, when, and why?

Breaking free suggests a clear militancy as we organize and act for social justice. Our search for social justice is political.

> "And don't be afraid of using the word political. I'm not talking about 'bossism' or 'politicking.' I mean politics in the Aristotelian sense; it should be good politics. Politics for justice. Politics for progress. Politics for peace."
>
> Orlando Fals Borda's closing words to the PAR Congress in Calgary, 1989
> (Pyrch, Morris & Rusted, 1990).

I refer to militancy with a strong sense of hope for the possibility of the impossible, a world of safety and dignity for all. As the culture of fear fades (Pyrch, 2007), we stand ready and able to facilitate processes of recovery and discovering, of connectedness and commitment to one another for social justice. Similar impulses have occurred now and then in Western traditions, commencing with Christian religious reformations of the sixteenth century, extending into the English political revolution of the 1640s, and throughout European revolutionary movements starting in 1848. British adult educator Tom Steele (2007) recently explored the rise and fall of European popular education movements following the great rebellions of 1848. These movements have affected much of the rest of the world throughout history, contributing to the formation of democracy in Canada and the US. All these radical impulses affected educational systems, and reforms were institutionalized and legitimized, making, some say, popular education movements redundant. However, as social movements succeed in influencing educational practices, ever emerging new social movements are keeping the radical traditional alive. Contemporary social justice issues include feminist, ecological, peace, disability, anti-globalization, and anti-war movements (Steele, 2007). These issues lead to and fuel other issues. As advocates for change within and across many diverse but related disciplines, we are guided by values and a belief system that focuses on learning opportunities within social movements. Consequently, we make social movements move (Pyrch, 2007). This shared focus is the heartbeat that guides and sustains adult educators and practitioners, wherever we may reside.

In the narratives collected within *Breaking Free*, I seek to critically recover history while preparing the ground for the future. Through the sharing of our stories in our own voices and documenting them in appropriate form, we resemble the Ganma rivers, free flowing in organic interaction while facilitating knowledge-making processes in preparation for future narratives, for future learnings.

Knowledge: *Healing the Split*

Interesting times. This may be both a curse and a blessing. Anglo-American philosopher of science Stephen Toulmin (1995), himself an advocate of PAR, captured the enormity of our challenge:

> Historically, the last time our ideas about knowledge went through such a deep change was the mid-seventeenth century. Between 1630 and 1690, a set of fundamental issues was framed which, for most of the next 300 years, defined the Received Program of epistemology and human sciences. Contemporary critics of this program refer to it as the 'Cartesian' program (p. ix).

The Cartesian program, based on individual knowledge, mechanics, rationality, and objectivity, led to great advances in material improvements while creating, along the way, a split between the rational and spiritual views of the world. The mechanical world-view produced great improvements in the material world of technologies and commodities, yet from the beginning in the seventeenth century in England, forces of resistance to the mechanical world-view were frequent and regular. According to American eco-feminist Charlene Spretnak (2000):

> Ever since THE (emphasis in original) Cradle of Western Civilization began rocking to a perverse lullaby about a thunderbolt-wielding sky-god, a desacralized Earth, and patriarchy galore; ever since the three curses of Western thought – the perception of a radical discontinuity between body and mind, between humans and nature, and between self and the world – were inscribed in our foundational philosophy; and ever since we decided to base Western knowledge on categories rather than process and Western religion on texts rather than the uncontainable fullness of being as it unfolds in and of the sacred cosmos, a resistance movement has been in play. (p. 34)

In our contemporary world, this "resistance movement," healing the split between the head and the heart, is gaining momentum. This momentum is clear in the language of a wide range of interdisciplinary inquiry. It is helpful to read these words at length on your own to experience their compatibility across disciplines. American palaeontologist Stephen Jay Gould (2003) argued that

> ...science needs the humanities to teach us the quirky and richly subjective side of our own enterprise, to instruct us in optimal skills for communication, and to place proper boundaries upon our competencies—so that we can all work together, for the best of humanity, uniting our factual skills with our ethical wisdom to form a shield and weapon in this age of immediate danger. (p. 143)

Gould's purpose could be well served by sociologist Silvia Gherardi's (2003) emphasis on passionate knowledge to improve organisational learning.

> The knowledge of the expert consists of mastery over canonical and non-canonical practices, over a body of knowledge acquired through social and cognitive learning processes. But it is also made up of passion, shared experience, collective identity—and the pride that accompanies it—pleasure and fulfilment and their opposites, pain and frustration. (p. 16)

We are well on the way to recovering a balance amongst the arts and sciences. In similar vein, British social psychologist John Heron (1998) defined sacred science as person-centred inquiry into the spiritual and the subtle. He wrote about a newly emerging and self-generating spiritual culture born from post-World War II expansion of adult and continuing education, of people-centred and peer self-help movements of all kinds, of the democratization of knowledge acquisition, of health care, and of psychological and soul growth. For Heron, "the human race stirs itself to fulfil the legacy of the Renaissance: the idea of the free and self-determining human person, active in all spheres of human endeavour" (p. 2). Like Toulmin, Heron connected our contemporary search to values in the pre-Cartesian world where we were still in tune with our spirituality. In a similar yet slightly different exploration into the human condition, Manfred Max-Neef (1991) suggested transcendence as the tenth fundamental human need common to all peoples. Vandana Shiva focused on how all life forms extend this collective inquiry even further. Her concerns and hope are in keeping with ancient "sights and sounds of Indigenous knowledge" (Pyrch & Castillo, 2001). Oneida sociologist, Apela Colorado (1988), founder of the Worldwide Indigenous Science Network at a meeting at the Nakota Lodge outside Calgary in 1989, explained the holistic philosophy of Native science:

> Through spiritual processes, it [Native science] synthesizes information from the mental, physical, social, and cultural/historical realms. Like a tree, the roots of Native science go deep into the history, body and blood of the land. The tree collects, stores, and exchanges energy. It breathes with the winds, which tumble and churn through greenery exquisitely fashioned to purify, codify and imprint life in successive concentric rings—the generations. (p. 50)

These words convey a sense of timelessness. Blackfoot scholar Betty Bastien (2004) connected this inquiry with the cosmos. For her, "knowledge is generated for the purpose of maintaining the relationships that strengthen and protect the health and well being of individuals and of the collective in a cosmic universe" (p. 2). These scientists/philosophers, women/men from several disciplines and traditions from around the world, are creating an emancipatory tone in the arts and sciences, a sense of **breaking free** of the controls of old and new and those yet to come.

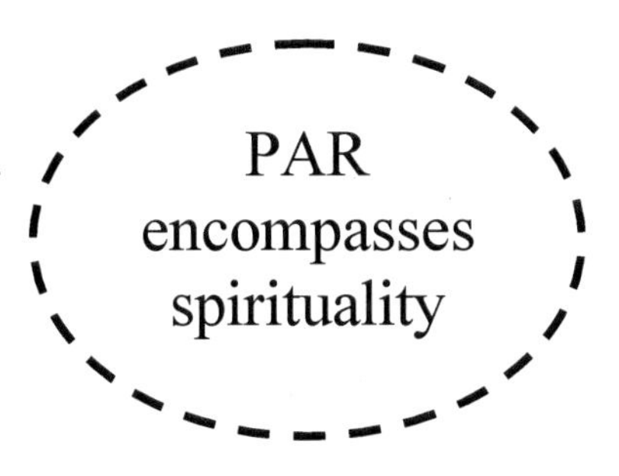

Although readers of this guide might share my metaphors, you are free to create your own. I wish to engage with you in a fluid and inclusive way, similar to Ganma. We are free to travel where our spirituality leads. For me, spirituality is my relationship with similar forms of energy —past, present, and future—for the purpose of acting together to transform our realities. Our work is to create spaces for our spirituality to flourish. In so doing, we facilitate processes for learners to do likewise, celebrating together our spirituality. Spaces of spirit are thereby co-created. This view of spirituality is similar to Larry Dossey's view of the "nonlocal mind." This American physician wrote:

> Nonlocal mind, being temporally infinite, reminds us that we are equally in touch with the past as with the present and future. While this may seem strange to us, for many native cultures this is a living reality. They go to great lengths to keep traditions alive and honour their ancestors. Through elaborate rituals they revel so thoroughly in the past that the past is made present. The wisdom of the ancestors is never far away and lends strength and comfort to the living. Marooned as we are in the present, we have amputated this reservoir of vigour from our lives, and we need desperately to restore it. (2004, p. 32)

Elders, those who have lived to see the wisdom of the ancestors, have traditionally played a critical role within First Nations communities in guiding individual and collective knowledge-making.

As a historically conscious adult educator, I am comfortable with the notion of a dynamic relationship between past, present, and future. The British historian E. H. Carr (1961) taught us long ago that history is a "dialogue between the events of the past and progressively emerging future trends" (p. 123). I would add to Carr's concept of dialogue the imperative of acting upon our dialogical inquiry in direct and purposeful action in the present. Not acting directly within our own reality reduces our inquiry to mere rhetoric, seemingly empty words with no direction. Dialogical inquiry plus action moves us away from a world of duality into a more fluid and organic understanding of how we might play with boundaries rather than be bound by them.

It is helpful to look back at other "interesting times" to see how our ancestors managed. American historian of religion Elaine Pagels (1979) interpreted Gnostic inquiry into early Christianity as processes similar to twenty-first century inquiry/revolt against orthodox institutions. The past has much to teach us and remains a valuable resource. For example, to better understand our contemporary global economic troubles, we might read Canadian economist John Kenneth Galbraith's (1954) *The Great Crash, 1929.* What we are experiencing now, we have experienced before, albeit differently. Examples of liberatory educational practices stimulated by national emergencies include: formation of the Danish Folk School Movement following the Danish defeat by Imperial Prussia in the 1860s; the 1919 Report emerging from the horror of the Great War; and the origin of the community development concept during the 1930s following the Great Depression. These examples are expressions of creatively liberating lifelong education. Implicit in these innovations is an acknowledgement of people's ability to live and work free from oppression and inequality. What innovations might we create to facilitate our movement out of our current international emergency caused by moribund capitalism? Are any of these innovations of use to the liberatory eruption in Egypt in early 2011? What can we learn from this enormous release of Egyptian people's power? Canadian journalistic perspectives on the first three weeks of the Egyptian experience with new found freedom of expression are located at (rabble.ca) – in particular an article titled "Egypt: 20 days of coverage" on 18 February 2011. Any coverage of the Middle East is incomplete without the Al Jezeera media network, so check there as well. Here's the point. There is a unity of purpose in the burgeoning grassroots democratic movement globally and the interdisciplinary movement to heal the Cartesian split. Our challenge is to tie these political and intellectual passions to a rich liberatory tradition in the adult education movement thus providing a sense of continuity in the disparate attempts to create a just society.

Liberatory Education Movement: *Equitable Justice for All*

Liberatory education respects the natural ability of all people to learn throughout life—a hopeful, democratic, and loving view of the world. However, as a historian of popular education writes, "the functionalist and vocational spin out on much state-sponsored adult education has evacuated it of the meaningful personal, cultural development and radical social purpose, which is sorely needed" (Steele, 2007, p. 280). In this liberatory education guide, I want to write about things we used to do and still can, about our passionate commitment to social action and the loving care we take helping others learn to learn, so that together we can act effectively to improve our lives. Our words reflect experiences of connection, interconnection, and relationship as we seek to recover our whole selves, as we search for meaning in a world dominated by "manic capitalism" (Greider, 1997), "turbo-capitalism" (Finger & Asún, 2001), and "disaster capitalism" (Klein, 2007). We require alternative images to guide the way. I take heart from Australian adult educator Michael Newman (1999) who argued, "we come by our moral sense through living, and we have a role in helping ourselves and others do this living as well" (p. 239). Furthermore:

> Moral learning is the process whereby we foreground our consciences, and give them space to develop. It does not involve the use of reason in its limited scientistic sense, but it does involve achieving a complete and passionate consciousness, and the continual making of radical choices.

Newman's notion of continually making radical choices in life is at the heart of the liberatory tradition. Moreover, his focus on morals reminds us of Aristotle's virtues.

Even with an extensive glossary of terms, we might pause to reflect on our language. Liberatory education, adult education, popular education, continuing education, recurrent education, and

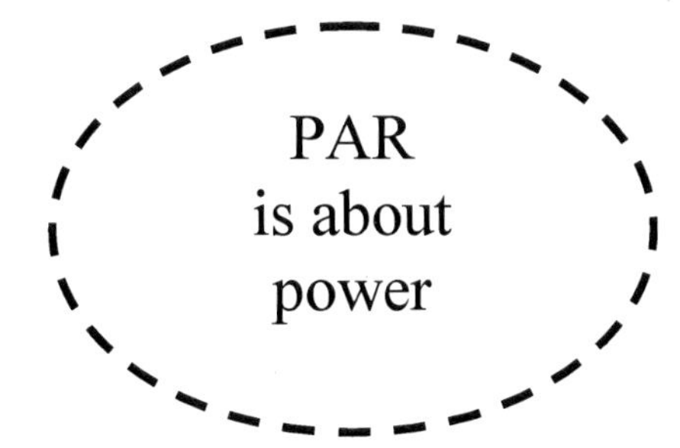

lifelong education describe processes that systematically organize resources to make learning efficient and effective beyond mandatory schooling techniques. This culminates in shifts over time and place, and terms frequently come and go. "Adult education" is the original term in English referring to learning facilitation outside mainstream educational systems. Mainstream education and learning is typically associated with and locked to formal, traditional schooling. The first history of adult education published in English appeared in the mid-nineteenth century (Hudson, 1851). Adult education is less about age and more about power. In its radical expression, it is about groups of adults working together to investigate reality in order to transform society into a harmonious place for all species. Adults, not children, control the political agendas of mainstream society.

Frequent international conferences and an expanding body of knowledge about PAR have tried to clarify terminology, meaning, and political agendas. As already noted, the third World Congress on PAR took place at the University of Calgary in 1989, the first university to host a PAR Congress. We did so with naïve enthusiasm since none of us in the Congress planning committee fancied ourselves as "experts." That may help explain our success. At that time we used the term "participatory research." Through negotiations between practitioner/scholars at meetings at Cornell University in the early 1990s, agreement had it that PAR expressed traditions from the Global South while participatory research would represent a similar approach in the Global North. The meetings had been called after publication of a book titled *Participatory Action Research* (Whyte, 1991) organized by Cornell scholars, which focused mainly on organizational research in the North rather than a commitment to radical societal change that pre-occupied scholars in the South. The first World Symposium on PAR was held at Cartagena, Colombia in 1977, organized by the Foundation for the Analysis of the Colombian Reality (Fals Borda, 1998). Albeit imperfect, clearly there have been efforts to clarify our terminology in the face of attempts by large organizations, the

World Bank for example, to co-opt PAR to their own purposes. Importantly, therefore, readers must be ready to query meanings behind all terminology in *Breaking Free*, especially mine.

Aiming to change human behaviour, liberatory and popular education arouses suspicion from education systems protective of their turf. This may account for the apparent fleeting influence of the concept of adult education as a distinct political force unable to access public education funds. Adult education in the liberatory meaning appears and re-appears in times of danger, when societal order has been shaken to its core. There are lessons to be learned in such dangerous times, times similar to those we are experiencing at present.

Exhibit 1.1: The 1919 Report (Pyrch, 1983)

The 1919 Report of the British Ministry of Reconstruction's Adult Education Committee is the starting point of the adult education movement in English speaking countries of the world. According to the Report:

> **The environment, intellectual, social, and political, is far more favourable to all kinds of educational endeavour than it was fifty, or even thirty, years ago. The consequence has been that adult education, though its origins can be traced back, has undergone in the last fifteen years something like a re-birth…Sporadic efforts have become a movement (Final Report, 1919, (p. 37).**

Some of those sporadic efforts in 19th and early 20th century in Britain included Adult Schools, the Co-operative movement, Chartism, Mechanics Institutes, and the University Extension movement. Additionally, there were the educational activities of the Y's, the settlement movement, and the many women's organizations. These combined with the large scale educational work among the soldiers of the Great War indicated the extent and diversity of adult education activities.

The Report focused on social reform and social justice and reflected a wide spread hope in Britain and beyond that the massive upheaval of the war would lead to general social reform. Hopes were short lived. The British economy slipped into a series of crises and calls for reform faded. The Board of Education had never welcomed calls for reform and disassociated itself from the recommendations even before the Report was published.

The Report was cited a few times in the early 1920s. It then disappeared from the literature until the 1950s when it was revived by Canadian and American adult educators. In retrospect, it became

an instant classic without ever becoming news. It had been effectively silenced in the country of its origin because of its radical call for educational reform and social change. (pp. 9-11)

The wisdom tree, appearing throughout the Guide, has leaves of all shapes and sizes. Each represents an insight gained if only we have the courage to step out from beyond its shade. The following lessons resonate for me. Please record your reflections as you wish. These reflections will evolve into your own Guide.

Lessons Learned
Exhibit 1.1

**Critical inquiry into societal issues is political.

**Times of emergency, struggle, and upheaval are fertile ground for radical innovation.

Your reflections

Historically, adult education has a strong commitment to democracy and freedom, to "power-with" and "power-from-within." Over time, however, the term has come to emphasize instrumental learning for job training and individual self-actualization. I settle on the term "liberatory education" to represent emancipatory processes located within the broader adult education tradition devoted to justice and dignity for everyone. My own practice was housed within the powerfully controlling academy which acts as guardian to professional knowledge required by all professions. Yet within the confines of the ivory tower, resistance to the practice of over-bearing control over knowledge-making practice is possible, as I demonstrate in *Breaking Free.* This resistance turns out to be trans-disciplinary as we are living in revolutionary times in terms of knowledge-making. Thomas Kuhn taught us that resistance is a vital part of any important paradigm shift.

Learning about and committing to this resistance creates that very empowering concept of resilience: the power of recovery.

We might expect the liberatory education movement to revive and flourish during the second decade of the twenty-first century as we face growing turmoil in all aspects of life. During fearful times, radical educators have come alive to their leadership responsibilities (Pyrch, 2002). I see signs of emerging leadership in our movement, helping us move away from oppressive fear and towards bountiful hope. Some of this leadership is reflected in the richness of *Breaking Free* and in reader engagement with its contents.

Creating Space: *An Invitation*

I invite you now to engage with me in this dialogue as we gather pieces of our own experience and order them into an image representing both ourselves and our worlds. Think of this as a work in progress as you add your own stories. An "exhibit" metaphor encourages us to share what we have while choosing from what others have to offer. What of the future? We must create spaces where ***we*** can prepare for learning epiphanies yet to come (Bateson, 1994). I hope to engage in a rich dialogue with you since we cannot face these challenges alone. Our social justice tradition encourages us to embrace and support freedom. What might this pursuit look like? What is freedom? One way to find out is to look back and see how we have responded to these questions in the past.

Where should we begin? We start with the present with an eye to the future so we might recover a past supportive of this promising future. I propose to do this by identifying late twentieth and early twenty-first century liberatory moments from a broad range of inquiry into the nature of knowledge-making taking place within all disciplines. Then we search back in time for similar moments in the liberatory education movement devoted to social justice. To this broad sketch of published materials, I add my own stories, drawing from a thirty-year practice as an adult educator in the field of practice and in academia. My invitation is that you add your insights and experiences so that together we may engage in a quest for liberatory moments. There is great potential here to actually co-create one of these liberatory moments through the very action of our collective dialogue. In this way we are co-creating as we engage together with the great Ganma rivers, meeting at the foam of our dialogue. This is within our power. Experiencing liberatory moments is an empowering experience in itself, and we are ready to support those we meet along the way to do likewise. How can we make our routine encounters with those we meet along the way empowering experiences for them as well as for ourselves?

Creating imagery: *Ways of presenting our knowing*

Our life's work, our vocation as social workers and adult educators, seeks to explore and celebrate alternative knowledge-making traditions. My intention is to explore a multiplicity of knowledge-making perspectives and traditions throughout *Breaking Free*. I would like to begin this exploration by considering "the arts" as one powerful pathway; a pathway that has proven to transcend many cultural borders and differences; a pathway with the potential to bring those who participate to a place of free expression. The Faculty of Social Work has embraced the arts in recent years, and the result has been wonderfully creative work by students and faculty alike, as this guide shows.

PAR
is inclusive of all
forms of knowledge

Arts-based inquiry provides a powerful lens for understanding the multiple ways of telling stories while expressing our knowledge freely. In keeping with contemporary times, we end this introduction with artistic flair. Twyla Mudry, MSW, drawing upon her passion for dance, makes a unique contribution to her understanding of PAR as part of a graduate course requirement in the Faculty of Social Work. Her unpublished essay follows with her permission.

Exhibit 1.2: Introduction to Dance (Mudry, 2009)

Dance is a universal phenomenon, with no end to the variety of styles, purposes and interpretations it has. From courtly dances, wedding dances and funeral dances to dances for healing, amusement, and arousal or to uplift. They have been used to welcome new seasons, praise gods and deities, tell stories, and create beauty and expressions that cannot be formulated into words. It is the universality, pervasiveness and attractiveness of dance that has set me on a journey to discover where the roots of the Western dance that I have become most familiar with stem from, how it has been suppressed and condemned in the past and how dance has and could be used in participatory action research.

The Roots of Western Dance

Our journey of dance will begin by exploring a culture where every aspect of life was in some manner related to dance, that was so captivating that it influenced almost every Western dance form that is practiced today. African people used dance to celebrate, mourn, during marriage and initiation rites, to prepare for war, to insure a good hunt and rich harvest, for healing and to make social statements (Knowles, 2002). Dance in African culture was so unique to communities and so pervasive that individuals' nationality could be determined by their particular dance. It served as an artistic means of communication where movement comprised a language, representing an entire community, where members could express religious and social issues, hostility, friendship and gratitude (Knowles, 2002). Music and dance were so indivisible of one another that they were considered a single art form, where drums directed the dancers' movements and connected them to the power of the Earth.

There are several characteristics of African dance forms that illuminate what a strong influence African dancing had on dancing around the world but most noticeably in North America.

**African Dancing was done bare-footed resulting in shuffling, gliding, and dragging steps, exhibiting many of the foot movements of modern tap dancing.

**It was done in a crouch close to the ground, bent at the waist with a relaxed body attitude. Dancing close to the ground is characteristic of hip-hop dancing, where relaxed body attitude can be seen in hip-hop, as well as jazz and ballet dancing.

**African dance heavily mimicked animals, which eventually became common place between 1910-1920 in American social dances such as the grizzly bear, kangaroo dip and bunny hug.

**This dancing was highly improvisational, which has been one of the major influences in Western dancing. Dancing was supposed to be an expression of the immediate experience and being creative, original, free and explorative were encouraged. It allowed them to move out of consciousness and move into the world of their ancestors. Both modern and hip-hop heavily incorporate improvisation into their dancing.

**African dancing involved the use of the hips and pelvis in an outward motion. This was adopted and made hugely popular in the 1960'sby Elvis Presley, which spurred outrage as well as a shift in acceptable mainstream dancing.

**Dancing was determined rhythmically instead of spatially, where beats of the drum informed dancers how to move.

**This is seen today in many forms of Western dance, where it is the music that guides the dance and influences the sequence of dance moves.

**African dancing has used swinging movements and accented the second and fourth beats, compared to European music which accents the first and third, which creates a bouncy feeling of stressing off beats. This influenced both the world of tap and swing dancing.

**This dance form used polyrhythmic body movements, where different body parts express different rhythms at the same time, requiring immense coordination and flowing movements. This was an important contribution to dances such as the Charleston and Black Bottom Social dances as well as contemporary and ballet dance.

**Satire, humour and mockery were used to make social commentaries and maintain traditional values. Parody was incorporated into such dances as the cake walk and corn shucking social dances in America.

** Instead of presenting dance in a conscious and controlled manner, African dance emphasized what was felt and dancers' lack of inhibition, control or elegance was admired. This is common in modern and contemporary dancing where dance is felt; movements are strong, rigid and challenging.

**African dancing is a combination of appearing wild and abandoned while also keeping composure and seeming nonchalance in the movements. This is a distinguishing feature of tap as well as modern dancing which can be busy and uncultivated yet strong and controlled. (Knowles, 2002)

It was through the world slave trade that African dancing and its characteristics were transported into American dance we see today. Africans were taken and shipped to the Americas as slaves as early as the 16th century, and over the span of four centuries an estimated ten million were enslaved (Knowles, 2002). Oftentimes Africans were lured to the ships with the promise of fame and fortune for performing tribal dancing for the ship crew's entertainment. Once finished their dancing they were taken below deck and given alcohol, where they found themselves at sea to the Americas when they awoke. Africans were kidnapped from their homes and taken to foreign lands, humiliated, beaten and dehumanized and even killed by the Atlantic slave trade. Every attempt was made to strip Africans of their cultural and artistic abilities and practices; however the ability to adapt to their environment and use dance as an outlet and means of communication allowed African dance to survive and develop new dance forms (Knowles, 2002).

When I travelled to Tanzania, Africa in 2006, I had the opportunity to view several dance performances and actually participate in some lessons. I was amazed by the commonalities between the dancing I was trained in and African dance, yet also how unique and challenging their dances are. These dancers were able to make even the hardest numbers appear effortless, mesmerize their audiences and engage people to dance with them. It is the collectiveness of African dance among other dance forms that is so captivating for me, the favourable reception all receive, the inclusiveness, the need to be together and the innate power in communal movement.

The Condemnation of Dance
"For where there is dance, there is also the devil." – Constantinople

Dance has a long and tumultuous history with the Catholic Church, a popular display by the faithful and a threat to the power of church officials. Christianity was born in the Roman-Greek basin of the Mediterranean at a time when an all-embracing empire was being formed. The loss of security, community and political instability that encompassed building an empire lead to the decay of local religious sects and subsequently left people hungry for a religion that offered high moral standards and power to attain them (Latourette, 1975). One of the moral filths assisting in the corruption of society was believed to be the art of dance, which had become associated with love, lust and even violence in early Rome. While distain remained about dance and its involvement in the new church, it was difficult for clergy to deny that dance was commonplace in the bible with references to the dances of David and Miriam in the book of Psalms and quotes by Jesus saying "we have piped unto you, and ye have not danced" in the book of Luke and Matthew (Jonas, 1992, p.42).

Rather that expecting parishioners to stop dancing the moment they converted to Christianity, the church found a way in which to "baptize" dance by making it more gracious and spiritually focused. The faithful were permitted to dance as a congregation in prayer, to celebrate the resurrection, and utilize it to aid mystical practice and other spiritual healing and cleansing (Jonas, 1992). Dancers would normally sing hymns, clap their hands and stomp their feet to the rhythm of the music, however the tendency of dancers to engage in more objectionable movements even on church grounds lead to church authorities opinions of dance to harden. One of the most influential authorities was St. Augustine who denounced all wild and abandoned dancing even when accompanied by prayer; his discouragement of dance was significant in that it compelled the war on dance with church councils regularly condemning improper dancing (Jonas, 1992).

By the 13th century the church's condemnation of dance had become a mechanism for social control. Church goers were required to confess their sins to their priest, one of which was dancing especially "lascivious" or "immoderate" dancing, which was promulgated as a confessable sin in the summa (a directory of sins) in 1317 (Ehrenreich,2006). The very fact that church councils condemned dancing during 1200-1500 A.D. indicates how prevalent the practice of dance really was (Jonas, 1992). In the church's denunciation, a variety of tactics were used to cast dance as a Pagan custom; a technique used by women to seduce men and lead them into temptation, and a practice of Satin used to possess and steal souls. Despite efforts to designate dancing as a pagan custom, there is sufficient evidence to suggest that dance was an established Christian custom, where even priests joined or lead the festivities (Ehrenreich, 2006). The very design of churches demonstrates what a fundamental component dance was to worship in that they were constructed with sufficient area for dancing in mind. As time went by, however, pews became prominent in European churches during the 18th century thus removing the traditional dynamic environment which had allowed for interaction, boisterous singing and dancing (Ehrenreich, 2006).

During the war on dance, the church had been successful in purging unruly and suggestive dance out of the church; however, knowing they would not be able to eradicate it from whole society, compromised allowing it only on holy days outside of the church (Ehrenreich, 2006). This only lasted for a short period as dancing at festivals began testing the limits of the church coming under attack, especially the holiday of Carnival. Carnival was a festival that preceded Lent which involved parades, comedy, music, drama, feasting, drinking, sports, dancing and often mass and church procession through town. One of the most attractive customs of Carnival was the mockery and parody of the authorities that took place, allowing people to escape from their social rank and dramatize the struggles between classes and gender (Ehrenreich, 2006). A similar approach was taken by the church to extinguish Carnival and other holidays as they did dance by expelling it from church property in addition to abandoning some holidays and secularizing others. This gradual ejection of drama, comedy and dance led to a world with regularly scheduled celebrations that we continue to see today including Epiphany, Ascension, Pentecost, and more recognizable Christmas and Easter (Ehrenreich, 2006).

The age-old debate about the appropriateness of dance was addressed by the Reformation and Counter-Reformation in the 1500's. In the effort to rid the church of everything that distracted people from worship, all displays of wealth and pomp were banished; poetry and music were allowed, however beautiful images and liturgical dancing were not permitted (Jonas, 1992). Carnival was brought under stern control of the church and most forms of dance were brought to a standstill.

There were several motivations for church control over dance; fear of possible disorder and property damage which has been heavily documented throughout history; fear of impoverished laity uprising with the accumulation of large concentrations of wealth in the church, and; fear of losing concentration of access to the divine and parishioners seeking god's presence through dance (Ehrenreich, 2006). Growing up in the Roman Catholic Church I was astounded to learn about how incredibly different the church was and how integral dance was in scripture, worship and to the parishioners of that time. Reflecting on it I wonder how different the church would be, how much more appealing would it be if dance was still present today and what a beautiful way to praise and celebrate your beliefs.

Dance and Participatory Action Research

Participatory action research consists of four techniques that make it an innovative and oftentimes rebellious methodology. The four are: the practice of collective research where studies are established and carried out by participants in a meaningful way; valuing and applying folk culture whereby account is taken for alternative and ethnic expressions and knowledge; the production and diffusion of new knowledge in various ways so that multiple audiences may learn; and, the critical recovery of history, where we recover events of the past that have oppressed others and guide our current climate.

Dance is representative of all of these aspects of participatory action research, practiced oftentimes collectively bringing people together and allowing them to define dance for themselves and learning and improving together. Dance in itself is a type of folk culture a means of expression that is often ignored as a form of knowledge. It also is an alternative channel to disseminate information telling stories and allowing the ability to express anger as well as joy in a non-threatening way. And lastly through this discovery, I have experienced the critical recovery of dance, its significance in this world, the interconnections between various forms, and the power it contains, enough to force the church to condemn it.

What I have come to a deeper realization about in this journey is that dance unifies us. It allows us to step outside of our roles, reduce the status and rank that seems to divide us and connect with one another in a more meaningful way. We as humans have an intrinsic need to be with others, it can be seen in our inclination to celebrate, break out in festivities and dance at rock festivals, parades and sporting events, where we experience an overwhelming state of solidarity and strength as a collective (Ehrenreich, 2006). Personally, I see dance as a mechanism to express the stories of oppression, to act in camaraderie with others and share in the challenges, as well as celebrate the successes in our struggle for knowledge, participation and social justice. Just as dance can be used as a tool in PAR, participatory action research also has a role to play in ensuring that dance remains a diverse and pure art form and does not come under monopolistic control by those who dominate the dissemination of communication and information. Participatory action research and dance share several commonalities: they are both about process, are incredibly personal, contain great meaning and value and are innately about people and collectiveness. It is my hope that participatory action research will continue to discover ways in which dance can be incorporated into its practice and be a useful instrument in transforming our society.

Control

One of the common themes that participatory action research continually is confronted with is the issue of control. Control over research, control of what is acceptable culture and knowledge and control over dissemination of information. I have chosen to incorporate a dance into this project that combines a song about power with strong movements which symbolizes for me breaking free of constraints and authority. Dance has played a central role in my life, a way to express my frustrations and joy, to maintain my health and has assisted in the formation of lasting friendships and experiences. I am pleased to share something so personal and powerful with others and hope that it initiates reflection and consideration about dance in itself and in the world of participatory action research.

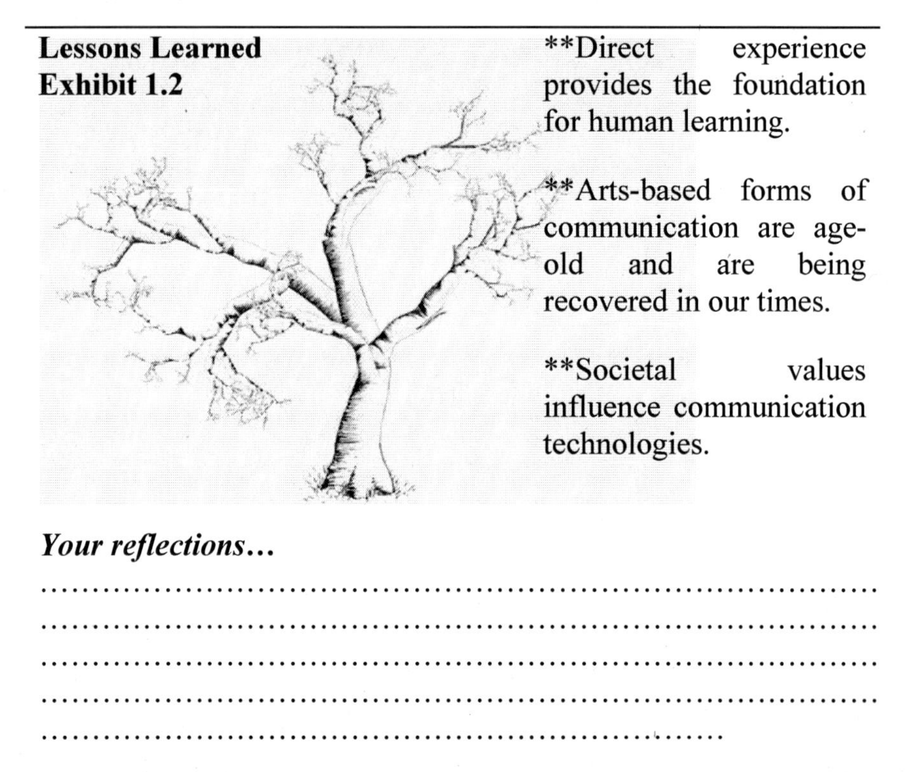

Lessons Learned
Exhibit 1.2

**Direct experience provides the foundation for human learning.

**Arts-based forms of communication are age-old and are being recovered in our times.

**Societal values influence communication technologies.

Your reflections…

……………………………………………………………………

……………………………………………………………………

……………………………………………………………………

……………………………………………………………………

……………………………………………………………

Coincidentally, Twyla's personal journey connected Tanzania and PAR. As it turns out, early activities of the International Council for Adult Education documented PAR activities in Tanzania beginning in the 1960s while inspired by Julius Nyerere, first president of the country after liberation from the British Empire. Canadian adult educator Budd Hall (1981), the former secretary general of the Council, was an early chronicler of PAR initiatives in Tanzania and throughout the Global South. These initiatives are recorded in the journal *Convergence*. Perhaps it is no coincidence after all bringing these expressions of liberatory education together in *Breaking Free*. It might be this is how our tradition is unfolding itself to us.

John Heron's (1992) fourfold typology of ways of knowing helps us appreciate Twyla's understanding of the knowledge-making imperative of PAR through dance due to his inclusion of "presentation" in the typology. Accordingly, presenting our experiences through dance and other performance is a knowledge-making process—dance as a form of knowledge, presentational knowing. This imagery resides at the very heart of the most recent *Handbook of Qualitative Research* (2005). The book cover features a photograph of whirling dervishes dancing in search of the inner strength needed to sustain their Muslim journey. In keeping with the liberatory tradition in the adult education movement, these knowledge-making processes are reflected in the Ganma metaphor of free-wheeling sharing of experiences, acknowledging the wisdom inherent in humankind. Similar to the dervish tradition, this free-wheeling sharing is disciplined and systematic in humankind's search for deeper knowledge by focusing on our spirituality.

There are creative signs of multi-media inquiry organizing narratives of resistance elsewhere in the social justice community. In 2009, the disability action hall joined in a partnership with the Calgary Sexual Health Centre and formed the Right to Love (R2L) group. R2L is a group of people with disabilities and their allies who want to change attitudes about the right to love and celebrate their sexuality. I have been granted their permission to share some of their narrative. In 2010, the R2L group created fourteen short participatory videos called "Love Bytes: Stories About the Right to Love." These videos include personal stories, why their right to love is important, and the history and barriers regarding love in the disability community. This project forms part of the doctoral dissertation by Kathleen Sitter, MSW, in the Faculty of Education. Here she shares some background about the process.

> Through discussions and doing a number of artistic games, the group identified six different topics they wanted to explore through film, as well as record

> portions of their individual stories about their lived experiences. After they spent time developing a storyboard and identifying themes, the group participated in a day-long workshop to learn about the filming equipment (e.g. everyone took turns with filming, directing, framing shots, interviewing each other, and so on. And then we watched the footage and discussed the topics). The group filmed, directed, conducted all of the interviews, etc. And we collaboratively edited the films together. The above process wasn't planned but grew and evolved through our time together.

To share these stories, the R2L group uploaded their films on YouTube, Facebook, and the action hall website. They have also screened their films at community venues in 2010, including an Art Gallery launch and an international film festival, and at a municipal government event on the International Day of Persons with Disabilities. To learn more about "Love Bytes: Stories about the Right to Love," please visit their website[2].

---

[2] www.actionhall.ca

Moving On

We—authors and readers alike—are now ready to continue in our knowledge-making journey. We have been introduced to the liberatory adult education tradition past and present with an eye to the future. We are finding we all have stories to share while presenting them in metaphor and through art, design, and imagery. We are recording our learnings in "lessons learned" to facilitate Freire's advice to re-write this guide for our own individual purpose. *Breaking free* is a hopeful process of shedding some of the societal constraints we have acquired in our formal education and, in doing so, preparing for renewing and refreshing ourselves through PAR. As we move beyond these constraints, we recover forms of knowledge cast off by academic forces aiming to control knowledge-making in the "positivist" ambition to emulate science's claim to be able to predict outcomes in measurable form. At the same time, we are acknowledging the knowledge each of us has within us. Together we are seeking that elusive balance between forms of knowledge so that new knowledge emerges like the Ganma rivers. We cannot do this alone. The next step in this journey is to begin breaking free of the narrow individualism constraining our collective efforts to work together for the common good.

Part Two

Breaking free of narrow individualism

We are so busy focusing in on our individual selves in research projects and in the classroom that sometimes we forget learning is a social process. Most institutional and organizational structures in Canada are based on individual initiative and none more powerfully than the academy. Rather than encouraging individual effort for the common good, the academy promotes the initiative of the individual to an extreme degree. For me, the commonwealth is neglected in Faculty of Social Work programs. For example, block courses are a convenience to instructors wishing to spend as little time as possible engaging with learners in the collective culture of a classroom instead of joining them in regular encounters over the thirteen weeks of the regular term. Curriculum is fragmented, isolated as a result. This hurts an already exhausted student body. We claim efficiency of time as we force undergraduates into Friday evening and all day Saturday classes, cramming them into already over-crowded classrooms. Additionally, technologies like Blackboard replace regular classroom contact with virtual connection. Where is all this heading? Is there a danger of deepening already serious individual isolation under the guise of efficiency and convenience? Who benefits? At what cost? What can we do about it? What are our undergraduate and graduate students saying about their learning? There is a rich, yet mostly hidden collective learning that both students and faculty are generating, and students should take the lead in locating and celebrating this richness. But how can this be done?

In the classroom. All of my courses are designed to introduce learners to themselves and to each other, both individually and collectively as equal contributors to our knowledge-making efforts. Canadian adult educator Virginia Griffin's guitar metaphor helps to demonstrate the richness of our collective power in the classroom (Exhibit 2.1). My learners are required to maintain a learning journal which they hand to me twice during the thirteen week term. The first journal is due after the fourth week of class. I collect them, "process" them guided by the guitar, and return the journals with my interpretation at the beginning of class the following week. They have about twenty minutes to skim the interpretation. Most are amazed with the richness of their individual and collective strength. Often they lose sight of their own words or claim the words of others. It becomes quickly apparent that a collective energy exists beyond the contribution of any one individual. The following exhibit comes from a graduate/undergraduate course on Popular Education and Social Justice completed during the winter of 2008 in Calgary. Everyone in the class had several chances to read my interpretation, comment, add and subtract words, and adjust meanings. *My* interpretation evolved into *our* interpretation. A consensus agreed the document was acceptable as it is presented here. I have added "bubbles" of information to clarify issues for the reader. Remembering Peter Mayo's advice about museum curator and visitor, I intervene as little as possible so as not to interfere with the rich experience we enjoyed while crafting the document and to present it in story-like fashion.

EXHIBIT 2.1: 6-string guitar (SOWK 551/699 Class, 2008)

Griffin, Virginia (2001). "Holistic Learning/Teaching in Adult Education: Would you play a one-string guitar?" in *The Craft of Teaching Adults* edited by Thelma Barer-Stein and Michael Kompf, 3rd edition, Toronto, Irwin.

Learning is like playing a guitar. Most of us have been trained by our schooling to play one string—our rational mind. However, we have at least five other strings, and if we learn to play them as well, and keep them properly tuned, we can make limitless music in our learning and can go on to help others do the same.

What are the other five strings in this analogy? They are the other capabilities we have as human beings, in addition to our rational, logical minds. They are our:

1. **Emotional Capability. If we accept our emotions for what they are, without judging them or being judged by them, we are free to move to take steps to change, or change the situation.**
2. **Relational Capability. We need others in order to learn. We need a "being with" and a "being alone" in a rhythmic pulsation to learn best.**
3. **Physical Capability. The more of our five senses—sight, hearing, smell, taste, and touch—we can use in learning something, the more likely we are to understand and remember it.**
4. **Rational/Intellectual Capability. Our ability to use words and sentences to convey our ideas, to read a book and understand its ideas, to analyze a problem situation, to gather information, and to decide on a logical solution and evaluate its effect all come from this capability.**
5. **Metaphoric/Intuitive Capability. The role of metaphoric thinking is to invent, to create, and to**

challenge conformity by extending what is known into new meadows of knowing.

6. **Spiritual Capability. Spirituality is an awareness, wonder, or deep sense of awe of the present, the potential of persons, or nature. It is awareness and awe of connectedness of what is and what could be. It includes your vision of what could be for yourself—your purpose in life—for others or for nature.**

Can you think of the missing seventh element in this analogy?

Words in quotes are taken directly from your journals.

Emotional capability. Acknowledging our emotions is a confidence builder. According to one of us, "I must admit, I was a little annoyed at the first assignment. All my ingrained assumptions about "how things are done" in a university course rose up to complain: the expectations are too vague, the weighting is too high, no one mentioned pre-session work when I registered, and how can I possibly know what to write when I don't even know what the class is about? Should I raise a concern or protest and risk starting by student/professor relationship in a conflict? Would it hurt my potential to do well in the rest of the class? The questions and complaints keep swirling around, but I finally convinced myself I should just take a stab at the assignment and see what happens.

Changing course mid-stream is not easy. "Now that there has been an election called, we are focusing on that. This is very scary for me as well but a little exciting at the same time. I guess I have no choice now but to get involved in politics."

Reference is to the Provincial election held in February 2008. We decided to take an active part by exploring issues and getting involved.

Our words reflect emotions that might not be readily apparent in the classroom. "Without being told, I could feel the freedom, the environment as less tense, and I was a free spirit—free to be me: unguarded."

Still another shared, "During school I learn about horrible things people don't have to deal with. The things that only happen to 'other people' especially if they are 'from away.' In school, we are not actually doing anything about it…in some ways I wonder if I am missing important parts of my world view. I am confounded by the simplicity of improving the world and the resistance to change."

Relational capability. If we listen carefully, we begin to hear one another. For one of us, "When listening to the presentation on the individual findings of what popular education is, I believe we were participating in the essence of popular education. We came together, brought our own perspectives, our own experiences to the group; some shared their own self reflection and passion on issues they desired to create change. I loved listening to everyone's findings as they were so different. This truly helps me realize we all have something different to bring to this class and to this world."

Another wrote, "When active learning is encouraged, infinite voices and resolutions can be heard."

Another wrote, "I feel affirmed and excited to discover that my own experience has a name and a language that others can relate to. I'm overwhelmed by the realization that there

really is a community of seekers in the world who are dreaming in the same images of peace, justice, and creativity."

According to another, "At the women's homeless rally, I realized this problem is not really being addressed properly, and what the women need are "mentors." I then thought if each woman took another under her wing and supported her in getting back on her feet with such a great program, problems would be solved.

Imagery helps uncover relationship. One of us said, "The class on Photovoice has inspired me. I thought this was a great tool to use and one I'll always remember. Photovoice really connects to the issues but also does not forget about the people who are experiencing the issue. I believe this tool can be more powerful than research alone; it has the ability to connect the issues to people, which can be much more effective when wanting to create change. I think it is effective because the visual helps the situation become reality."

While another joined in: "While the comics are short and provide humorous entertainment, they are also provoking. They can be provoking in the sense they challenge us to think about our own personal attitudes, beliefs, values, and behaviours as well as society's. As a visual person, I truly believe art and images can and do provide an outlet of expression that often is more powerful and impactful than mere words. While admittedly I read the comic section for the basic entertainment it provides, I also read the comics because they so often reflect general life experiences and the day to day happenings and beliefs in society. I often find I am challenged to think critically about the issues and concerns brought forth in the comic strips."

Physical capability. The classroom environment is important to learning. One participant wrote, "This (Stage Left) was by far the most enjoyable class for me. Creating images with our bodies was an *extremely* powerful process; we all came together as one, all walls and biases were gone, and we were just people with one common goal. It was very cool to see my colleagues behave in a manner so unlike what we've been taught, losing sight of the 'professional boundaries' we've been force fed and identifying with a problem, making it our own." Another wrote, "To be comfortable with your body and to use our bodies to make a change is an amazing concept. Even in watching the movements going on around me, I was so moved, and I kept paying attention to the feelings and thoughts going on within me and thought that there is no way someone could watch this and not feel compelled to listen and make a change."

We draw from one another's energy. In the words of one student, "Myles also talked about fear.

Myles Horton co-founded the Highlander Folk School in the hills of Tennessee in 1932. It has been the very essence of liberatory education ever since.

Fear is an emotional response to tangible and realistic dangers, yet in all his dangerous encounters with the law, he knew no fear. If you let your fears plant their roots in you, you defeat yourself before you even set out on your journey. Myles tied this in with his brush with death. He talked about a vehicle of death with its occupants as they stared him in the face. He expressed with ease his not so easy ordeal with the tyrants and how he overcame with his words and his resolve to live."

All of our senses need caring. For one of us, "Music is a tool that can reach many and a tool that can capture feeling, perspectives, hope, and the injustice in the world." For another, "Painting garbage cans in brilliant colours adds so much more life to an inanimate object that blends into the ho-hum environment we live in every day."

Rational capability. Critical thinking skills fit here. One of us wrote, "One of the more uncomfortable comments for me I noted in the film was Horton's take on the current state of democracy. He said, 'We don't have democracy, only the trimmings of democracy.' What is disturbing about that comment is the challenge to those of us who take refuge in the appearance that we live in a free and democratic society. If we believe all is well with democracy there is no need to demand change. Horton's comments challenge us to look at how power is shared. Who has it? Who is denied it? To what extent do we support an unequal distribution of power? To what extent do we support the structures that maintain the status quo?"

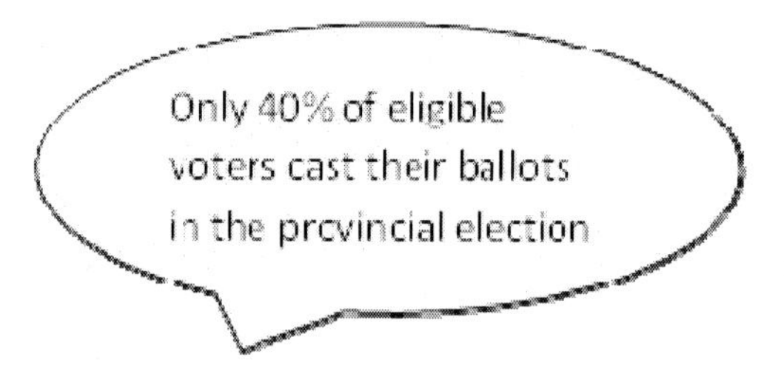

And where is our democracy? One of us felt that "the right to vote is a fundamental democratic right, and it's such a shame that 60% of our population found reasons not to exercise it. People throughout history have died in pursuit of that right, and Canadian soldiers are dying right now so that people in Afghanistan can have their right to democracy as well. I know that it feels hopeless when we live in a province led by the same party for well over thirty years. One vote doesn't make a difference on its own, but it is an important symbolic act in support of a governing system that hears the people. Even if people feel so strongly that there are no decent candidates, I think they should spoil their ballots instead of not voting at all. To vote is to acknowledge support of a system that can be (and must be) influenced ordinary people in lots of ways. I am afraid of what happens when democracy isn't supported. If we aren't there already, I fear we are dangerously close to a system of government by corporations instead of people. In addition to deepening corruption, rising religious fundamentalism, increasing disparity between rich and poor, and ecological destruction, I am afraid of

the dangers this alternative may have that we are not yet aware of... that is why I vote."

Meanwhile, another questioned, "What can be taken from this dismal report on the health of our democracy. If you are the party in power you can claim, as our premier did, that the state of the province is strong, citizens are satisfied; all is good with the world. 'Not so fast Mr. Premier!' I want to scream. How can you have a healthy democracy when most people remain silent? Just like the Iraqi government, how can you claim to rule legitimately – in principle—when 60% of the voices have not been heard? The silence is deafening. So Albertans have no issues with their government? They are silent because they are happy? What about the road blocks that have been strewn across the province. They aren't as easy to spot as burned out vehicles, tanks, and armed soldiers. Road blocks can be made of paper—like voters lists that are not complete. Road blocks can be inaccessible voting stations that keep out the elderly, the infirmed. Road blocks can be invisible—the lack of information about where to vote, the invisible and inaccessible candidates—the incumbents who do not want to face tough questions. Road blocks can come in the form of eligibility rules and polling stations supervisors who don't know the rules. All these and more were encountered by our class as we tried to jump start our democracy." And another wondered, "I think I can say with some assurance that there are a lot of people in Alberta or even Canada that do not understand the political system very well. As a result, why doesn't the government make an effort to educate people or even find out why there are such a large number of people that are not going to the polls? It also makes me wonder why it was so hard for many people in our classroom to find where the information sessions of each political party was going to be held. There seems to be too many coincidences here in order to not shout out 'Foul play!'"

Metaphoric capability. It is helpful to keep things "fluid." One of us wrote, "What I enjoyed the most about the sharing was making connections between my understandings and others' understandings. Now, a couple of days after the class, I have had time to reflect upon the sharings of my fellow students as well as what you had to say about the class and the class assignment. I

have begun to make some connections between the course and the class assignment. So far what I have come up with is that not knowing about what the assignment will look like is an educational experience in itself. By not having a plan or a clear and definite expectation for an assignment handed to us students by a teacher, we are encouraged and challenged to direct our own learning. Instead of being the traditional students we are student teachers. In a sense, my unexpected surprise is popular education in action."

Metaphor implies multi-media imagery. For one of us, "Art gives students a change to be themselves, create, and use their imagination. These elements are powerful tools for later participation in the society and can be very helpful to set the path to real democracy." And another drew this image:

We move on despite our fears. One of us wrote, "Fear can make people sometimes action driven but too often paralyzed. When we learn how to face our fears and control them, we should be able to act more inspired. Learning to overcome fear comes over time and with knowledge. This knowledge can be obtained by using popular education tools such as adult education, participatory action research. Because popular education wants to make us actively participating citizens, it brings the elements of fear into the open and lays out its tactics to a thorough examination. As soon as we feel afraid we should realize that there is an issue or concern that needs our attention. In fear there is no room for knowledge, and where there is knowledge it illuminates fear.

One day while walking with an Indian friend, Malaquìas, he told me the story of the five friends and the five enemies.

The first enemy of human beings is fear. If you live in fear, you will live like a mouse in a dark corner and never see the light. Fear will become your enemy and you never will grow up. But if you are not afraid of the fear you will have, then you can live in light, and fear becomes your friend.

If fear is your friend, then you are able to look around you with clarity. But if you think that you can see all things clearly, then you are really blind, and clarity becomes your enemy. If, however, you strive to see clearly, then clarity becomes your friend.

If fear is your friend and you can see clearly, then you will have power. But if you keep power to yourself, you will become weaker and weaker. If, however, you share the power, you will become strong, and power will be your friend.

If fear is your friend, you see clearly, and you share power, then you will be wise. But if you think you have all the wisdom, then in reality you are ignorant, and wisdom will be your enemy. If, however, you admit that you do not know everything, answers will come to you, and wisdom will be your friend.

If fear is your friend, you see clearly, and you share power, and you have wisdom, then you will meet old age. But if you sit, doing nothing and denying your history, then old age will be your enemy. If, however, you meet old age with grace, having met fear, seeing with clarity, sharing power, and making wisdom your friend, then you will live forever.

- Mexican popular folklore as told by Arturo Ornelas (cited in *Nurtured by Knowledge* (1997) edited by Susan Smith, Dennis Willms and Nancy Johnson, Ottawa: IDRC).

If fear still exists within the realm of the knowledge, however, it has become our friend as mentioned in one of our articles. When you have a friend, you become powerful in a way because you share something that belongs to the both of you. You and your friend (fear) can create an alliance of trust and understanding. You will question your friend in a more caring and understanding way, and you will take time to listen. And when you listen, you will hear. You might hear the silence of an oppressed inner part of yourself or from another person, group, community you work with. Fear all of a sudden becomes a source of active wisdom which will not paralyze but activates."

Yet another asserted, "I find the more I listen to others discuss their understanding of popular education the more I scratch my head in worry. Let's hope my grasp on Popular Education is budding under the surface of the soil. I do feel confident in knowing that no matter what cause draws us in and motivates our action, it cannot thrive in isolation...Dignity can be found in one's marginalization. The mutual respect and understanding that comes alongside dignity helps lead and encourage self-worth. Fear is a perspective which can be managed, coped with, and stood up to in order to bring about change. Rather than trying to overcome it, we can use our fear and turn it into fuel rather than keep it as a barrier... Why is it that our fear is so often at the front of our minds? Do we only feel this when challenged? Do we only recognize how common it is from person to person when we compile and share our thoughts? This classmate's thought said it best, 'If you let your fears plant their roots in you, you defeat yourself before you even set out on your journey.' I am glad experiencing fear and letting fear take root are not the same thing."

Spiritual capability. We search the world deeply and find hope. One of us wrote, "Hope is a collective responsibility to inspire and stay positive for those who are facing a world of heartache. We need to constantly remind each other what we can become if we have hope. Hope is so important, despite being very difficult to have. But personally it is what keeps me going." Another wrote, "The future is not a result of choices among alternative paths offered by the present, but a place that is

created—created first in the mind and will, created next in activity. The future is not some place we are going to but one we are creating. Paths are not to be found, but made, and the activity of making them, changes both the maker and the destination.' This has really influenced me to think differently. I think it challenges me to look at the future as something I want it to be, not just something that is going to be...I have realized this is a key ingredient in change; you need to believe it is possible, yes sometimes hard to do, but if you don't believe in it then what are we striving for?"

And yet another reported, "Although we all are adults in this class and you hope that you know yourself, I found that are some areas that need a deeper look in relation to social issues. One of these areas is to find out more about my own history. As a worker I found it even harder to listen to popular education because it places the entire social workers field and practice in a different context. One where we have dared to make choices in the social and political context that we work in. I realized even more that our work is politically ingrained and that it is time for change."

We see things holistically. For one of us, "Learning should be fun and scary at the same time. It should evoke your whole person to respond. I think that in our march to be professionally respected as a science we are sacrificing the heart and soul that started the best profession, social work."Another student went further, stating, "One thing I thought about that could be explored/clarified further in the paper is the overlap and interaction between the six –'strings;' it's clear that some of our classmates' words could easily be applied to more than one string, and reflections from one string category would not be able to exist without one or more of the other strings. To extend the metaphor, to create melody, chords, and harmony (building blocks for music) requires the simultaneous and/or progressive use of multiple strings."

We will not be discouraged. One of us declared, "Even though I felt very frustrated, politicians will not force me into being silent. Even if I am not able to change a lot, I at least have a voice during elections, and I will not have this taken away from me no matter what the government tries to do to prevent it."

We commit ourselves to action. For one of us, “It is not okay for people to be sleeping on the streets in this weather and for society to think it is no big deal. And yet I feel so useless and helpless in the whole situation, and I am just as much to blame because I do nothing. What can I do? It’s times like these I lose my hope and sit back and do nothing because I am at a complete lose of what to do. Therefore I need to switch this around and rebuild my hope. Yes, I did nothing in the past, but here is what I could start doing in the present. Volunteer at shelters; bring someone a coffee; help advocate for people for somewhere to stay. I could work with the bigger picture and advocate for social change. These things that seem so small could make a very big difference. As I have learned over the past few years in school and in my own experience, one person can definitely make a difference.”

For another, “When we make our path rather than find our path, or even when compared to the expectation that others will pave it for us, we are then able to take pride in our accomplishments, something we couldn’t have experienced any other way.”

And what about the missing seventh element? One of us felt, “Well, it must involve the hope felt, the fear turned fuel, the seeds planted, the journeys travelled, and the voices put into action. The word harmony embraces both the unity and variety of all the voices from this class into one academic choir. It is our synchronization capability.” Or is it simply that the missing element is our “hands?”

An ending gift from one of us illustrates the power of our hands.

“Last thoughts on the guitar

My daughter plays the guitar. She got interested after watching a movie in which girls were playing the guitar. For Christmas that year, I broke down and got her one. She was incredibly excited. Soon she practiced and played almost every day. She learned very fast. Now she can play quite well, having learned the intricacies of the instrument. When, in this article,

playing the guitar was an analogy to learning, it caught my attention immediately. I personally find it quite difficult to think of myself playing a guitar. I would like to, but I don't have the patience to learn until I can play to my own content. Here is where I started thinking of the question around the missing element. I wondered what it could be. As I was thinking through those weeks, I quickly figured out that it must be the person itself, the learner, who is the missing element. The person self must be the one directing, inspiring, creating and shaping his learning. The will must be there. When I watch my daughter playing the guitar, beginning the moment she got it, I understand that she really wanted, needed to learn to play. I also saw her going from very excited to less excited and not motivated. But… She learned. I try to analyze what elements made her learning to play so successful. If I think of the different capabilities mentioned in the article and look back on her learning journey, I'll next try to see if I can identify them in her experience.

Emotional capability: Her enthusiasm was an incredible motivator. When she got the guitar, she immediately started putting all the elements together to start playing. She was very happy and pleased with the gift, the guitar. I did not stop her curiosity to find out how it would sound, work or not. She herself found everything out on her own, each day bringing new discoveries. She would ask her father for help with instructions that she could not understand. She was completely wrapped up in this. I gave her complete freedom, but I was sure to watch from aside.

Relational capability: Soon my husband and I suggested she take classes. She was okay with it. I guess she understood that she needed someone else to guide her further in her learning. Faithfully she would go lessons and still practice at home. Soon she learned the basics, and shortly after a few months of classes, she could play full, complete songs. She could read music and get harmonious sound out of her guitar. She liked her instructor, and that made it quite easy for her as well.

Physical: The fact that she put every part of herself into learning to play the guitar gave her a chance to use her senses. I would watch her admiring the smoothness of the beautiful electric guitar. Her body language was all in accordance to what she was doing. In my mind it was quite impossible to start learning on an electric guitar. According to the teacher it was not a barrier, certainly not for her. She wanted to learn to play an electric guitar since the film, and whether it was an electric guitar or acoustic one it did not matter to the teacher.

Metaphoric or intuitive: She did create new ways of knowing by using what she had learned and practice on songs she liked. She did so well that she was asked in the church to join their musical band. At a certain point, she stopped with the lessons at the music centre and is now exploring the world of guitar on her own.

Spiritual: I know that my daughter envisions herself playing the guitar in an amazing way. She is so much in tune with her guitar and very focused on her playing. She admires many guitarists in different bands; she is totally in awe of their skills. I also know that she has made her own a choice to master this instrument. In school, however, the instrument was chosen for her; she plays the bassoon…And she is not so much in love with it.

With this I hope that the analogy 'learning is like playing the guitar' can be seen as a whole symphony of the learner starting a journey in which one tries to make the experience as pleasant and meaningful for not only oneself but also for the journey self. The enrichment that it brings together while learning must be seen as a very intense route of playing not only *the one* string but automatically force the learner to touch either intense or playfully the other capabilities."

Lessons Learned
Exhibit 2.1

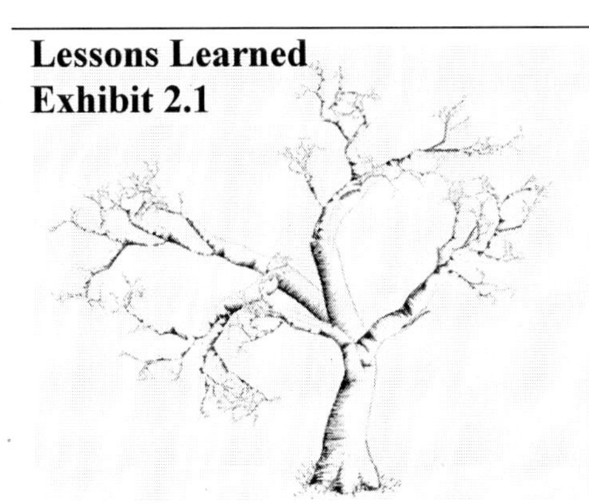

**FSW learners have a critical eye and encourage each other to use it to their mutual benefit. This indicates a deep sense of trust in our classrooms.

**We are not alone.

** We commit ourselves to social change. FSW learners are ready, willing and able to engage in democratic citizenship if encouraged. This is social action aiming to change a weak sense of social responsibility.

** FSW learners possess rich 'human capabilities'.

** FSW learners are creative, artistic and musical.

** We are recovering our interconnectedness.

Your Reflections…

....

....

....

....

As my class was discovering our individual power and collective strength, I added historical vignettes, introducing them to similar processes from early in the twentieth century. We learned socially conscious Canadians have been, throughout history, committed to reasoned inquiry into current events while searching for balance and coherence in face of national emergency. Canadians were challenged by fierce ideological competition during the Great Depression in the 1930s. An editorial in the journal *Adult Learning* in 1937 captured the mood of the age, "In days when democracy seems to be steadily retreating before the advancing forces of Fascism and Communism, the self-imposed discipline of voluntary study appears to offer some hope of maintaining the individual liberty which underlies political and intellectual freedom" (Plumptre, 1937). Even during the Great Depression, Canadians were seeking a balance through their independent study. The liberatory education movement seeks this heightened state of balanced inquiry. One of the principles of the 1943 Manifesto of the Canadian Association for Adult Education declared, "Planning must be combined with such local and community participation and democratic vigilance as to prevent the regimentation and frustrations of the human personality" (Manifesto, 1943). Another principle stated,

> Neither the old individualism nor the newer mass-collectivism but a relationship of voluntary co-operation, which balances rights with responsibilities, is the basic pattern of the emergent social order. Such a relationship of voluntary co-operation has a place for central planning and control as well as for the legitimate liberties and enterprises of the individual. (p. 4)

These words were written following a decade of depression and three-and-a-half years of war as socially conscious Canadians rallied to democratic principles of voluntary cooperative action in local communities. Barack Obama's 2006 call to action in *The Audacity of Hope* is in keeping with Canadian values established sixty-three years prior to publishing. In the face of current global economic and political uncertainty, Obama's call and our small scale democratic traditions hold some promise. Do we have the courage to recover a similar spirit in Canada? How are we playing this out in the Faculty of Social Work? Should we care?

As course instructor, I still have a role to play, though it is more a role of facilitation. We start with individual experience in our educational journey. In itself, however, this is insufficient. We need one another in the classroom and community in order to enrich and interpret our individual experience. Still not good enough. The Ganma rivers are stimulated and enriched by many streams; the foam fed by abounding waters. These streams include "the literature." In class, we learn how to share and expand our own lived experience with challenges and wisdom from other disciplines, other times, and other cultures. These streams are located in what we call "the literature." We cite "the literature" to build upon what has come before, to show respect and to acknowledge the experience of others. These "others" become our irreplaceable partners in our journey of knowledge-making. Together we create foam and interact with it in a dynamic process, thus avoiding the notion of foam as a commodity; we are content living in this process—an infinite game.

It takes confidence to function in dynamic processes of knowledge-making. The rich words from my class captured in Exhibit 2.1 reveal efforts to connect past experiences of critical citizenship in face of upheaval with emerging critical awareness of the demands of democracy. My class was socially aware. In his study of physical actions in the performing arts, Canadian dramatic artist Mike Unrau (2008) notes three competencies in social awareness that can shed light on relating to others: empathy, equity, and service. Unrau goes on to describe empathy as "the ability to view other cultures, religions, and social structures with cross-cultural sensitivity, relating to diversity without discrimination" (p. 85). Various students in my popular education course displayed their empathy in the activity, but one in particular appropriately noted,

> "In our society, sometimes even in social work, people assume a person in distress needs help from others to find a solution; but more often than not, those individuals have an idea what needs to be done to solve the issue. Often it just takes time to listen to them and let them explore while they explain what is going on, what could be done".

Taking time to listen is required behaviour in American economist and activist Jeremy Rifkin's (2009) notion of "empathic extension" whereby we respond to and experience each other's condition as if it were our own, and our engagement loops back to deepen our self awareness. Through critical reflection and dialogue, we continue to grow stronger both together *and* individually; this creates a magnificent feedback loop. Readers of this guide are invited to join this "empathic extension." As we engage together and with the many voices joining us along the way, we will grow stronger individually while strengthening our broader community and collective narratives. Collectively we discover our ability to empathize and to act upon this empathy in our daily routine.

Following empathy in social awareness competencies comes equity. Unrau delves into this second of the competencies, stating, "The competency of equity enables us to view situations through a lens of fairness in diverse contexts, to ourselves and to others in an individual as well as a societal manner" (p. 87). Equity is reflected in these words from my course, with one student noting,

> "We, as a society, are disconnected from other people and their problems because we like our safe place/comfort zone where we don't have to be socially responsible for our neighbours. I talked about inner city schools and how the school board wants to close them, but also that they make great accommodation for the homeless in smaller numbers throughout the communities. Again, someone in the community would adopt someone and commit to investing time in this person by supporting them to get back on their feet. When I say support, I don't mean money. I mean emotional and just plain old caring for your fellow wo/man".

Equity is felt intuitively for another student who remarked,

> "Oh my goodness, I don't even know where to start with this journal! I've only heard of "popular education" very recently, and since then my whole world has been spinning like crazy. The thing is, even though I didn't know that something called "popular education" existed, I found out I've been doing it all my life! It's as if all the threads of my life's passions—story, spirituality, community, justice, creativity, grassroots activism, ecological sustainability, mysticism, etc.—have finally woven themselves together into a recognizable pattern".

It might be no surprise to discover, eloquently or not, a deep reserve of equity in our classrooms.

Service is Unrau's third competency in social awareness. For him, service is an empathetic identification with what is equitably fair and offering assistance to another without self-interest, a competency requiring expanded social consciousness and the transformation of the barriers that constrain them. These service qualities are clear for one member of my class who argued,

> "Popular education has a lot to do with change, protest and resistance, liberation, empowerment, and adult education. On the other hand, the academy (formal education in structured institutions) moulds and produces educated people in specific fields of employment in society for the benefits of national economies, some, if not all, of which are intertwined with globalization. I think this kind of learning process keeps intelligent and educated people locked up in a cocoon of economic and social "rat race" (endless, self-defeating or pointless pursuit), and fear of the unknown in life. In this pursuit of happiness, social justice and humanity are trampled upon. I think this is where popular education comes in. A popular education informal learning circle provides a stress free learning environment and power balance, which is liberating and empowering. Therefore, popular education is a knowledge that helps people to surpass that state of fear, economic/social gains and make ultimate sacrifices to improve life for grassroots people and to bring about meaningful change for the common good of society".

Indications of deep understanding and commitment to service in the students come as no surprise in Faculty of Social Work classes.

We were learning how to listen to self and others more deeply, and together we began hearing new things. We were finding ways of speaking and listening while recording these findings in collective documents. An added bonus awaited another of my classes during the winter of 2007, this one in a course on PAR. We had the opportunity to publish our collective document in a scholarly journal. The following item was published in 2008 in *Educational Action Research*, 16/3, 335-44.

Exhibit 2.2: Recording action research in a classroom: singing with chickadees

Ramona Beatty, Judy Bedford, Peter Both, Jennifer Eld, Mary Goitom, Lilli Heinrichs, Laura Moran-Bonilla, Mona Massoud, Hieu Van Ngo, Timothy Pyrch, Marianne Rogerson, Kathleen Sitter, Casey Eagle Speaker & Mike Unrau
University of Calgary, Canada

This is a collective interpretive record of a graduate course in Social Work on participatory action research (PAR) offered during the winter of 2007. It is written by fourteen individuals including the instructor. It was inspired by the image of a chickadee bird borrowed from Jonathan Lear's (2006) book *Radical Hope*. The chickadee is a powerful metaphor for aboriginal peoples of Western Canada as she thrives in the bitter winters despite her tiny frame. She does so because she is gifted with deep listening in her environment wherein lies all she needs to know. The class of fourteen met in a circle, read articles, kept learning journals, argued, ate together, practised popular education techniques and presented our emerging knowledge in multi-media forms. We related our experience to recent articles in EAR and to other PAR literature. The chickadee facilitated our deep listening to writings and to our own stories. Collective power emerged from our relationships and our diversity.

Keywords: Participatory action research; radical hope; deep listening; diversity; relationships

---

Journal editors had this to say about the article:

> This account provides us with a resource to think rigorously about the cultural politics of action research, and who we are individually and with each other through the action research process. The delightfully titled 'Recording…chickadees by Remona Beatty…in Canada is an intriguing and original attempt to produce a

> collective interpretative record of a graduate course in Social Work on PAR. It has been written by all 14 individuals, including the teacher, and inspired by the hopeful image of a chickadee bird. The writers explain that this fragile little bird is a powerful metaphor for aboriginal peoples of Western Canada because it thrives in bitter winters, aware of and listening to its environment. The article details the way in which a Social Work class of diverse cultures and genders worked together, struggles with knowledge forms, recording their experiential knowing and their opening to each other. They present here an inspiring and thought-provoking story of individual songs, voices and collective power. (p. 292)

The editors applauded our collective power emanating from our rich diversity and profound goodwill. Their words acknowledged our knowledge-making success. The "chickadees" ordered their knowledge-making journey, creating Ganma-like foam, by borrowing John Heron's four ways of knowing: experiential, presentational, propositional, and practical. We will draw upon these four ways of knowing throughout this guide.

Similar richness and goodwill appear in other FSW courses. The highly successful integrated course in our BSW program is one example. The three instructors who conceived the idea of the course have taught it for several years, involving a staggering time commitment of one thousand hours over the duration of the five blended course offerings. One reason for this success is the rich diversity and profound goodwill of the instructional team.

Exhibit 2.3: Team teaching in social work: sharing power with BSW students (Zapf, Jerome & Williams, 2011).

This volunteer teaching team featured diversity across many demographic categories: gender (one woman and two men); age (40s, 50s, and 60s); racial/cultural background (two Caucasian and one Aboriginal); community of origin (one grew up in urban London, England; one grew up in the Duck Mountain region of northern Manitoba; one grew up in a military family moving across Canada). In addition, team members exhibited a range of political orientations and values, a wide variety of social work field and research experiences, and very different experiences with oppression (both as oppressors and oppressed). What they had in common was commitment to BSW students, belief in the value of generalist practice, openness to sharing their personal stories and reflections, willingness to commit classroom and planning hours beyond the norm, and a keen sense of adventure about this new approach to classroom relationships with each other and students…

Guidelines from the literature suggest that assignments in team taught courses should be inquiry-based with an emphasis on individual expression and integration across content areas. Collaboration and thoughtful planning of assignments over the term has proven to be one of the major strengths of the team taught BSW integrated course. Rather than being overwhelmed with the busy work of disconnected assignments and conflicting due dates, students are faced with a focused and more manageable pattern of one assignment due each week. Students are encouraged to write in the first person voice for all assignments. This does not negate academic rigor or competent use of the literature, but students take responsibility for the selections they make and the implications for themselves as developing social workers.

The first piece of graded work is due in late September. Following from Mullaly's (2002) question of "what makes you angry?", students identify an injustice or oppression in society that disturbs them, possibly a motivation for entering social work in the first place. They explore the issue from the perspective of all five courses (What developmental or environmental issues are involved? What policies serve to create or maintain the injustice? Whose values are at play? What is known about the frequency and experience of the issue? Does generalist practice offer a meaningful way to approach the issue?). Called the Social Justice Assignment, this paper makes up 25% of the final grade in all five component courses. Each paper is read by all three instructors who meet to determine grades. Students receive three sets of comments on their work (three different colors of ink!) along with their grade.

The final assignment, in early December, is called an Oral Reflection and similarly is worth 25% of the final grade for each component course. The format here is much like an oral examination, a new experience for most undergraduate students. Each student has 30 minutes with all three instructors to respond to the general question "Tell us about your learning." The student presents for 15 minutes followed by 15 minutes of responding to questions from the instructors. The emphasis here is not on a summary overview of content from the term. Instead, the emphasis is on significant moments for the student. What spoke to them? How were their ideas or values challenged? How are they different now than in September? Students demonstrate their ability to integrate material from the course with their own experiences and knowledge as they begin to develop their own practice models…

Student resistance, as anticipated in the literature, has been apparent during the first month of the team taught BSW Integrated Course. Based on past academic experiences, many students want to know the specific requirements to get an "A" grade. Many have difficulty expressing their own opinions and reflections in the first person voice after years of learning to use the objective third person passive voice for academic writing. Others are looking for what they need to memorize rather than engaging in reflective dialogue with themselves and others. Overall, there is a cautious suspicion of the process, a hanging back to watch the instructors interact, until some students begin to participate actively in the dialogue and others follow their example beginning to trust in the process. Particularly helpful in this transition from suspicion to participation are the monthly anonymous formative evaluations (especially the first one at the end of September) which allow students to comment on the process and asses their learning. Grouped data and themes of concern from the evaluations are discussed in class where changes or improvements can be negotiated and, as a side benefit, links can be made with the theoretical concepts taught in the research class…

There are also hidden rewards for teaching team members. The opportunity to learn from colleagues, to respond to others' material and to have them challenge our own, develops all of us as teachers and as people. We have learned much from each other's grading practices and priorities, teaching styles, and life stories. A level of trust and respect has developed among team members which keeps the work fresh, interesting, and fun.

As a concluding thought, it should be noted that the organization of this discussion does not parallel the real world development of our team taught BSW Integrated Course. This paper began with a systematic overview of the process and issues of team teaching from the literature. We were not that proactive or efficient when we began our course. We jumped into something we believed in but knew little about, amazed after a few years of experience to discover that much of what we had discovered and developed together in fact had a foundation in the literature. Reported experiences and lessons learned in other places were very similar to our own. We hope this paper might serve as a resource for other social work educators considering team teaching, possibly providing direction and saving them some time. Or, as Beavers and DeTurck (2000) concluded in their discussion of team teaching, perhaps "the best approach to finding one's way is to revel in the getting lost" (p. 3).

Lessons Learned
Exhibit 2.3

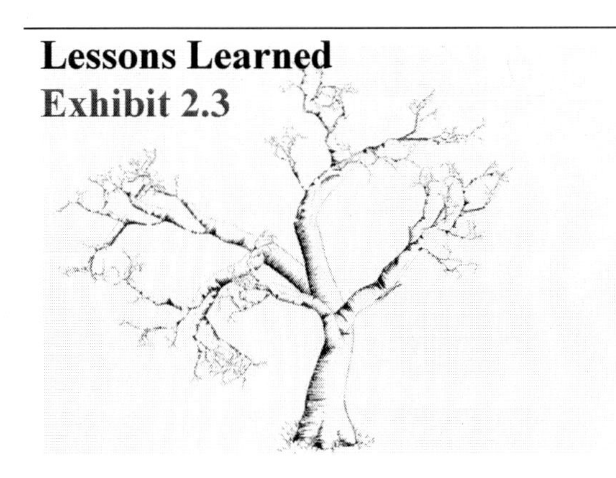

**Collective support enhances individual strength.

**A sense of mutuality inspires confidence.

Your Reflections…

……………………………………………………………………
……………………………………………………………………
……………………………………………………………………
……………………………………………………………………

A spirit of adventure, good humour, and a commitment to fairness—not to mention many years experience in the classroom and in the field of practice—have given this trio of instructors the courage to learn together with all the uncertainties and challenges always included in learning. As it stands, they are modelling many attributes of liberatory education practice, whether they know it or not. How well did they reflect the values of the liberatory education movement listed in the glossary of terms of this guide?

- Direct experience provides the foundation for human learning.
- Everything we need is near at hand.
- We commit ourselves to social change.
- Knowledge-making is a democratic collective relationship of equals.
- Acting knowledgably is empowering.
- Clarity of language and purpose.
- Disciplined, thoughtful hope.
- Liberatory processes are holistic, intertwined, and mutually dependent.

Perhaps the trio used different language than mine, but I see these values in the undertones of their words. They modelled teamwork at its best as they treated one another and their learners with respect and care, and it worked, for them at least. For those of you wishing to emulate this teamwork in your practice or instruction, be aware of a downside to this approach. American sociologist Richard Sennett (1998) writes widely about the "corrosion of character" of work in capitalism. He cautions, "Teamwork might seem to be just another example of the bonds of group conformity" (p. 108). Group conformity, when disguised as teamwork, can eliminate rather than foster the individual creativity of each person involved. It is a tough outcome to avoid. Clearly, however, Kim Zapf, Les Jerome, and Margaret Williams are not the "group conformists" Sennett warns us about in the contemporary workplace. It might be useful to read their story closely again to see how they avoided group conformity. I'll wait here while you read it again. Go on, take your time.

How could the students themselves have been blended more clearly into the course record? Is this blending—perhaps like the chickadees and guitarists—possible or desirable? Do the three instructors capture the individual and collective learning experience sufficiently in their account? In the spirit of "democratic collective relationship of equals," can something more be done to facilitate liberatory education practice? Food for thought.

Similar questions can be addressed to other Faculty of Social Work innovative teaching practices. Recent collaboration between the Faculty of Social Work and the Faculty of Nursing expands the notion of blending all learners in a course including students, community activists, and instructors. An added touch in this community-based research initiative was to locate the course in a unique community setting. The following exhibit contains the abstract and final paragraph of the article authored by two professors from Social Work and Nursing along with a Social Work graduate student.

Exhibit 2.4: Fostering Inclusivity Through Teaching and Learning Action Research (Walsh, Rutherford & Sears, 2010).

Abstract

In post-secondary curricula, the introduction of research paradigms that emphasize community inclusion and social action is increasingly valued by scholars. However, there is only a modest amount of scholarship regarding how the delivery of such material should be structured, or the challenges and/or successes with various course models. In this article, the authors synthesize the existing literature on developing and implementing courses on alternative research paradigms, and use it to analyze the development and implementation of an innovative undergraduate course taught on community based research in the spring of 2007. Taught in the setting of a local homeless shelter, course learners included undergraduate students of social work and nursing, staff members from the homeless-serving agency, individuals from the homeless community, and the course instructors themselves. The authors present the challenges and successes of this particular course model in reference to the suggestions gleaned from academic scholarship, and make recommendations to those involved in teaching models of action research.

Given a context that facilitates the development, implementation, and maintenance of such a course, we feel that this course model has immense potential to enrich the knowledge of all learners involved. The topic of instruction (in this case poverty and homelessness) can be adjusted according to the needs of any agency or community, and any alternative research paradigm could be used in place of [community-based research] CBR. As academics, we need to do more than do [action research] AR, and teach students to do AR. We need to learn and teach AR "in and with" community. It has been made clear from the literature, from our own experience with the course, and from student evaluations, that any innovations that can increase inclusivity and a diversity of learners, or create a community-based or community-immersed setting, will contribute positively to the learners' experience in a CBR or other AR course. We must continue to develop meaningful and effective ways to co-learn with the community in undertaking CBR and similar AR frameworks. It is only through knowledge and skill acquisitions that communities can really participate in developing solutions to their complex problems, or in changing social relations to foster equity, inclusivity, and social justice.

Lessons Learned
Exhibit 2.4

Your Reflections…

……………………………………………………………………
……………………………………………………………………
……………………………………………………………………
……………………………………………………………………

A sense of community is an integral part of PAR

These first four exhibits in breaking free of narrow individualism display profound learning experiences in the liberatory tradition being practised creatively in our classrooms with commitment and passion by instructors and students—both learners in this system—in continuing critical inquiry often hard to see through the noise and pace of contemporary times. When we take a moment to look around us, we see evidence of respectful, democratic, and cooperative knowledge-making activities everywhere. The Ganma Rivers are producing rich foam, and when engaging playfully with this foam, the rivers themselves are becoming stronger and ready for new spiralling iterations. We need to gather this dynamic process together in a place where we all can partake of its empowering nature.

Moving out of the classroom, even when it includes community settings, enables us to introduce the rich fieldwork undertaken by our students who are endeavouring to include collective learning experiences into social justice work. One of our graduates, Lilli Heinrichs (MSW, 2007), wrote a case study of her lived experience as a post-tsunami aid worker in the Aceh province of Indonesia while employed by the International Red Cross. The case study is titled "Blending Voices: Facilitating a search for collective meaning." With her permission, I present one section of the case study in order to exemplify the practical power of Ganma. The "bubbles" are my thoughts.

Exhibit 2.5: Formation of a Village Committee – Collective Research (Heinrichs, 2007)

The communities were clearly frustrated, tired of all the delays and excuses. I couldn't blame them - I was frustrated, too! The reconstruction process, involving the reallocation of land and in some cases, relocation of whole villages had become a long and legally complex issue, fraught with tensions and difficulties. Having either permanently lost their land to the sea or had their land destroyed and damaged, filled with debris and sedimentation and/or infiltrated with salt when the water from the tsunami receded, many required new land in order to rebuild. While the government of Indonesia promised assistance to all those who had lost their house in the tsunami, it did not guarantee access to free land.

Reconstruction was further complicated by Indonesian law, which only recognizes land registered with the National Land Registry (BPN) in Jakarta. However, in Aceh only a small fraction of all land was registered with the BPN before the tsunami. Most land ownership was either in the form of traditional land or communal land, obtained through

inheritance or certified by local authorities. When the earthquake struck, land title records were swept away in the ensuing tsunami. Neither the Indonesian government nor NGOs were willing to build permanent houses until ownership was clarified. To compound the problem, many individuals and communities did not have the funds to purchase new land that was needed for resettlement to replace the lost or unusable land. Although the communities and the government looked to NGOs to fund the purchase of land, in most situations, NGOs they could not due to the legal ramifications. Given this reality, the Indonesian finally determined that financial assistance would be provided by the BRR (Aceh and Nias Rehabilitation and Reconstruction Agency) to assist people to purchase land from the local government in a resettlement site. However, local governments in Aceh did not have the capacity or the resources to acquire land and without any clear policies or guidelines, no real progress had been made. Communities were expected to wait for the BRR to settle their problems, but there was no indication when land would be acquired.

As the field program manager, responsible for implementing the reconstruction and recovery program in partnership with five tsumani-affected communities in Lamno, I did not know what to do next. Although billions of dollars in funds had been pledged, slated for relief and rebuilding aid in Aceh, unless land was secured, houses could not be constructed. Many NGOs had already started to build houses for communities that did not require new land. Seeing these houses constructed while neighbouring communities remained confined to government barracks or tents, resulted in even greater frustration. Instead of everyone benefiting, the reconstruction effort was creating winners and losers. I was emotionally attached to these communities. No longer strangers, I had to do something.

After much discussion and debate, a village committee was formed, comprising of community representatives who would work with the local government (camat and bupati), BRR, and BNP, to facilitate the process of acquiring land for resettlement. Together with local field officers, I offered to facilitate meetings with local authorities and BRR, provide

assistance in recording minutes, writing letters, and transporting members, as well as coordinate with other villages experiencing the same challenges. In this way, rather than wait and rely on the words and decisions of government and experts, the communities themselves could take an active role in the negotiation process of land acquisition and thus, regain control of their lives. Relieved to finally be able to channel our frustrations creatively, we were hopeful that this kind work would be helpful in speeding up the over all process of land acquisition and land titles.

The community's direct involvement and participation in addressing the problem of land acquisition demonstrated a process of collective research, the first of Fals Borda's (1988) techniques for engaging in PAR. Fals Borda (1988) describes collective research as "the use of information collected and systematised on a group basis as a source of data and objective knowledge of facts resulting from meetings, committees, fact-finding trips, etc." (p, 102). Even before the establishment of the village committees for land acquisition in Aceh, community members had already begun a group process of data collection. Together, they had determined how much land they required for resettlement and identified the land most desirable. They had also collected information from the landowners and negotiated a price. In the village, sometimes the landowners were willing to give part of the land as a gift to the members of the village. Other times, if landowners did not want to give the land free of cost, then they would sell the land. Furthermore, the community leaders had taken the initiative to consult with local governmental authorities and held informal meetings to exchange information with each other.

Fals Borda's 4 techniques resulting from the practice of PAR: 1. Collective Research; 2. Critical Recovery of History; 3. Valuing & Applying Folk Culture; and, 4. Production and Diffusion of New Knowledge.

According to Fals Borda (1988), the "group-and-oral" content of this research work, directly related to immediate community usefulness, gives PAR two of its special characteristics, "collectivity" and "informality", which are not found in other methodologies (p. 61). PAR incorporates valuable knowledge acquired from the collective experiences of people and with people, using the same social mechanisms which serve to transmit the culture and basic values of a community, such as story-telling, daily activities, dances, and games. Moreover, Fals Borda (1988) contends that with PAR, these mechanisms achieve another dimension: "they reappear in meetings and assemblies where the same informality and spontaneity of the other events are maintained" (p. 62).

While the communities in Aceh seemed naturally inclined towards a collective research process, it struck me how unusual the notion of collectivity, let alone collective research, is in our culture. Western culture has become increasingly marked by individualism, associated with personal alienation and loss of community and social relevance. Sources of collective support evident in Aceh, such as reciprocities and responsibilities towards others and the Earth, seem to be dissolved here. Rarely do we engage with each other in a dialogical way, in storytelling and collective dance; these activities are deemed too trivial for our busy and important lives. Too often we rush through our days, failing to take the much needed time to listen and learn from each other. I propose that our participation in a mutually respectful process of collective inquiry could help us to re-establish essential inherent connections with each other and our environment, unleashing the collective power necessary to change unjust realities prevalent throughout the world and within our own backyard.

The formation of a village committee, which began to meet on a regular basis to deal with the problem of land acquisition, helped to systemize the information collected. The committees contributed their knowledge of the issues at stake and together we worked to systemize this knowledge, beginning with where the communities were at and moving along with them. The process was based on mutually respectful dialogue and the direct exchange of information collected from everyone. According to

Fals Borda (1988), this collective and dialogical method not only produces data, which may be immediately corrected or verified, but also provides a social validation of objective knowledge. In this way, confirmation is obtained of the positive values of dialogue, discussion, argumentation, and consensus in the objective investigation of social realities. Additionally, people's experiences are affirmed in the search for practical applications of knowledge, and experience essentially becomes a valid way of knowing. This combination of thoughtful reflection on reality corresponding with informed action forms a kind of praxis, "a repetitive, transforming process of reflection-action, action-reflection…[with] spiralling moments of 'think, discover/recover, and do'" (Smith, 1997, p. 186).

When people begin to research their own problems, they begin to feel they have some control over the information and their lives (Lewis, 2001). This type of genuine participation can shift people's inner consciousness. People's ownership of decisions reflects a belief in their capacity for self-direction. Moreover, the results obtained through a PAR process tend to reflect reality more effectively because the participants bring to the research exclusive knowledge and understanding that would not otherwise be available (Fals Borda, 1988). As a result, people begin to value and trust their own experiences rather than the words of leadership or experts. This kind of "countervailing power" was needed when the frustration in Acehnese communities over land acquisition mounted.

Through collective research, people begin to feel a sense of hope, excitement, cooperation, and ownership about the future. As such, the process of collective research enhances people's capacity to decide, act, and potentially transform themselves collectively, strengthening their search for justice and enabling them to exercise their rights with greater effectiveness and power. Though the Acehnese communities with whom we worked were not able to acquire the land they needed for resettlement during my short stay in Aceh, their direct involvement and participation became a step towards empowerment.

Lessons Learned
Exhibit 2.5

**Living with other cultures encourages us to self-examine our own cultural values.

**We do not have time to be in a hurry.

**We commit ourselves and our work to global solidarity for peace and justice.

**Everything we need is near at hand.

**Disciplined, thoughtful hope.

Your Reflections…

....

....

....

....

Learning is a social process where a balance between individuality and collective cooperation can produce meaningful experiences for each person and the community—the power of balance. We see evidence of this power in the exhibits in this part of *Breaking Free*, all drawing from our classrooms, formal research, and informal inquiry. When we slow down and listen—perhaps to the chickadees— we find many empowering stories nearby. We have known this for many years, yet for whatever reason we seem not to register it. Our colleagues at the Université de Montréal during the 1980s engaged creatively and with discipline in "community care" and participatory research, or *solidarités* in French.

> We are witnessing, as one of the paradoxes of our time, the concurrent emergence of a new emphasis on individualistic values and the formation of new forceful solidarities. But the contradiction between the pursuit of individuality and the rebirth of solidarity is more apparent than real. While individualism is often denounced as self-serving, it merits a closer look, as behind such conduct often lies a quest for authenticity, for identity. And as each of us becomes more aware of our own aspirations, values, talents and limitations – in short, our distinctiveness – do we not become more sensitive to those of others? And is it not in this recognition of individual differences as well as common desires that true solidarity takes root? (Alary, 1990, p. 11)

I suggest true solidarity emerges as we break free of narrow individualism and record our stories of individual and collective learning, as we have begun to do in *Breaking Free.* While doing this, we need always to ask ourselves, If we understood the power of individual and collective balance in the 1980s in Québec, where is that understanding now? What forces in the last decade of the twentieth century and the first decade of the twentieth-first have turned us away from this understanding? Have we been silenced? Or have we silenced ourselves? Why?' Without self-inquiry and self-examination, we can scant understand our motives, drivers, and abilities.

Lessons learned in part two. Faculty of Social Work learners and colleagues in the broader community are articulate, curious, and courageous actors. They exist together in a collective exploration of themselves as individuals in mutual relationship with each other, both in the classroom and in the field. While discovering ourselves in the world, we come to listen to others deeply while finding our own voice and hearing the voices of others more clearly than before. In fact, we might not have even been aware of these other voices when we began our journey. We take heart in this discovery and commit ourselves to collective action and solidarity to improve local conditions. We also take heart in knowing our efforts are respected in international scholarly journals. Often hidden by a veil of silence, these local success stories are crucial in the face of the current global economic meltdown and popular grassroots people's movements globally, and these accounts must be heard. Within them lies the resilience needed to sustain our hope, the driving force of PAR and liberatory education.

Part Three

Breaking Free of Silence

We struggle to be heard in a world overflowing with information, a world controlled by agendas counter to liberatory education. Powerfully creative and passionate voices in the liberatory tradition struggle to be heard, drowned out by the din of excessive stimulation. Can you hear them? dian marino (1997) spoke about the language of silence:

> Those who want to understand injustice, or be in solidarity with the silenced, must learn to *listen carefully to the language of silence* (emphasis added). Silent resistance needs to be transformed into stories of resistance. Hidden cracks in our social consent need to be made visible. Personal stories and social histories of resistance and change, the failures no less than the successes, need to be widely shared. Otherwise we are left with the impression that community issues and struggles are born out of nothing—or that only extraordinarily heroic people can get involved and make a difference. (pp. 30-1)

It has been especially important for me to learn the language of the silence we attribute to aboriginal peoples effectively silenced by our universal policies of exclusion and oppression. Sometimes we feel silenced by an inability to find the right words to express ourselves, especially when sharing our spirituality. This is another reason why the "Glossary of Terms" remains open at all times. British action research advocate Peter Reason (1998) reflects on what he calls the "disconnect" between the dominant mechanical paradigm and the realities of practice. "This puts us in a strange situation, almost in a classic double-bind, because we know, deep down, that the official knowledge is breaking down, doesn't represent everyday life, yet we don't know how to comment on it" (p. 43). As a result, we seek new ways other than written language to express our knowledge. Within *Breaking Free*, we are exploring artistic forms of expression in our knowledge-making and incorporating them into our discourse. There is emerging strength and confidence in arts-based and collaborative research methods offering new forms of expression in trans-disciplinary inquiry (Liamputtong & Rumbold, 2008). American management guru Bill Torbert (2004) resorts to alchemy to resolve this emerging world of expressive knowledge.

> The very essence of the Alchemist action-logic is that it cannot be stated as a settled truth in words or numbers but is open instead to new revelation, new shadows, and new wonderment on a continuing basis. The transformation from the Strategist action-logic toward this most elusive and flexible of action-logics is, like all other developmental transformations to a later action-logic, a movement from being *controlled by* something to having a peer *relationship with it*. (p. 189)

Torbert's imagery of "timely and transforming leadership" resembles James Carse's concept of the infinite game. There is reference to the infinite game throughout *Breaking Free*, and it is the focus of Part Seven, *Beginnings: the infinite game*. The timelessness of our life work reflects the very essence of my spirituality, my continuing relationship-making with similar forms of energy of the past, present, and future for the purpose of acting together to transform our realities. As readers of this guide, you are free to express your spirituality as it suits *you*. You might have to recover abilities and sensitivities quietened by the dim noted above.

Have we forgotten how to listen to the language of silence? How can we come to listen deeply? If we are indeed an empathic civilization as Jeremy Rifkin (2009) would have us believe, we must be able to listen to one another as a prerequisite. Are there different kinds of listening? Let's listen in to a social justice experience of dramatic artist Ian Prinsloo, who is contributing creatively to dramatic expression on the margins of society while learning about the creativity of American philosopher Otto Scharmer (2007). While working on his MFA, Prinsloo wrote the script and directed the production of the story of a place called ExCel, a half-way house for young offenders, amongst the most silenced of our citizenry.

Exhibit 3.1: The Infinite Game of Story (Prinsloo, 2008).

In the course of research for plays I regularly interview people: seeking to understand their point of view and motivations so that I can bring that sense of life to a production. On entering into the ExCel research project I thought I was prepared for the conversations and what I would hear. I was mistaken. Looking back, I can understand the reasons why this situation was different from previous interviews. In past interviews the safety net of the play I was creating insulated me from being taken by surprise. There was specific information that I needed, and certain questions I wanted answered. The people I was interviewing knew what I was interested in and the focus of their conversation stayed on those points. In this way there was nothing unexpected about what I was to discover; there were no real surprises or revelations, only confirmation of an established idea. When I began meeting with participants of the ExCel project I had no expectations of what I was seeking. My purpose was to open up a connection with the people I was meeting and to see if I could bring forth their story. I had no idea what I would find once I entered into contact with their way of being. For these reasons, everything I encountered was a surprise and a revelation. In addition I was attempting to engage with the participants using a new listening technique in order to deepen the connection between us. In *Theory U*, Otto Scharmer (2007) describes four types with which people can engage. The first two levels of listen—"downloading" and "factual" (11-12)—are the normal range for most interactions. As someone speaks to us we download our response while they are talking and simply wait to unload it on when they finish speaking. The next level of

listening is to simply identify the new facts that are present within what is being conveyed. Scharmer then outlines two deeper and more significant styles of listening: "empathic" and "generative" (12-13). In empathic listening we move our attention away from ourselves –we stop observing facts that are interesting or new to us - so that we can open our hearts to the living person with whom we are in contact. "If that happens, we feel a profound switch; we forget about our own agenda and begin to see how the world unfolds through someone else's eyes." (Scharmer, 2007, 12) Yet as profound as this shift in our listening can be, generative listening takes us even deeper. In this listening we are seeking to not only connect openly with another person but to also allow for new paths or possibilities to open. "On this level our work focuses on getting our (old) self out of the way in order to open up a space, a clearing that allows for a different presence to manifest." (Scharmer, 2007, 13) By listening at these deeper levels to the stories that expressed the way of being of the participants, the revelations and surprises took me unprepared. At times, what I heard cut deeply into myself. On one occasion I could not get the images out of my mind for days and felt uncomfortable with my family. Heron and Reason (2006) highlight the need for skills in managing distress and developing emotional competence with the members of the inquiry group. "The very process of researching the human condition may stir up anxiety and trigger it into compulsive invasion of the inquiring mind" (150). I was able to reflect on my experiences in the sessions with members of the research team so that the situation did not become overwhelming, but for future projects I see the need to build in more measures for developing and maintaining the emotional lives of all participants, as well as methods for managing distress as an inquiry group throughout the process. The deeper styles of listening that Scharmer describes are absolutely necessary in order to connect to the infinite story that captures each person's way of being. As well the ability to stay consciously naïve is a productive mental space to occupy in the inquiry process. In reflecting over the work I conducted with the participants, I think these two conditions were critical to the success in bringing forth the infinite story. But these abilities can take

their toll on the inquiry participants. This style of investigation requires that all aspects of our selves be available, healthy and strong. Central to that is preparing individuals for the emotional nature of the work and ensuring that the group develops practices by which to sustain itself throughout the inquiry.

Lessons learned
Exhibit 3.1.

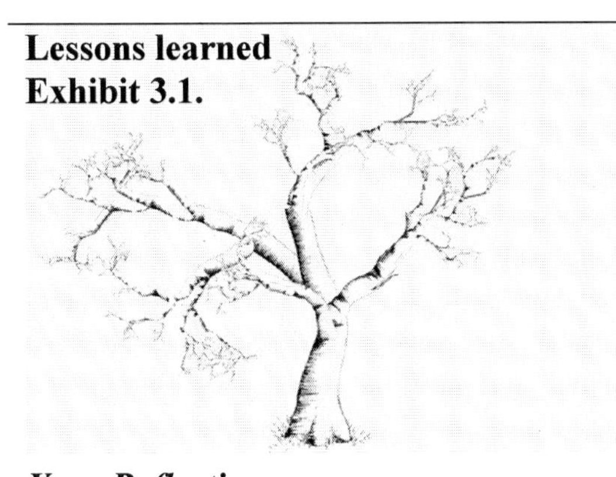

**Deep listening can reveal empowering possibilities.

**Deep listening activates all six strings of the guitar metaphor.

**We don't have time to be in a hurry.

Your Reflections…

....
....
....
....

PAR
is based on
trust

Ian wrote about the processes leading to the presentation of the ExCel story at the Faculty of Social Work Second Annual Social Justice Encounter held at the Calgary campus on 1 May 2008. For further inquiry into the art of listening, see Louise Dunlap's *Undoing the Silence: Six tools for social change writing* (2007). Also, throughout this learning journey while creating your own guide, keep drawing from the rich and deep well in Exhibit 2.1 and from your own experience. If we listen carefully, we begin to hear one another. Reflections taken from Exhibit 2.1 follow:

> "When listening to the presentation on the individual findings of what popular education is, I believe we were

> participating in the essence of popular education. We came together, brought our own perspectives, our own experiences to the group; and some share their own self reflection and passion on issues they desire to create change. I loved listening to everyone's findings as they were so different. This truly helps me realize we all have something different to bring to this class and to this world".

Are you experiencing something similar to these experiences as you carefully craft your own guide?

While reflecting on the democratizing imperative of PAR, MSW learner Erin McFarlane is discovering the latent strength of youth's capacity for understanding life's complexities. Focusing on the intrinsic abilities of youth rather than on perceived limitations of young people too often found in mainstream research, McFarlane contributes to the breaking free of silence imperative. Reproduced below in Exhibit 3.2, this paper was part of her contribution to the emerging guide resulting from my PAR course in 2009.

Exhibit 3.2: Research with Youth (McFarlane, 2009).

In many ways, the following is largely a reflection piece. All papers have a personal side to them, regardless of whether their writers are conscious of this reality. In this case, I am choosing to be particularly explicit in my use of "I." I am expressive about the ways that my own life filters into this paper, and I have opted to discuss feelings I encountered while exploring my selected topic. To begin, I have considerable interest in working with children and youth.[3] This has been a relatively recent development in my life. It was not all that long ago that I still bought into the "dominant media narrative" mentioned by O'Toole (2009, 1) which paints youth as being generally apathetic and in particular, disengaged from political life. Fortunately, I have been

[3] Hereafter, "children and youth" will be subsumed under the general label of "youth."

granted opportunities to work with youth in a variety of different capacities in recent years and have come to view them as potentially powerful agents of social change. Sadly, the wonderful capabilities, ideas, and creativity possessed by youth remain largely unnoticed. The common adage that "children should be seen and not heard" remains current in our culture and this view even extends into the ways youth are treated in research. Inspired by the tremendous work of Candace Lind (2007, 2008), I became interested in exploring the ways youth can engage in Participatory Action Research (PAR). In the following discussion, I will look at a few different examples of PAR projects which have tapped into the potential of youth. To begin, however, I give further consideration to the dominant ways youth are perceived in our culture and contrast these images with some of my personal experiences involving youth. In addition, through my exploration of this topic, I gained a deeper understanding of how different PAR can look from project to project and the troubling way that some of what is being passed off as PAR may not be PAR at all. I will discuss this later on in the paper.

Camino and Zeldin (2002) argue that dominant characterizations of youth focus on "resistance to adult authority, conflict with parents, risky behaviour, identity confusion, and conformity to negative peer influences" (214). It is no secret that our most readily available images of youth are overwhelmingly pessimistic, and ageism towards youth is widespread. Youth are frequently ridiculed by adults and their efforts are often quite simply overlooked.

Unfortunately, youth often internalize these ideas, which can actually result in a self-fulfilling prophecy (O'Toole, 2009). I experienced this first hand growing up. While I was lucky enough to have had a number of supportive adults in my life during my teenage years, I still did not perceive that there were all that many avenues open to me to participate fully in society. As a result, I felt alienated and detached from political life. It was not that I was inherently apathetic; I did have opinions and questions, but I remained unaware of

available spaces where I could genuinely explore these. I always had the sense that I was in some sort of transitory state between childhood and adulthood, and that this state had little meaning in and of itself, other than being en route to the ultimate goal of becoming an adult. The focus was on getting through high school, for it was after high school that "freedom" would occur. This was the general sentiment amongst the people I knew, and I suppose most of us could not wait to be "free" from adult constraint. This is so much of what adolescence currently is in our society; an in-between stage. The vibrancy and energy of youth is wasted in so many ways.

As Camino and Zeldin (2002) perceptively point out, in our culture at least, "youth are marginalized because they are portrayed as *other*, and they continue to be portrayed as other because they are marginalized" (215). This may seem like an impossible cycle to overcome. Luckily, there is reason to be hopeful, if my personal experiences with youth are any indication. I can honestly say that I have been nothing short of amazed by the enthusiasm, dedication, creativity, and insight I have witnessed on a number of occasions over the past few years, in situations where opportunities are provided to youth for them to thrive. I worked for the YMCA this past summer coordinating a program called Kids in Motion. This program involved taking a group of "higher needs" youth, aged 9-12, into the community for part of the day to work on various projects for non-profit organizations and local businesses. The other half of the day involved "fun" activities such as games, arts and crafts, and fieldtrips, which were earned by participating in the community projects. While there was certainly some complaining along the way, I was continually surprised by how seriously many of the youth took their work and the ways they were able to link it to a bigger picture. Some made the most perceptive comments and often remarked on issues and situations which I had not even begun to consider until I was in university. This is something I have experienced on more than one occasion. While volunteering for the 2008

Global Youth Summit, I was struck by the enthusiasm and drive of many of the high school students in attendance at this day-long event which involved participating in workshops conducted by local NGOs, discussing what had been learned, and then creating concrete action plans. Hearing their ideas and some of the things they had already done in their lives was genuinely inspiring. I lost count of the number of times I asked myself, "Why haven't I ever thought of that?" In short, when given a chance, youth are concerned, youth are involved, and youth do dream of a better world.

Adding to the complexity, even survey data suggests that youth are largely uninvolved. However, the most obvious limitation of this sort of research is that it does not consider the ways that youth themselves make meaning of their lives and define "the political." Rather, it imposes on them a traditional and confining view of what being "politically active" means (O'Toole, 2009). Youth will inevitably fare poorly when these sorts of mainstream conceptualizations of the political guide research, since as the discussion so far has suggested, few avenues exist in the mainstream for them to participate in the first place. If one looks beneath these exceedingly limiting surface meanings, however, it turns out that youth *are* involved, albeit in somewhat unconventional ways, which is in line with my personal experiences. When we broaden the meaning of the political, a much different picture emerges. For example, Camino and Zeldin (2002) name "five contemporary pathways of civic engagement" (215) which have gained momentum over the past decade and a half. They are: public policy/consultation, community coalition involvement, youth in organizational decision making, youth organizing and activism, and school-based service learning. I would suggest that PAR could be added to this list. It could be seen as a pathway in itself, or it could serve as the basis for some of the other pathways. In this way, I believe that PAR is able to serve as an extremely effective way for us to move away from the perpetual cycle of negative youth images and

limited space for youth voices to be heard.

It has been a gradual process, but PAR has slowly started to break through the barrier of silence which has characterized the place of youth voices in knowledge creation. This is quite the feat, as according to Lind (2008), "adolescent knowledge may be devalued or ignored by mainstream society, and consequently not shared with others or even recognized as a form of knowledge" (223). It is telling that even given my passion for working with youth, it was not until very recently that I even considered the possibility that youth could be active in PAR; I focused solely on the ways adults could be involved. Apparently, I am still unlearning some of my own previously held assumptions. Luckily, there are researchers who have been doing a wonderful job of engaging youth. In my review of the literature, I was fortunate enough to quite quickly come across a fascinating initiative online known as Voices of Youth in Chicago Education (VOYCE). After exploring the group's website and accompanying report, it became readily apparent that this was one of the strongest examples of PAR I had come across to date.

VOYCE arose in a truly grassroots way, as a result of significant concern by students over the abysmal drop-out rate in Chicago Public Schools; five out of ten students do not graduate (VOYCE, 2008). What emerged was a "youth-led organizing collaborative comprised of students from 7 community organizations and 12 Chicago Public High Schools working in concert with them" (VOYCE project). The group held the primary goals of keeping students in school and increasing college enrolment rates. A year-long study was embarked upon which involved students in every phase. In collaboration with a PAR research consultant and a report consultant, students developed learning questions, created surveys and interview questions, interviewed students, parents, and teachers, conducted site visits at various schools, analyzed data, and finally, compiled and distributed an impressively comprehensive

report of findings and recommendations. Additionally, the group is currently working with Chicago Public Schools to put its recommendations into action in the form of student-led pilot projects. Importantly, VOYCE is committed for the long term. The group recognizes that this is an ongoing endeavour and that student voices need to become entrenched within school reform.

Whether they are aware of it or not, I feel that VOYCE demonstrates Orlando Fals Borda's four techniques quite well. The research is most definitely collective. The group has worked very hard to understand how students define their own realities and the ways in which education can be transformed in order to make it more relevant to the lives of students. This has served as the basis for their recommendations for change. New knowledge has certainly been produced and diffused. The "critical recovery of history" piece may initially seem less apparent, but I would suggest that it is evident in the way that commonly held perceptions of why students drop out of school were refuted during the project. VOYCE (2008) found that "students in Chicago Public Schools have internalized the problem of the dropout rate and believe that they are the ones to blame for the failures of the school system" (7). In other words, students have individualized systemic causes. The hard work of VOYCE has served to re-write these individual and collective understandings. More than anything, I am delighted by the ways that the multiple capacities of the youth working with this project have been enabled to flourish. This reaffirms my belief that PAR can serve as a powerful means for youth engagement.

While VOYCE spoke to me because it seems to be a quintessential PAR project in many ways, two other articles I came across drew me in more due to the way in which they expanded my understanding of PAR processes and the additional questions they incited me to ask. One of these articles was "Participatory Action Research: Creating an effective prevention

curriculum for adolescents in the southwestern US" (Gosin, Dustman, Drapeau, & Harthun, 2003). I was struck by how different the PAR process looked in this instance. This article really had me pondering over what exactly "counts" as PAR. To summarize, the project began as a means to correct the limitations of current school-based drug prevention curriculum. As Gosin et al. (2003) state in their introduction, there is a "need for an implementation process that allows schools to benefit from expert knowledge in addition to community/teacher input" (363). They argue that PAR has the potential to satisfy this need. The result is the *keepin' it REAL* Drug Resistance Strategies (DRS) curriculum. In stark contrast to VOYCE, members of the school community (teachers, students) were *not* involved in all stages of the project design. In fact, they were hardly involved in the design at all. As is pointed out, the experimental design and most of the survey items used were created by the research team. It is exceedingly important to note that a very strict distinction is made in the article between the "community members" and the "research team." Input from community participants was obtained mainly through the use of focus groups for the areas of lesson modifications, evaluations, suggestions for supplemental activities, and the production of instructional videos. In other words, community members were not co-researchers by any means but instead supplied information sought after by the research team. I seriously question the extent to which this project was actually participatory in any meaningful sense. In their defence, the researchers admit to only using *components* of PAR. The question remains, however, of why they elected to indicate in the title of their article that this represents a PAR project. Perhaps what I find most troublesome is the justification provided concerning the question of why community members were not more involved. I would suggest that the attitude of the researchers demonstrated in the following quotation places

them somewhat in opposition to the essence of PAR:

> **Because of the theory-driven experimental design, researchers initiated the full scope of DRS with the intention of partnering with the school community to develop the intervention and to implement the experiment within the schools. Given that adherence to theoretical underpinnings, rigorous methodology and systematic evaluation are essential to effective programming, researchers controlled these functions while simply guiding other phases. While the experimental design and some methodological constraints served to limit school community involvement in some phases, the immersion of the school community, i.e. teachers, principals, middle school students and high school students, was crucial to creation of the curriculum, videos and supplemental materials. In these efforts, participants played a pivotal role; their decisions regarding the instructional materials were adopted, reinforcing the expertise of the students and teachers. (364)**

At its core, PAR seeks to break down barriers between researchers and researched, and yet the researchers here seem determined to maintain a certain distance. I would suggest that at best, this is an example of a diluted form of PAR. The question arose in my mind while exploring this article of "when precisely does PAR stop being PAR?"

One final article of interest is titled "Constructing meaning about violence, school, and community: Participatory Action Research with urban youth (McIntyre, 2000). It presents the experiences of a group of grade six students from "Blair Elementary and Middle School" in the northeastern United States who live within contexts of violence and marginalization. What I found most fascinating about this article was that it provided me with an introduction to what PAR can look like when a considerably younger group of youth is involved. In a similar vein to the article just described, youth were not

used as co-researchers in this project per se. Rather, a "research team" consisting of the primary researcher and a group of graduate students was in charge of the research design. However, this is perhaps understandable given the ages of the youth. Nonetheless, the youth were heavily involved in the direction data collection took. In this way, the process was much more flexible than in the previously described project. A variety of creative techniques were used including collage making, storytelling, symbolic art, and community photography. A significant weakness of this article, however, is that McIntyre remains vague in her description of what constitutes the action piece of the project.

> **In this paper, I present the experiences of a group of young people who live in contexts of violence and marginalization in hopes that educators will pause, listen, and allow the young people's stories to generate new ideas for connecting schools and communities, for evoking critical conversations among educators about how we can better understand the multidimensionality of violence and its impact on young people, and for building bridges to schools and communities that enable urban youth to succeed and thrive. (126-127)**

It is unclear how exactly these bridges will be built or how the findings can contribute to this overall goal. It is also unclear what potential, if any, exists for the youth to become involved in this endeavour.

As I have attempted to convey in this discussion, exploring the literature for this paper has benefited my learning in a few different ways. First, it helped me to gain an introductory understanding of the versatile ways PAR is being used with youth. The VOYCE project in particular provided me with what I had wanted to gain: hope that the creative energies of youth are being put to good use, and that PAR is able to serve as a pathway for youth to affect positive social change. Finally, it allowed me to see that definitions and

interpretations of PAR vary. It is more evident to me now that PAR forever exists in tension with a mainstream, positivistic methodology, and its position is tenuous. As Gosin et al.'s (2003) article demonstrates, components of PAR can be uneasily mixed together with elements of positivism, and inaccurately labelled as PAR. This is something we must always be on the lookout for.

I will end off for now with two quotations from students involved in the VOYCE project which I believe truly encapsulate the benefits of PAR for youth, including the ways it breaks free of the constraints on their individual and collective voices, and the avenues it opens up for participation:

> **I agree that the VOYCE project has had an effect on me and my education. The type of research that we are doing is what college students do and proves that youth are capable of doing great things if adults believe in them. By participating in the project I got a better understanding on how the Chicago Public Schools is working. I learned that it isn't easy to make education reform, but it is not impossible. (VOYCE, 2008, 26)**

> **On a personal note, we learned to communicate with others better and speak our mind. We learned a lot about the real world and to become more open-minded. And the most important thing of all - that if we feel something is important and we do something about it, our actions, our voice, will be heard. (VOYCE, 2008, 26.**

Lessons Learned

Exhibit 3.2

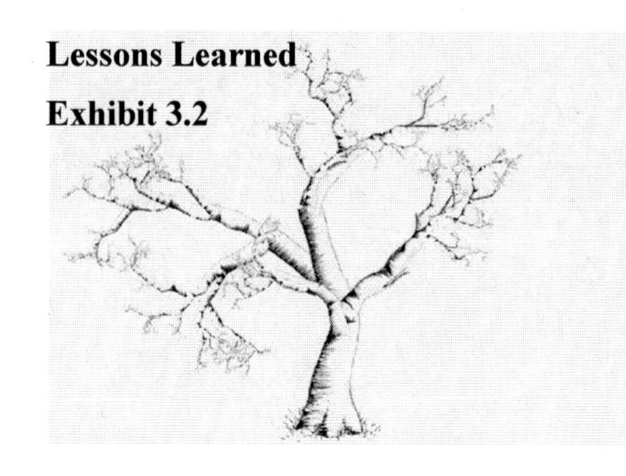

** Knowledge-making is a democratic collective relationship of equals.

** Direct experience provides the foundation for human learning.

**If we listen deeply, we hear strength in ourselves as youth.

**Disciplined, thoughtful hope.

Your Reflections

....

....

....

....

Freedom within the margins. Here we focus on the dignity lying within the people we marginalize so easily, writing them off as people of little worth. Brigette Krieg (2008) devoted her PhD dissertation in Social Work to a critique of the concept of marginalization while engaging in a PAR inquiry into the lives of Aboriginal women in Prince Albert, Saskatchewan. She found marginalization largely a negative concept in the literature, and when she commenced her Photovoice project, that negative concept coloured her initial expectation.

> The bulk of the literature on marginalization has been dedicated to examining marginalization from the perspective of individual and community shortcomings, whereby certain people and communities experience greater opportunity for social and economic adversity. Writing from the perspective of oppression disregards the experiences of those who have demonstrated resilience and resistance in the face of adversity. (p. 41)

As her research evolved, Krieg began finding emancipatory possibilities in the marginal experience of the women. This discovery led to a framework for resistance and social change. The following exhibit contains the concluding section of her dissertation. Like Ian Prinsloo, she learned how to listen more deeply than she had before the research project commenced, and she began hearing new things as she progressed through the research. It takes confidence to recognize our evolving learning as we are crafting knowledge, even during the rigours and strains of doctoral research.

Exhibit 3.3: Freedom within the margins (Krieg, 2008, pp. 170-9)

As social workers, our professional mandate requires we commit ourselves to social justice and social change. This is especially important in Canada where Indigenous clientele dominate. If social workers are going to work effectively with Indigenous peoples, they have to balance their professional values and principles with the values and principles of Indigenous communities. Social work practice, inclusive of emancipatory values and principles, appears to present the necessary connection between theory and practice to successfully work with Indigenous communities. This marriage between emancipatory values and social work practice is as essential to practice as it is to the creation of knowledge intended to guide social work education and practice.

Although the intended outcome of the Photovoice project, Marginalization of Indigenous Women in Canada, was to advance understanding of the concept of marginalization through the perspective and voice of women defined as marginalized, the potential impact of research findings is far-reaching, with significant implications for social work education, practice and research. Adhering to guiding principles of emancipatory research and practice, the outcome of this project creates a different perspective from which to examine the role of the social worker that appears to be in-line with the work of Indigenous scholars and practitioners promoting social work practice which values equity, inclusion, empowerment, and community (Campbell, 2003).

This final chapter examines the Photovoice process and outcome within the literary reflections of Indigenous scholars, promoting emancipatory social work education and practice as an appropriate framework for guiding practitioners who work with

Indigenous communities. Further, Photovoice as an emancipatory research method embedded within the methodological values of participatory action research is advanced as a research process complimentary to Indigenous forms of knowledge creation.

Implications for Social Work Education

In Canada, client demographics in social work practice are primarily Indigenous women and children. In current schools of social work, students are offered training in emancipatory practice which reflects a cross-cultural or culturally-sensitive approach (Sinclair, 2004). A critique of the current approach distinguishes between culturally-sensitive and culturally-appropriate practice (Morrissette et al., 1983). Where culturally-sensitive practice promotes awareness of issues relevant to Indigenous communities within the context of involvement with an ethnic minority, culturally-appropriate services integrate core Indigenous values, beliefs and healing practices into program delivery (Weaver, 1999). Emancipatory social work education and practice that is delivered in a culturally sensitive way, therefore falls victim to complacency, claiming awareness to issues without upholding the primary goal of action and making the personal political. As such, Sinclair (2004) argues:

> Awareness without legitimate action is a cognitive ploy that risks passing for [emancipatory] pedagogy and practice in social work. It contributes to silence and inactivity about tangible issues of racism and oppression in the field of social work and in society. Contemporary [emancipatory] pedagogy does not address the culture of silence because it does not require anything beyond a theoretical grasping is issues. (p. 52)

To this end, the foundation for social work education and practice should be a "decolonizing

pedagogy" in which the educator and student, worker and client, are involved in a "process of healing, learning and developing along a path guided by Aboriginal epistemology" (Sinclair, 2004: 55). Decolonization is a process whereby oppressed peoples and communities regain social, economic, political and cultural self-determination and independence (Verniest, 2003). McKenzie and Morrissette (2002) believe reclaiming cultural identity is the key to the healing process of Indigenous peoples, both individually and collectively.

Reclaiming cultural identity was the backbone of the unique definition of marginalization set forward by the women who participated in this project. However, identity, as defined by the women, was more than cultural claims to heritage; it also involved a process whereby cultural identity and social circumstance were separated, where Indigenous women were not seen as potential victims, but as potential leaders. The women clearly identified the oppressive feelings they associated with practitioners engaged in prescriptive responses to their social circumstances, and alternatively, the sense of empowerment derived from practitioners who sent messages of encouragement.

For the Photovoice photographers, identification as an Indigenous woman emphasized family and community over individual needs. It indicated an alternative perspective from which to base social work education, from a position both culturally-appropriate and culturally-sensitive. That is, future social work education must be inclusive of locally identified issues in the Indigenous community to inform program policy and development steeped in Indigenous values and beliefs.

This can only be achieved in partnership with Indigenous communities through direct dialogue, which promotes collaborative response to locally identified issues. As such, social work education harmonious with Indigenous communities will emphasize more community-based

skills, with practitioners learning more dynamic ways to interact, which are more proactive rather than prescriptive and reactive.

The future of social work education, both appropriate and sensitive to Indigenous communities, lies in community-based interventions and teachings in-line with our professional mandate directing social workers to be "sensitive to cultural and ethnic diversity and strive to end discrimination, oppression, poverty, and other forms of social injustice" through activities such as "direct practice, community organizing, supervision, consultation, administration, advocacy, social and political action, policy development and implementation, education, and research and evaluation" (CASW, 2004).

In dialogue with the women, key values aligned with emancipatory education were identified, suggesting future social work education should be inclusive of teachings emphasizing empowerment through Freirean pedagogy, which holds people experiencing oppression should be active participants in understanding their community issues and should become agents of community change through the process of critical consciousness and sharing of mutual experiences (Freire, 1970; Pennell and Ristock, 1999).

Critical consciousness would involve teaching practitioners to critically evaluate their own role in maintaining oppressive societal structures by learning about issues of power (Williams, 1999) and oppression in the delivery of social work services and in the lives of marginalized and oppressed clients (Pollack, 2004). Examples of power imbalance were evident in the women's dialogue regarding interactions with social work practitioners and the community, limiting the women's interactions with services and service providers.

Essentially, the women's call for more community-based efforts suggests social work education should be directed towards emancipatory teachings. Social work is seen as a profession with the potential to contribute to, or challenge, oppressive societal structures, which are reality for many people. The marriage of emancipatory social work practice to Aboriginal value systems, along several key points, promotes the potential of social work to attend to social justice issues, which challenge inequality and empower communities to create lasting and positive change. Promoting social work education that creates a connection between professional mandate and emancipatory and Indigenous values impacts how education will translate into practice with Indigenous communities.

Implications for Social Work Practice

Social work theory and practice appear to have come full circle for community-based social workers, and this is evident in several commonalities with the outcomes of the Photovoice project. First, community action is striving for social justice and humane treatment across the boundaries of gender and race. Second, we are recognizing, relatively quickly, that approaches characterized by their individualistic nature are ineffective. Therefore, political agendas are calling for responses inclusive of community direction and involvement. Third, women are at the center of social change, at both local and government levels (Mizrahi, 2001).

Emancipatory practitioners believe social work is a professional body with the potential to challenge and transform oppression because of the profession's presence on social, political, and cultural levels (Campbell, 2003). This is apparent in the professional mandate espousing the potential of social work to challenge and transform oppression, through direct work with diverse individuals, groups, and communities and mired in the voices of the women who made direct claims to leadership potential of Indigenous women at local and societal levels. As emancipatory social work practice encourages connections to be made between individual action and social structures, practitioners are trained to critically

evaluate existing differences at individual and societal levels and how these influence each other (Dominelli, 1998).

Such an understanding of social relations and structures forces practitioners to critically examine the socio-cultural group location of both practitioner and client to challenge dominant understandings and structures and how they create and maintain oppressions (Fook, 2002; King-Keenan, 2004). In doing so, practitioners move away from social work practice promoting client stereotypes to "understand the meanings and practices of culture and power within the worker-client relationship" (King-Keenan, 2004: 540) and derive practice activities more inclusive of different interest groups (Fook, 2002). Through dialogue, the photographers made several recommendations for social work practitioners they felt would improve access to services, which appeared to be in-line with emancipatory practice.

Firstly, promoting leadership opportunities among Indigenous women emphasizes the personal as political, thus creating a connection between individual concerns and societal inequality. As such, social work practice with Indigenous communities should not individualize or pathologize personal issues, but view the community or society as failing the individual. The relationship between the social worker and the individual, then, is non-hierarchical as there is an understanding of each person's expertise in their own lived experience. The role of the social worker, then, is to advance this local expertise and incorporate the knowledge shared into critically examining the social, political, and cultural processes which create inequality.

That being said, social work practice reflective of emancipatory values and principles employed with Indigenous communities should incorporate decolonizing methods of practice. Decolonizing social work practice empowers oppressed peoples and communities to regain social, economic, political and

cultural self-determination and independence. By doing so, social work practice challenges power imbalances present in dominant society, in terms of resources, including the monopoly on knowledge creation through research, which informs theory and eventually practice.

Implications for Social Work Research

The theoretical foundation of this method makes Photovoice appropriate for knowledge sharing with individuals and communities who experience marginalization. The connection between the experience of marginalization and the employment of research methods addressing, rather than reinforcing, the status quo in knowledge generation is essential to understanding Photovoice as an emancipatory research method. Research historically conducted *on* rather than *with* oppressed and marginalized populations maintain imbalance, as the knowledge generated through this process is not a shared process, nor does it benefit the community (Dodgsen and Struthers, 2005; Heron and Reason, 2001).

Co-researching with marginalized individuals and communities requires a process inclusive of participation and ownership. The research outcome should be a locally-generated community response to a community issue (Potts and Brown, 2004). The theoretical underpinnings of Photovoice are in-line with emancipatory research. Photovoice is research with a political purpose and commitment to social justice (Potts and Brown, 2004). It recognizes research as a process of resistance, it embraces socially constructed and subjective knowledge, and it involves constant and critical reflection on internal and external power relationships (Kovatch, 2004; Potts and Brown, 2004).

Further, the research principles of ownership, control, access and possession (OCAP) should be promoted to highlight the right to self-determination through the stages of

research -- "ownership" of the research process and products; "control" of the research process itself; full "access" to and use of research information; and "possession" of the findings of the research and determination of the use of results (Ermine et al., 2001). Photovoice attends to all principles of OCAP.

Essential to the theoretical underpinnings of the Photovoice process is the ownership of the project and its outcome by the photographers. Photovoice aims at giving voice to marginalized populations in political arenas, who become the catalysts for political and societal change, creating images to challenge dominant opinion (McIntyre, 2003; Strack et al., 2004; Wang and Burris, 1997; Wang, 1999; Wang and Redwood-Jones, 2001). This means the presentation and voices behind the images are those of the women who dedicated their time to exploring and understanding the issues and effects of marginalization (McIntyre, 2003; Strack et al., 2004; Wang and Burris, 1997; Wang, 1999; Wang and Redwood-Jones, 2001).

Lessons Learned Along the Way

Perhaps one of the most essential benefits of the Photovoice process is that it has the ability to stimulate discussion and motivation for social action at the community level. Photovoice can be an effective means of shifting the power balance, encouraging local people to become advocates in their own reality by organizing community members to prioritize their concerns and discuss problems and solutions (Wang and Burris, 1997).

In this project the primary presenters were the photographers who shared their photos during community displays and led discussions about the issues related to poverty. The strength of the individual presenters and the group as a whole was apparent; demonstrating the potential to empower co-researchers through enhanced self-esteem and increased political efficacy during the Photovoice process (Wang,

1999). Photovoice values the knowledge shared by its co-researchers as a vital source of expertise. This source of expertise shared through the Photovoice process helped the Photographers to document their community resources and strengths (McIntyre, 2003). Through the power of visual image, Photovoice enabled the co-researchers to share powerful stories about their community's strengths and limitations.

Further, the project was not done through a pathologizing lens, presenting the community as deficient but as one of strength with the capacity to take action. In this, Photovoice was helpful in documenting the successes and failures of community activities and interventions. This allowed the photographers the opportunity to assess policy and program strengths and weaknesses and back this up with evidence from their views on how these policies and programs had or had not benefited them (Wang, 1999).

Outside of concerns of academic merit was the incredible potential of Photovoice to create opportunity for individual growth and transformation. In being given the opportunity to have their voices heard, the co-researchers and researcher alike found the confidence to locate their voices regarding issues that impacted their well-being. The experience of being part of the Photovoice process was one of tremendous growth for all involved. In being part of the Photovoice process, we became friends and comrades working towards a shared goal. We recognized the individual strengths each possessed and worked together to create a living, breathing work of art to be shared with others.

Summary

The potential of Photovoice to understand issues of marginalization in Canada is just beginning to be realized. Using Photovoice to understand marginalization will demonstrate that local knowledge and abilities can affect necessary change at all levels. It emphasizes community involvement and ownership, where the end

result of the process is not simply for knowledge generation, but also to develop a community response to a community issue. The theoretical foundation for Photovoice is echoed in the emancipatory research traditions emphasizing the inclusion of community voice in its decision-making process. Further, the goal of Photovoice in placing local knowledge in the forefront of the process of action and critical reflection upholds the position that all voices in the community are important.

Lessons Learned
Exhibit 3.3

**Emancipatory practice demands immediate and practical action.

**Education is most meaningful if grounded in local conditions and culture.

**Photovoice is an effective method for stimulating community-based action.

**Integrity and dignity lie within the margins of society.

Your Reflections…

....
....
....
....
....

PAR builds self-awareness

Here again, the 2008 Popular Education and Social Justice class intuitively understood the latent power on the margins. In the words of one student,

> "I find the more I listen to others discuss their understanding of popular education, the more I scratch my head in worry. Let's hope my grasp on Popular Education is budding under the surface of the soil. I do feel confident in knowing that no matter what cause draws us in and motivates our action, it cannot thrive in isolation...Dignity can be found in one's marginalization. The mutual respect and understanding that comes alongside dignity helps lead and encourage self-worth. Fear is a perspective which can be managed, coped with, and stood up to in order to bring about change. Rather than trying to overcome it, we can use our fear and turn it into fuel rather than keep it as a barrier... Why is it that our fear is so often at the front of our minds? Do we only feel this when challenged? Do we only recognize how common it is from person to person when we compile and share our thoughts? This classmate's thought said it best, 'If you let your fears plant their roots in you, you defeat yourself before you even set out on your journey'. I am glad experiencing fear and letting fear take root are not the same thing". (Extracted from Exhibit 2.1)

These words reflect a deep understanding of the dignity to be found in the margins, enabling people not to fear the fear they have. It might help to recall the wisdom of the five friends and the five enemies noted in Exhibit 2.1:

> If fear is your friend, you see clearly, and you share power, and you have wisdom, then you will meet old age. But if you sit, doing nothing and denying your history, then old age will be your enemy. If, however,

you meet old age with grace, having met fear, seeing with clarity, sharing power, and making wisdom your friend, then you will live forever.

Brigette Krieg's research process relied on a circle metaphor to create a place of safety so the women who were her co-researchers felt comfortable to express themselves freely and safely. The "talking circle" is central to Aboriginal traditions of knowledge-making and individual healing. In her doctoral dissertation in Social Work, Sharon Big Plume explained at length the protocols and processes of a talking circle in her exploration of the concept of warrior for the practice of social justice work.

Exhibit 3.4: The power of the circle (Big Plume, 2007, pp. 90-4)

The circle is a sacred and important symbol in many Aboriginal cultures. Many things in nature are round, such as human beings, rocks, the sun, and the moon. The circle is also symbolic of circular life cycles found in all of creation, such as the seasons or the course of human being's existence. For this reason, many Aboriginal ceremonies are conducted in a circle to represent connection to creation as well as to immerse participants in the powerful, circular patterns of the universe. Both the power of the creator and transformational power may work best when connected to other souls such as occurs in Aboriginal ceremonies, talking circles included. Learning to access and share this place of power and love as often as possible, and certainly when it is most needed, is part of the Warrior way of life.

A talking circle might be seen as a kind of traditional focus group and there are indeed some commonalities, such as a group of people working together on a certain topic; but there are also some important differences. In my experience, talking circles take the participants to a place of intense love and joy – the centre of the universe – where one is, in effect,

wrapped up and filled with the Creative Power found in every living thing. This is essentially the holy place where the people live and where Warriors acquire their strength.

Talking circles are places for human beings to share and speak about their experiences, joys or struggles, and are also places to learn and listen to life lessons others have been learning. Talking circles can be conducted in several ways depending on the need and the task at hand. Some talking circles may be private for a particular set of participants, but more often than not, all people are welcome to participate. There can be any number of participants, but smaller groups can have some advantages in that some may feel more comfortable sharing in a smaller group. Many talking circles are intended for healing, while others may be intended to focus on a given topic, as was the case for the talking circle in this study.

Generally, but not always, Elders or Medicine People act as facilitators for the talking circle. Facilitators explain the process to participants, including the need to respect one another's confidentiality. The proceedings usually begin with prayers and smudging, which help to calm and slow things down. Smudging consists of burning sweet grass, buffalo grass (sage), cedar, or some other kind of material used for this purpose. As the smudge burns and is passed around, participants symbolically wash and bless themselves with the smoke. Smudging acts to purify the people as well as the space, and acts to protect participants from any negativity. Smoke from the smudge is believed to carry prayers upwards to Creator. Like all ceremonies, talking circles are to be approached with a good heart, clear mind and clean hands, i.e. the right intentions.

Participants sit in a circle, facing each other, and are free to say whatever they need to say. Everyone can express themselves, though they are not required to do so if they choose not to; but if they do share, each person is allowed to speak without interruption until they are

completely finished saying whatever they wish to say. Participants take turns speaking and an object, such as an eagle feather, rock or talking stick may be passed from one speaker to another, which they hold while they speak. In my experience, speakers usually go in order from the ceremonialist to the left, clockwise, the way the sun moves; although at other circles, speakers may pick up the object or share in any order whenever there is an opening, and they have something to say.

When people are not sharing, they are asked to be actively listening in acceptance and respect, with no criticisms or adjustments either spoken aloud or in thoughts. There is no fixed time limit for talking circles; they are finished whenever they are finished, meaning after everyone has said all they wish to say. Participants are asked at the beginning not to leave until the proceedings are finished because it is important for everyone present not to break the circle. A closing prayer is usually said and may also include smudging. Afterwards, participants may hug or shake hands, but it is important to acknowledge everyone in the room in some way.

Talking circles are very powerful experiences. Typically, when people are sharing, their level of honesty is remarkably deep and may be very intense. There can be many tears and there may also be much laughter. Accountability in a talking circle is almost unavoidable because honesty and courage demonstrated by one individual can often stir and motivate others to do likewise. In truth, even though talking circles take place in a group setting, people are really speaking with their Creator and not necessarily with other participants; although something said by an individual may trigger or inspire different thoughts in others. Taking part in a talking circle is an incredibly powerful and important experience hard to describe. Somewhere during a talking circle, a shift occurs and the circle seems to take on a life and force of its own. This is the transformational power of the circle…

Despite its decidedly therapeutic aspects, taking part in a talking circle is different from taking part in a therapy group in its design, intent, results and the way it feels, both during and after the event, possibly because of its focus on speaking to the Creator, with the presence and assistance of the Grandmothers and the Grandfathers (the Spirits) who have been invited in and asked to help. Honesty and strong bonds are promoted among the participants as a result of the shared experiences, as well as shared tears and laughter. Participants become closer and stronger together. Talking circles advance, reinforce, and demonstrate that "we are all one."

After first connecting with the sacred energy that is always present, individuals can more easily see and feel how all living beings are connected to that same sacred energy, and hence how all living things are connected to each other. Committed individuals who can feel and see their connections to one another may be more likely to have a sense of kinship, union, belonging and relationship. This inspires devotion and strengthens commitment, which is one necessary part of the Warrior way of life. In this way, talking circles make strong Medicine for the community.

Lessons Learned
Exhibit 3.4

**Circles can be the site of powerful learning.

**Circles insist we listen carefully and quietly to one another and to our own thoughts.

**Circles have their own protocols and integrity.

**We don't have time to be in hurry.

Your Reflections…

PAR
demands time

On historical inquiry. In unfolding the liberatory tradition in the adult education movement, my purpose is to encourage us at present to attend to the fundamental human need for freedom. How do we celebrate this fundamental human need? We can do so by breaking free of the inhibiting satisfiers of freedom like paternalism, overprotective family, and authoritarian classrooms (Max Neef, 1991). In historical research, inhibitors of freedom include an ingrained belief that certain evidence is more credible than others. For example, government documents and legal records are prized above stories and legends of the people. It is only recently that "history from below"—another aspect of the democratic ideal of acknowledging the worth of all citizens—has been accepted as legitimate inquiry in historiography (Hobsbawm, 1985).

> Whatever its origins and initial difficulties, grassroots history has now taken off. And in looking back upon the history of ordinary people, we are not merely trying to give it a retrospective political significance which it did not always have; we are trying more generally to explore an unknown dimension of the past. (p. 65)

According to British historian Eric Hobsbawm (1985), in order to understand the present we must understand the past. Moreover, he argues, "understanding how the past has turned into the present helps us understand the present, and presumably something of the future" (p. 73). We have to demonstrate an understanding of present conditions and trends related to the need for freedom in order to explore the past while preparing for the future.

Engaging in historical interpretation democratically is explicit in PAR. "Critical recovery of history" is one of four techniques articulated by Fals Borda (1988), resulting from many years working with colleagues in Colombia, Nicaragua, and Mexico. Their work was inspired by Freire's notion of conscientization, the English form of *conscientização* roughly translated from Portuguese as consciousness-raising—that included the opportunity for common people to create their own individual histories. One of the amazing examples of the power of people's memory is Fals Borda's (1979-86) "double" history of his home province in Colombia. It is a double history in the sense that it comprises two versions of the past. On the left side of each volume is the "people's version" that tells the story using the folklore collected by Fals Borda during many years of talking with *campesinos* (peasants). On the right side, carefully documented according to the rules of historiography, is the "official version." Fals Borda's history has been acknowledged as a major contribution to Colombian scholarship in a collection of essays analyzing his life's work published by the Colombian Sociological Association (Catano et.al., 1987). It had taken years of research to prove the existence of and the enormous value of people's knowledge so often ignored or devalued by expert knowledge. One example he provided was about a certain president that the *campesinos* remembered, but the alleged president had not appeared in any available history books. He investigated and indeed found the missing president, apparently left out of official history because he was mulatto. Room had to be found in the portrait gallery of Colombian presidents in the National Assembly in Bogotá to fit the dark face into the white crowd (Pyrch, 1996).

Making meaning helps in finding our own voices. We have been inspired since the early 1970s by the thoughts and actions of the Brazilian Paulo Freire, whose experiences in his home country and elsewhere in the Global South showed us how to help people trapped in silence imposed by colonialism and neo-colonialism (Freire, 1970, 1994). By looking at the world through their own eyes, by naming the world in their own words, learners shift from a naïve consciousness to a critical consciousness. Learners can cease being "objects of social history" and becoming "subjects of their own destiny." At this point, it is important for Canadians to mention Father Moses Coady's *Masters of Their Own Destiny* (1939), a classic statement of innovative community adult education for social and economic justice growing out of severe economic depression in Atlantic Canada. Coady and the priests of Antigonish, Nova Scotia, drew the economically depressed people back to their roots to find their resilience. Although the priests were committed to facilitate gradual social reform and Paulo Freire was more radically inclined in terms of socio-economic change, their practice of liberatory adult education was similar to Freire's in its empowering possibility. Recalling the Ganma rivers, blending Freire and Coady, Brazilian and Canadian, 1960s inquiry with 1930s hopes, is helping create the foam-like quality of *Breaking Free*.

Metaphors abound in all my courses. I rely on the "Tree of Life" exercise to encourage everyone in the class to share their lives deeply in a celebration of our richness. The exercise is a simple introduction to "history from below," and the instructions are minimal.

Tree of Life

Roots represent our own roots:

- The family from which we came,
- Strong influences which have shaped us into the person we are now, and
- Traditions.

The trunk and branches represent the structure of our life today:

- Job,
- Family, and
- Organizations, communities, or movements to which we belong.

Leaves represent our sources of information:

- Newspapers,
- Radio, TV, Internet, and

other electronic sources,

- Books, and
- People.

Fruits represent our achievements:

- Projects we have organized,
- Programs in which have taken part,
- Groups we have started or organized, and
- Materials we have produced.

Buds represent our hopes for the future.

I encourage readers to pause for a few minutes and list out attributes of your own Tree of Life...
....
....
....

In all my courses, we present our trees to each other during class with a clear understanding of the importance of roots. A PAR class (See Exhibit 2.2) explained the tree exercise to the readers of *Educational Action Research* as follows:

> We shared our "Tree of Life" on coloured paper with pastels and crayons when it seemed our number was settled: roots, our origins; trunk and branches, how our life is structured; leaves, our sources of information; flowers, our accomplishments; and buds, our hopes and dreams (Hope & Timmel, 1984, vol. 2, p. 36). Metaphorically, each of us dropped a seed from the fruits of our past experiences and knowledge. We planted our seeds and came together to nurture what we sowed as a collective throughout our classes. Rooted in our rich personal histories and enriched by our diverse cultures, we came together co-creating, re-covering, and re-creating knowledge. Our seeds began to sprout into a tree of shared experiences and unified voices, forming the trunk. Chickadees began appearing on some

> branches. As we continued to come together and share on a weekly basis, the trunk supported the development of branches. Our journals and conversations in class allowed us to develop strong branches, which in turn grew in various directions. It became apparent through our shared words and common thoughts that our branches were actually intertwined, growing in a common direction. We became united like a great Banyan Tree, one group with many far-flung roots. In a gentle manner, the tree eased us into the critical recovery of our own histories. This is in keeping with Fals Borda's (1988) insistence that we must acquire language and imagery to convey our meanings to all levels of literacy. The trees appeared on a wall each class as if to remind us of our rich diversity and evolving relationships. A forest appeared. We drew from many forms of expression, multi-media displays, to create our safe place. (Beatty et al, 2008, pp. 337-8)

Reflecting on our roots encouraged us to share our own histories in a playfully respectful yet demanding way as we came to acknowledge our own collective "history from below." Sharing individual trees and placing them in the classroom created a sense of collective identity, a forest of selves. The forest remained visible throughout the course and became a metaphor of the interconnectedness of life in its holistic strength.

Recovering our own stories is a way of countering the hegemonic intentions of the modern nation state which have grown enormously after 9/11 as the War on Terror led to growth of the surveillance industry, which continues to thrive globally as well as locally. Who benefits from such scrutiny? In his critique of the modern nation state, James Scott (1998) argues that many forms of "high modernism" have replaced a valuable collaboration between practical skills and formal knowledge with

> …an "imperial" scientific view, which dismisses practical knowledge as insignificant at best and as dangerous superstitions at worst. The relation between scientific knowledge and practical knowledge is part of a political struggle for institutional hegemony by experts and their institutions. Taylorism and scientific agriculture are, on this reading, not just strategies of production, but also strategies of control and appropriation. (p. 311)

Our liberatory tradition connects us with earlier times and earlier forms of resistance. German educator Max Stirner wrote about the concept of "ownership of self" during his critique of all forms of education in the mid-1800s. His influence on contemporary times is acknowledged by liberatory educator Joel Spring.

> The real source of power in a society was the institution which owned the inner life of the individual. In the past the church fulfilled the mission of guiding and dominating the mind. In the world of the nineteenth century the dominating influence was becoming the politics of the state. Religion and politics gained power by their ability to establish imperatives directing the actions of the individual. Stirner wrote, "Under religion and politics man finds himself at the standpoint of *should*: he should become this and that, should be so and so. With this postulate, this commandment, every one steps not only in front of another but also in front of himself."
>
> The power of the modern state lay in its recognition of the importance of domination of the mind. In the modern state, laws were internalized within

> the individual, so that “freedom” merely meant the freedom to obey the laws that one had been taught to believe. It was the dream of the nineteenth-century schoolmasters to end disobedience through the internalization of law in the public schools. (Spring, 1975, pp. 39-40)

Technology has given the modern nation state many more tools of control just as 9/11 gave the state another reason to silence opposition to its control—the American Patriot Act. Who benefits? Who doesn’t? Should we care? Are we on a similar path in Canada?

At the same time, there are technologies enabling us to express ourselves in colourful, multitudinous ways while engaging in rigorous discourse countering the hegemony often established through technology. Twyla Mudry in Part One of *Breaking Free* demonstrated the power of dance while Barbara Ehrenreich (2006) sketches the history of dancing as a meaningful form of expression for all citizens commencing in the early Christian church. In his personal guide for practising popular education, BSW learner Tyler MacPherson included a section on “rebel music.”

Exhibit 3.5: Rebel Music (MacPherson, 2009)

The following will concentrate on certain types of rebel music, which were born out of a repressed state, to express the revolt of the people contrary to dominant societal values and ideologies. The music of Rock and Roll, Punk Rock and Hip Hop immersed from traditions of underground rebellion, mainly through people who were disempowered politically, socially, and economically. All three types of music mentioned were later converted into the mainstream and utilized for popularity, status and

monetary value (which went against the grain of what the intentions of the music stand for, but exemplifies how the power of authority and the structure in place can annex even contradictory forms of art and music for the purpose of the dominant value system). The rebelliousness and freedom against oppression still stands true in much of the underground forms of the music today. The following paper will examine the origins of Rock and Roll, Punk Rock and Hip Hop as expressions of the struggles to freedom against the oppressive societal structures of control over the people. It will also discuss how the oppressive structures worked to maintain control over the music (but were unable, in the end, to capture the true essence of the music, but rather an approximation of what the music meant to the dominant culture when used as a part of the mainstream).

Rock and roll is a type of music of rebellion posed against oppressive authority, which originated from African slaves who were brought to the United States by British colonists. Of the approximate 40,000,000 slaves transported to America over many years, it is estimated that only 1,500,000 survived the trip across the Atlantic Ocean, as living conditions were so poor (abuse, murder, dehydration, asphyxia, and disease etcetera). The enslavement of African people, and the metaphoric and literal enslavement and silencing of all people has been a tradition of colonists throughout time to decide what is right for others by exploiting people for the benefit of those with power. The Africans brought with them some musical instruments, such as Senegambian barafoo drums, flutes, and some precursors to the American Blues guitars (African bowed lutes, two-stringed plucked lutes and monochord zithers). As the slaves worked, many sang to lift up the hopes of the people against such horrific oppression. The only songs allowed by slave masters

were work songs. Sacred spiritual songs and African drumming were banned as the masters felt that such music may conjure up revolution (they were correct). As Christianity was forced upon the slaves, many slaves used it as their own way to sing spiritually (even though it was forced upon them). The spirituals expressed the powerlessness and the despair of the people.

The cotton fields were the birthplace of the music entitled "The Blues." The Blues encompassed elements from the spirituals and from the secular work songs. "Oftentimes, Blues songs voiced agnostic feelings towards an afterlife, which was a rebellion against the Christian spirituals that many slaves had adopted as their own." The monochord zither, which used the slider technique prevalent in Blues, was transformed into a western-style, one string guitar called a Bo Diddley (with a Whiskey bottle neck as a slider). Later the steel string acoustic guitar became the main foundation of The Blues. The Blues was seen as the devil's music by the whites in power, as it often was depicted as against white, Christian values. It is a type of music of relative physical simplicity, but grandiose profoundness and depth simultaneously (similar to early Punk and Hip Hop). With artists such as Howlin' Wolf, Ma Rainey, Bessie Smith, Robert Johnson (of the Mississippi Delta Blues), the music began to move towards the use of the electric guitar (and a shift towards Rhythm and Blues <Rock and Roll> began).

In the early stages of Rock and Roll, the government, religious and education spokesmen alike felt that Rock and Roll was immoral, sinful, and turned the listeners into juvenile delinquents. Musicians Chuck Berry, Fats Domino, and Little Richard were instigators of the music which was reportedly turning people's children into improper deviants (and un-American). However when Elvis Presley began his Rock and Roll career, there were changes made in the perception of Rock and

Roll. As a white man (and good to his mama) had taken on the role of the King of Rock and Roll, the dominant view of Rock became more mainstream and eventually became more of a tool of big-business capitalism and record sales.

Punk Rock arose from the tradition of Rock and Roll unofficially in the late 1960s, early 1970s (officially around 1976, to the mainstream). It came from the sentiment of misfits rebelling against the system and authority (some incorporating anarchy into their way of living). Crypt Records in the 1960s signed many raw, unpolished garage bands, with a harder, heavier sound which expressed feelings of being proud to be misfits and failures in the prevailing system of oppression. Iggy and the Stooges worked with the same idea in the early 1970s (with influences such as The Velvet Underground), with their Album "Raw Power." To paraphrase Iggy Pop: when The Stooges started playing college venues, the kids therein did not understand the complexity of their music. To oversimplify and over-generalize, I believe that may have been partially due to the mass majority of kids in college at the time (who may not have experienced the feelings of failure and exclusion to such as extent as was the connection to Punk Rock association). The New York Dolls continued the hard, kick-in-the-face music, with the complimentary use of cross-dressing. The Misfits, The Ramones, The Clash (bringing more political standpoints) all raged against the machine, by speaking out against injustices, poverty, authoritarian corruptness, and against the volatility of mainstream (record sale prioritized) music. Punk Rock was a lifestyle of living freely against the system. It was about kids who came from rough streets and poor areas, with poor quality equipment and a D.I.Y (do it yourself) mentality to recording and producing (so as not to have to deal with major labels, and to have full creative control and independence).

Punk Rock in its true forms exists in many present day garage bands, however much of the genre (like that of Rock and Roll) was annexed by the corporate design (and made for radio) with pop punk bands like Blink 182, and Sum 41.

Hip Hop music (rap, break dance, DJ turn-tablism music) originated in the 1970s, from the Bronx in New York with originators such as Kool Herc. Kool Herc claimed to have taken the idea of improvised poetry over a musical background from Jamaican traditions he had experienced in his youth in Jamaica. Kurtis Blow, Run DMC, Public Enemy, Grand Master Flash and The Beastie Boys (who were initially a Hardcore Punk band from Brooklyn) were a few groups that originated the genre. The music was another profoundly deep and completely unique and moving style of music, with some simplistic elements, such as a beat, a hook, and a rapper (or several rappers). With the evolution of the spoken word of hip hop, lyrics became complex and intricate (my personal suggestion would be to hear groups like Blackalicious and K'naan (Canadian refugee from Somalia), as well as the amazing groups listed above) and the evolution of turn-tablism created insanely complicated "scratching" techniques on records and "beat juggling" and "beat boxing." DJs and MCs began a whole new style of instruments and music making which spoke of hope, despair, and the desperate living situations in slums (mostly populated by black and Latin American populations in the U.S.A.). Hip Hop is a new fight against oppression from a subjugated, disempowered people. Much of rap music in the mainstream has been used to market cars, brand names, exploit women, and prioritize record sales.

Rock and Roll, Punk Rock and Hip Hop are a few types of recent musical genres which expressed the feelings of disempowered, oppressed people, rebelling against the system in place. As each genre gained popularity among the people, large portions of the genres were assimilated into

the mainstream to become simply another extension of the system of power and control in place. However the real Rock, Punk, and Hip Hop still exist and can never be fully dissolved into the system, because they hold ideologies of resistance and rebellion which will always hold true for people who wish to creatively explore them.

Lessons Learned

Exhibit 3.5

**The soul of a people can be found in their music.

**Resistance to oppression resides in the sounds, words, and presentation of music.

Your Reflections…

…………………………………………………………………

…………………………………………………………………

…………………………………………………………………

…………………………………………………………………

…………………………………………………………………

"Rebel music" forms a part of James Scott's (1990) arts of resistance whereby enslaved peoples throughout time have been remarkably creative and agile in retaining dignity, reflected in their music despite their enslavement. "Bread and roses too" was a restorative banner to the Industrial Workers of the World and captured beautifully in the music of the Wobbly bard Joe Hill[4]. Modern folk music grew out of the despair of the Great Depression of the 1930s, a process currently being revived in the hope for better times during our contemporary upheavals. This musical legacy is an integral part of radical adult education traditions located in the hills of Tennessee where we now venture.

---

[4] www.iww.org

Homage to Highlander. My classes get a chance to meet on film the "Radical Hillbilly," Myles Horton, one of the founders of the Highlander Folk School. In its radical best, adult education has been living at Highlander in Tennessee since its founding in 1932. The Highlander magic strongly influenced an early book on Canadian and American participatory research, *Voices of Change*, and three of its chapters come from Appalachia (Park, Brydon-Miller, Hall & Jackson, 1993). Unlike the Cornell University led *Participatory Action Research* published in 1991, *Voices of Change*, in focusing on "participatory research," clearly falls within the PAR traditions I privilege in this guide. *Voices of Change* draws richly from the Global South and from Aboriginal experiences while blending them, in the spirit of the Ganma rivers, with similar stories from Canada and the US.

Albertans have benefited from the Highlander tradition in numerous ways over the years; two contributions will be noted here. We invited three community activists from Highlander to the PAR Congress in 1989. Their personal strength and commitment in their stories was matched by strategic shrewdness in combating environmental degradation throughout Appalachia in the eastern United States. In a way, this was not new to us since there is a substantial literature about their work spanning seventy-five years. What I had not clearly realized before was the holistic trans-disciplinary understanding of the Highlanders, firmly founded on traditional ways of knowing of the Appalachian mountaineers. One of the presenters explained their purpose as always "to provide an educational centre in the South for the training of rural and industrial leaders and for the conservation and enrichment of the indigenous values of the mountains." Indigenous values of the mountains resemble the Aboriginal values celebrated by Big Plume and Krieg. Another member of the audience at the Highlander presentation picked up on these concepts and made them central to his focus on spirituality. According to Leroy Littlebear, Blood elder and a professor at the University of Lethbridge,

> What we mean by spirituality is not necessarily anything to do with church or beliefs and so on, as much as it has to do with the whole notion of people togetherness. Secondly, spirituality has to do with a holistic view. A holistic view implies respect for nature very similar to indigenous people's belief about everything being related. In some ways, we can look at PAR as a spiritual movement if we go by our definition as togetherness and a holistic view. Everything has a spirit in it . . . environmental movements can be seen as true respect for nature and can be seen as a spiritual movement. . . Highlander is a spiritual movement . . . All this includes a growth in knowledge . . . Spirituality breaks down boundaries between us. In some ways, we can look at PAR as a spiritual movement if we go by our definition as togetherness and a holistic view. (Notes from Pyrch's learning journal)

Littlebear's words, strongly resembling Ganma thus warranting the watermark, help me make some connections for myself. I had read a good deal about Highlander and actually had the opportunity to meet Myles Horton on one occasion. Nevertheless, it had never been as clear to me before our Congress that Highlander had survived various attacks, moving from championing one constituency to another while continuing to serve the oppressed first and foremost. Highlander had done all of this out of strong faith—a commitment to participation, openness and simple democracy.

PAR encompasses spirituality

Highlander passion impacted another event in Alberta. The first general assembly of the North American Alliance for Popular and Adult Education (NAAPAE) gathered at a rustic guest ranch near the town of Rocky Mountain House north of Calgary in 1994. The Alliance was formed in 1993 by representatives of thirty-five popular and adult education organizations originating throughout Canada and the United States.

By the time of the first assembly, representatives from Mexico had joined the fray, thus making the alliance more representative of the North American continent. American, Canadian, and Mexican colleagues, comrades, and *compañeros* came to my home province to witness an event largely organized by a group of Calgary volunteers. The Alliance chose us for the privilege because of our track record organizing numerous workshops and smaller conferences on PAR-related topics in the years after the Calgary Congress of 1989.

There is a published record of the conference (NAAPAE, 1994) containing outlines of the many workshops and meetings on various issues typical of a gathering of adult educators concerned with social justice. Those present, borrowing from the *educación popular* tradition in Latin America, refer to us more often than not as popular educators as well as adult educators. According to NAAPAE's co-ordinator, María Elina Dufau-Kramarz (1994),

> Registrants at the First General Assembly included 170 popular and adult educators who work in a variety of sectors. These are: anti-racist groups; grassroots organizations; university related groups; First Nations and Native Americans; youth; gay and lesbians; women; people of colour; environmentalists; labour educators and farmers. The 112 women and 58 men present was representative of all these groups. The overriding tone of the Assembly was participation, openness and true democracy. (p. 3)

These ideals inspired some creative organizational decisions such as the division of the continent into five political entities for purposes of representation on the co-ordinating committee: Indigenous/First Nations, Mexico, Québec and Francophones outside Québec, the rest of Canada, and the USA. The then current reality of an imminent withdrawal of Québec from the Canadian confederation was reflected in these entities. Part of the reasoning in separatist Québec was a perceived neglect of French cultural values in the Canadian confederation. As with Indigenous/First Nations peoples, NAAPAE seemed to be focusing on urgent social ills. Moreover, seeing the United States boasting the same representation as Indigenous peoples suggested the Alliance was focusing on a unique balance of interests and general rights. Listening to Mexican concerns expressed by activists from Chiapas where rebellion had been underway for several months put us into direct contact with realities facing some of our *compañeros*. We were in touch with major world trends and tensions. The unique balance of interests reflected in the five political entities in NAAPAE resembled Murray Bookchin's (1989) "equality of unequals," a maxim forming the foundations for his ideal of freedom.

Dufau-Kramarz suggested another reason for choosing Alberta as the site of the Assembly, writing,

> The theme of the assembly was: "Resistance and Transformation: Popular Education —challenging the new global economy." Alberta seems aptly chosen for the assembly as Premier Ralph Klein's neo-conservative "slash and burn" approach to fiscal efficiency reverberated in and out of our discussions on workers' struggles in many sectors of North American Society. (NAAPAE, p. 3)

My home province was engaging in practices I have seen and criticised in other countries—environmental irresponsibility, power imbalance, and fiscal policies widening the gap between rich and poor. I was immediately sensitive to the oppressive conditions around me since I had been in close contact with similar conditions elsewhere. I was taken aback to find what I had seen abroad but had never before noticed at home: overwhelming *fear*. I had seen it in the streets of Bogotá, Colombia. I had felt it in rural villages in Mindanao in The Philippines. I had understood it in the Zapatista revolt in Chiapas in Mexico. And now I was seeing it in the faces of many Albertans experiencing the destruction of a social welfare system that took many years to put into place and only a few months to completely undermine. Being near Rocky Mountain House with several Albertans representing a variety of frightened and concerned groups was revealing, and I was immediately immersed in current conditions after having focused on global issues for so long.

It was clear the fear was much deeper than just in the hearts and minds of minorities, be they racially, culturally, sexually, physically, mentally, or economically oppressed groups. The growing attack on the health and education systems removed the security we had fought so hard for over the years while the number of traditional jobs was dwindling rapidly. Not that reform was unnecessary. Changes were needed and most people understood this. It is the process of this change that can be so cruel. The arrogant uncaring approach of the political elite was best described as a "slash and burn approach." These approaches are reverberating even more deeply with the global collapse of manic capitalism in 2008 and the upheaval in the Arab World commencing in 2011.

The Rocky Mountain House conference was well seasoned with the Highlander sense of faith. In part, this was due to the fact that many participants—especially the Americans—had either visited Highlander or had been taught the Highlander way. The president of NAAPAE at the time, American sociologist John Gaventa, was a former director of Highlander, having replaced Horton. The Highlanders reflected the emerging spiritual quality of PAR as a global phenomenon, revealing itself through a renewed awareness and valuing of Indigenous knowledge. The Rocky Mountain House conference acknowledged those values explicitly by regarding Indigenous/First Nations peoples as a major political entity in the world of popular education, a previously undone action. The conference itself commenced with a celebration of aboriginal knowledge. Cree elder, Mike Merrier, led one hundred people in a circle in a sweet grass ceremony:

> It was an unusual experience to observe so many educators in one room remaining quiet for about an hour. An awareness for the need for quiet seemed to permeate the room after awhile and people began to become comfortable with the ceremony and the accompanying peacefulness (NAAPAE, 1994, p. 4).

Initially, it was hard for some of us to remain still, to take the opportunity to meditate, being stuck in a chronic malaise of manic capitalism and social media. The next day, Merrier introduced us to the meanings of the Medicine Wheel:

The Medicine Wheel starts with the centre, a mirror, reflection. What you reflect is what you'll get back. The centre belongs to the creator, the centre of all living things. All living things need our prayers every day - mountains, grass, trees, rivers, two-legged creatures, four legged creatures, the wings of the air, the planted ones, the finned ones, and the creepy crawling ones. We need all of them to survive on mother earth. (Notes from Pyrch's learning journal)

He started us off in a patient reflective way. This experience is very much in keeping with Sharon Big Plume's understanding of the power of the circle and is akin to Brigette Krieg's practicing respectful listening. These processes create safe places where we can overcome the fears around and within us.

PAR is based on trust

Overcoming fear. The twenty-first century commenced with a flurry of violent acts in response to collective fear. Elsewhere I called for creating alternative responses to the fear generated immediate reaction to 9/11 (Pyrch, 2002) and ever since to the ever deepening manufacturing of fear (Pyrch, 2007). The culture of fear has been brewing for some time. Charles Elliott (1999) writes,

> It is almost a truism that this is an anxious age. From fears of job loss and subsequent prolonged unemployment to fears about death (still one of the great taboos of our culture) and failure (another great taboo in the culture of success), the generalized anxieties that beset us tend to get focused in two key areas: our families and our work. (p. 62)

He advances the concept of "appreciative inquiry" to withstand such fear, a concept full of hope. Elliott deals with criticism that this concept is "undisciplined" and "soft" by arguing,

> I think that it's an extremely disciplined process which can, at times, look a bit chaotic but which at a deeper level is highly structured. It's fundamentally about constructing reality. And people have to be very disciplined, very organized, very committed if they are going to construct that reality concretely as well as conceptually. (p. 177)

Fear must not be hidden and its symptoms must be addressed directly. We must, for the benefit of ourselves and others, face our fears. Fear becomes more like a friend in the sense imagined by Malaquías in Exhibit 2.1. Elliott was an early voice to champion "hope" as a disciplined guide to practical politics. Many others followed, including the philosopher Lear (2006), the oral historian Terkel (2003), the chickadees of Exhibit 2.2 (2008), and American President Obama (2006). Writing in *The Observer* two days before

Obama's election, Andrew Rawnsley (2008) said, "The big lesson is that the politics of unity and hope can still beat those of division and fear." We are still working on the possibility of the impossible as we work on creating our own guide—peaceful humankind.

In earlier times, adult educators responded directly to societal fears. Joseph Hart's (1927) comments on American society and the aims of adult education make sense to us today (Pyrch, 2007). He made it clear that adult educators have to confront fearful forces of oppressive control as part of our routine work. Elsewhere, William Kilpatrick (1929) spoke of our challenges at the first world conference on adult education held at Cambridge, England in August 1929. "The Crash" was to come in October the same year. I present his words at length as they resemble closely the language of contemporary times.

> With authoritarianism weakening, not a few among us face moral chaos. Youth asks very difficult questions, which perplex the older people, who in their turn find new situations for which old ways of behaving do not suffice. A permanent problem arises of keeping moral responses and the moral and the oral outlook abreast of the changing times . . . In any event, continuous moral education in the life of each one is thus indicated, and again must the education be essentially different from that type of authoritarian preparatory indoctrination hitherto dominant. Morals based on a philosophy of change may to some appear a contradiction, but this seems exactly what must obtain (Kilpatrack, 1929, p. 60)

In 2012, we face an equally powerful crash of the financial system and growing dissolution of young people as we prepare to engage actively in our communities. Kilpatrick continued,

> All hitherto abiding civilisations have stressed unchanging elements...If difference there be for different ages among us, the education of the generation in actual control of affairs seems perhaps of all the most essential...It is hardly an over-statement to assert of our own times that there are multitudes among us who are disturbed, restless, uneasy, rushing hither and yon,

> trying this and that, but at heart seeking they know not what. And many also of deeper character are ceaselessly but more consciously seeking to find some cause, as yet unknown, that shall be worthy to call out and unify their best and full effort…The degree to which this unrest exists will be differently appraised. But to the degree that it is in fact present, to that degree is our civilisation sick and diseased. It needs no words of proof to argue that such a malady cannot be adequately cared for by education of merely the younger ones of us. (pp. 61-5)

These words might describe contemporary global society as we move to the abyss. The adult educator Kilpatrick reflected a "moral aspect" of learning articulated more recently by Michael Newman (1999) as noted in Part one of *Breaking Free*.

> Moral learning is the process whereby we foreground our consciences, and give them space to develop. It does not involve the use of reason in its limited scientistic sense, but it does involve achieving a complete and passionate consciousness, and the continual making of radical choices. (p. 239)

Newman's sensibilities sound very much like Barack Obama's audacity of hope before, as president, becoming overwhelmed by realities. Yet he remembers the narrative of hope and is constant in his vision. Nobody said our transformative work is easy.

At the end of the twentieth century, American sociologist Richard Sennett (1998) argued that one indicator of our corroded character is our unwillingness or inability to deal with conflict—our fear of conflict. And yet

> …there is no community until differences are acknowledged within it. Teamwork, for instance, does not acknowledge differences in privilege or power, and so is a weak form of community; all the members or the work team are supposed to share a common motivation, and precisely that assumption weakens real communication. Strong bonding between people means engaging over time their differences. (p. 143)

The key point here is that we must engage with one another for the long haul and not fear our fear of the conflicts that will occur along the way. Conflicts are bound to happen, but how we address them is our own choice. Are we listening deeply to one another and then engaging together in dialogue? Dare we then act together to improve the human condition? American philosopher Michael Sandel (2009) encourages us to try. He concludes *Justice: What's the right thing to do?* with these words:

> Rather than avoid the moral and religious convictions that our fellow citizens bring to public life, we should attend to them more directly—sometimes by challenging and contesting them, sometimes by listening to and learning from them. There is no guarantee that public deliberation about hard moral questions will lead in any given situation to agreement—or even to appreciation for the moral and religious views of others. It's always possible that learning more about a moral or religious doctrine will lead us to like it less. But we cannot know until we try. (p. 268-70)

As global conditions remain on the brink of chaos and revolution, we must create conditions of trust and integrity so we can learn our way out of this mess.

How might we engage similarly in our classrooms? Liberatory educators have long claimed the ability and willingness to create spaces of trust to facilitate deep learning. As we are learning in Part Three of this guide, a circle image reflects the very essence of our spiritual selves. We are forced to spend much of our lives in boxes—a job box, discipline box, nation-state box, and so on. At times it is comfortable and secure in these boxes. We feel safe and sheltered from the fear housed in other boxes. They also can be suffocating and prison-like. A circle metaphor might help. Imagine a circle in between the boxes. Occasionally—especially when like-minded people meet—the boxes lower their walls, and each of us enters the circle to share what we can. Sometimes the circle is large; although the larger it gets, the less contact we have with each other. In keeping with Max-Neef's (1991) advocacy of human scale proportions in all aspects of life, the circle might be smaller than larger. Iranian scholar Majid Rahnema (1990) also contributed to this notion when he suggested that "long-term and serious processes of social and individual transformation are, essentially, the work of small groups of individuals awakened to the world to which they relate" (p. 220). Commenting on the failure of "development" models in the Global South, he sees those small groups meeting in "new spaces of freedom," where mutual sharing takes place and a sense of community established. This new space of freedom may be the circle we choose to enter when we venture to leave our boxes. Like Aboriginal Canadian Medicine Wheels, the circle is always there when needed, a safe space for community.

We move on despite our fears. It is heartening to record how we deal with these fears in our classrooms. Listen once again to the learners in Exhibit 2.1:

> "Fear can make people sometimes action driven but too often paralyzed. Fear comes from intimidation but also from the unknown. A lot of times we see in the world that we are living that those we fear the most are those who intimidate relentless with a sense of entitlement. When we learn how to face our fears and control them, we should be able to act more inspired. Learning to overcome fear comes over time with knowledge. This knowledge can be obtained by using popular education tools such as adult education, participatory action research. Because popular education wants to make us actively participating citizens, it brings the elements of fear into the open and lays out its tactics to a thorough examination. As soon as we feel afraid, we should realize that there is an issue or concern that needs our attention. In fear there is no room for knowledge, and where there is knowledge, it illuminates fear".

These words reveal a confidence within university learners to get involved in life and practice and fear not the fear we have so we can teach others do to likewise. Our work becomes transformative for self and those we encounter along the way. Another student from Exhibit 2.1 remarked,

> "I find the more I listen to others discuss their understanding of popular education, the more I scratch my

head in worry. Let's hope my grasp on P.E. is budding under the surface of the soil. I do feel confident in knowing that no matter what cause draws us in and motivates our action, it cannot thrive in isolation…Dignity can be found in one's marginalization. The mutual respect and understanding that comes alongside dignity helps lead and encourage self-worth. Fear is a perspective which can be managed, coped with, and stood up to in order to bring about change. Rather than trying to overcome it, we can use our fear and turn it into fuel rather than keep it as a barrier… Why is it that our fear is so often at the front of our minds? Do we only feel this when challenged? Do we only recognize how common it is from person to person when we compile and share our thoughts? This classmate's thought said it best, 'If you let your fears plant their roots in you, you defeat yourself before you even set out on your journey.' I am glad experiencing fear and letting fear take root are not the same thing."

These reflections on marginalization by learners in the Popular Education course in 2008 resonate with Brigette Kreig's findings on the concept reported in her dissertation. Skilled facilitation and passionate commitment reawaken voices in the margins.

There are techniques in the liberatory education toolkit to prepare us to face our fears directly. We introduced Theatre of the Oppressed, another contribution to liberatory processes by a Brazilian, to one of our classes by the Calgary-based Stage Left ensemble.[5]

One participant wrote, "This (Stage left) was by far the most enjoyable class for me. Creating images with our bodies was an extremely powerful process; we all came together as one, all walls and biases were gone, and we were just people with one common goal. It was very cool to see my colleagues behave in a manner so unlike what we've been taught, losing sight of the 'professional boundaries' we've been force fed and identifying with a problem, making it our own." Another wrote, "To be comfortable with your body and to use our bodies to

---

[5] www.stage-left.org

> make a change is an amazing concept. Even in watching the movements going on around me, I was so moved, and I kept paying attention to the feelings and thoughts going on within me and thought that there is no way someone could watch this and not feel compelled to listen and make a change." (Extracted from Exhibit 2.1)

There is no doubt of the liberating power of arts-based research in our liberatory quest. Once again, Canadian traditions are rich, and we need to go back no further than the CBC's Challenge for Change initiatives in the 1960s.[6]. We pause to note the passing of Augusto Boal in May 2009, the Brazilian founder of Theatre of Oppressed. He died the very same day Americans honoured Pete Seeger's ninetieth birthday with a celebration of folk music traditions that grew in places like Highlander during the 1930s. Those traditions are reviving the hope we require to practice liberatory adult education.

---

[6] www3.nfb.ca/collection/films

Lessons learned in part three. In order to encourage listening to, and engaging with, one another, our classrooms must be arranged respectfully and thoughtfully. A circle works best. Canadians are richly endowed with various Aboriginal traditions of the circle. We are also gifted with Stage Left's talented ensemble of popular theatre players. These advantages teach us that learning our way out of silence is a global and timeless pursuit. Listening is an art and a science in itself. Through listening deeply, we can find hope and make it a way of life. In this, we are on the cusp of global trends. All of this means we are more than well prepared to take a lead in restoring democracy to a place of citizen control similar to community development initiatives in the 1930s and 1940s. We need to do this to replace our superficial democracy with passionate engagement and make it responsive to the real needs of all the people. Our resilience is being enabled by song and dance, by music and movement, by democratic involvement and leadership in our communities as well as in our classrooms.

Part Four

Breaking free of apathy

The power of a swarm of mosquitoes starts us off. We think we are weak and powerless in face of overwhelming force. In response, Manfred Max-Neef (1998) devised this allegory which he presented at the Seventh World Congress on PAR in Cartagena, Colombia in 1997:

> If you were in an open field with an angry rhinoceros about to charge at you, the silliest thing you could do would be to imagine you were a rhinoceros too. The outcome would be obvious. What can you do faced with a rhinoceros, to get the better of it eventually and come away unharmed? What is the one thing, in this case, that is more powerful than a rhinoceros? Why, a swarm of mosquitoes. (p. 76)

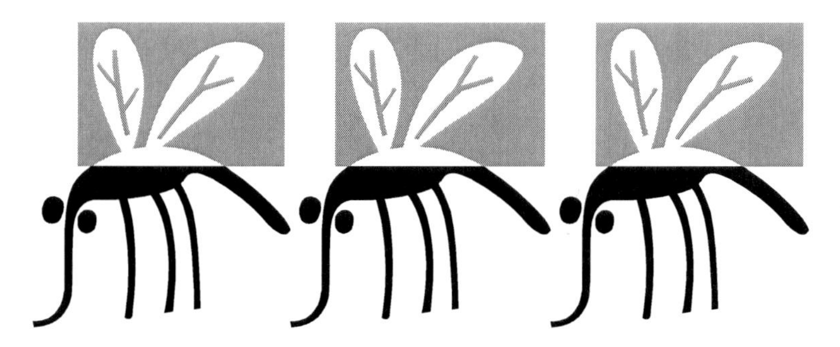

With some encouragement, my class in Popular Education in 2008 showed a real willingness and energy to take an active role in a provincial election.

> One of us remarked, “I am glad we have a chance due to the Election coming up and our involvement through this class. It feels a little scary to me to become involved because I feel I don’t have enough knowledge and speaking skills to challenge politicians. But I hope I will get over this and learn to find the right words and make my opinion heard.” For another, “With the upcoming election, this is our chance to take a stand and address an issue that politicians never face. We are going to attend meetings and ask the same questions of each candidate. I think there is a lot of work to be done with this project, and although it terrifies me, I think this is my push to do something bigger. This is my chance to stand up with shaky knees and make a point. I am terrified but at the same time eager because I have never done anything like this…I am excited yet nervous to begin this class.”

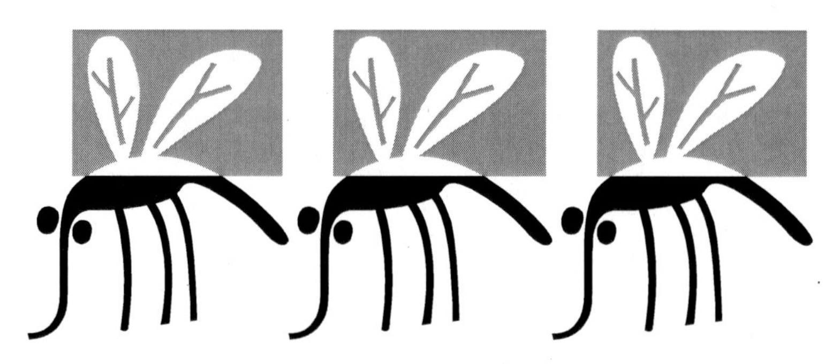

Mosquitoes can be effective even with shaky knees. Our challenge is not with a rhinoceros, at least not directly. Our challenge is with an electoral system impossible to figure out and perhaps negligent even if unintentionally. Who benefits from this broken system?

What does it say about our democracy if university graduate and undergraduate students in a caring profession like social work are uncertain about meeting one of the basic acts of citizenship? At the same time, we asked some hard questions of our system.

> I know others in the class encountered other issues with being sent to the wrong polling station, not knowing

what kind of ID they would need, the Elections Alberta computer-system being down, etc. My own experience was easy: a "mobile poll" was set up in my apartment building (which happens to house a lot of seniors, who happen to be fairly affluent), so I didn't even have to go outside... I don't like to be cynical, but I wonder how many lower-income housing units or apartments were blessed with their own "mobile polls?" These are the voters that might not be so happy with the status-quo and would likely vote accordingly.

Perhaps some of the apathy we see is more apparent than real. Faculty of Social Work programs and courses require all learners to be active through very demanding practicum requirements. Maybe it's less apathy and more simply being overworked and wracked with exhaustion. At the same time, it may be we don't know how to gather together our harvest of action accomplishments; or we don't want to or won't make the time. What is my responsibility in this? Should we offer mosquito lessons? Is this in fact what *Breaking Free* is all about?

Call to action. Recovering our voice and fearing not our fear are processes requiring direct and regular participation in our communities and neighbourhoods and in our classrooms as well. For this we need courage. Editors of *We are Everywhere* (2003) tell us how to proceed.

> So let's have the courage, let's have the heart that lies in the root of the word courage, *le coeur*—the heart to build a rebellion that embraces, the heart to insist on an insurrection that listens, the heart to create a revolution that when it looks in the mirror understands that it's not just about rage, but that it begins with the word "lover." Let's have the courage to demand nothing for us, but everything for everyone; the courage to keep the spaces that this movement of movements has created radically open, rebelliously inviting, and profoundly popular. For when "we" are truly everywhere, we will be nowhere—for we will be everywhere. (p. 8)

Is this the kind of courage that exploded in the Middle East commencing in January 2011? Faculty of Social Work learners I've met would agree with these sentiments from *We are Everywhere*. Compare the previous statement from *We are Everywhere* to what Faculty of Social Work students had to say.

> "We need to start connecting with each other again in order to care for each other and what is happening to our neighbors and us. Only then, I believe, we can make additional positive changes in our lives, our society, and the world around us." ...According to another, "I remember my first year at the University, and the students were protesting the tuition hike. The Students Union decided to protest by camping on campus for three nights until the morning of the tuition meeting where the students would gather and protest. I was so

> excited to be a part of this, and I slept on campus and attended the rally and shouted and waved my banner. But when the decision was made that tuition would go up, all of the students including myself went home. When I told my father that I had participated in a protest and what the result was, he told me that he was amazed at how easy it was for the government to push people around and how people quickly stop objecting when they are told no. This occurs in our society over and over again, we are told 'No' by someone, and we quickly shut down and walk away; we don't raise our voices and make ourselves heard. It would be so interesting to see what our society would be like if we were to adopt the passion and strength of our Latin American neighbours; what would our country and our society look like then?"

At times we look abroad to be reminded of our local responsibilities. Reflecting on the possibility of the impossible after the collapse of the Soviet Union in 1989, Canadian author and activist George Woodcock (1992) urged us to action.

> In Canada we shall only have changes of lasting value if we make sure that the people are involved, and for that to be achieved, the people must awaken from the condition of things done for and to them, to that of doing things for themselves. If the politicians refuse us a constituent assembly where all views can be talked out, we should arrange it ourselves. If the government will not hold referenda on various points of the constitution (as is already customary in Switzerland and some other countries), we should recruit the technicians and the facilities and proceed on our own. And if the government does not effectively return power to the people, we should strike and march and fill the streets and clog the roads with cars and tractors until our peaceful manifestations secure a political arrangement that satisfies us. The peoples of Berlin and Leipzig, of Prague and Budapest, of Moscow and St. Petersburg, have given us an example abroad; the native peoples

> with their non-violent confrontations are giving us examples at home. They have acted according to the ancient right of dissent against governments that fail to meet their responsibilities to guard the rights and freedom of the people. (p. 203)

Though he supported their methods, Woodcock would have been disappointed with the results of those hopeful actions in Eastern Europe. Instead of a new era of democracy and social justice, unfettered global capitalism emerged after the demise of the Soviet Union, and it remains with us even into 2012. The upheavals in the Arab World, commencing in Tunisia and Egypt in January 2011, have been interpreted as another people's movement similar to 1989 and have been equated with the great European rebellions of 1848 (Nazemroaya, 2011). Will these new expressions of people's unfettered democratic urge for freedom make any inroads into manic capitalism? Should we care? What is to be done in Calgary?

As liberatory educators, we commit to action. Listen to my class:

> For one of us, "It is not okay for people to be sleeping on the streets in this weather and for society to think it is no big deal. And yet I feel so useless and helpless in the whole situation, and I am just as much to blame because I do nothing. What can I do? It's times like these I lose my hope and sit back and do nothing because I am at a complete lose of what to do. Therefore I need to switch this around and rebuild my hope. Yes, I did nothing, but here is what I could start doing in the present. Volunteer at shelters; bring someone a coffee; help advocate for people for somewhere to stay. I could work with the bigger picture and advocate for social change. These things that seem so small could make a very big difference. As I have learned over the past few years in school and in my own experience, one person can definitely make a difference." (Extracted from Exhibit 2.1)

This ties in nicely to what *Breaking Free* is all about. We want to be socially relevant. However the question remains: what is social relevance? It might be we are more socially relevant than we credit ourselves. It might be our routine activities in our daily jobs contribute more to societal well being than we realize. How so?

Let me share some of my own experience which, now that I think of it, might have contributed to the commonwealth. I am not offering "exemplary" behaviour; rather I am sharing what I know best while inviting you to do likewise in your stories for your own guide. I look back on my own practice during the 1980s to see how I functioned as a liberatory educator. Working for First Nations organizations over a number of years brought me close to oppressive conditions within my own country, and I struggled to maintain a hopeful yet realistic and critical eye. I participated in community-based adult education initiatives in Saskatchewan while working at the Gabriel Dumont Institute of Native Studies and Applied Research, and I had some success in encouraging small scale micro-projects and a critical recovery of history. The latter included re-interpretation of official history—Riel resistance rather than Riel rebellion—and its translation into curriculum for the regular educational system and non-formal adult education events at informal gatherings. The Ganma metaphor fits here. Mainstream history of Métis rebellion blended with people's history of resistance, creating foam in the shape of new knowledge transformed into curriculum. The process was one of dialogical inquiry always creating new interpretations, new possibilities, perhaps even the possibility of the impossible.

PAR translates knowledge into action

I experienced a similar blend of formal and non-formal education as community education co-ordinator at the Westerra Institute of Technology in Stony Plain, Alberta (Pyrch, 1989). I analysed the experience using Stephen Brookfield's (1983) conceptual model of community adult education. This model includes three categories: adult education for, in, and of the community. Programming *for* the community meant determining the interests of the people, so they would attend our courses. My team came to be seen as careful listeners and first responders. A telephone call from a local parent resulted in a day-long course on first aid for babysitters, a course we were able to offer cheaply because one of our staff was willing to work for a very low fee on a Saturday as a community service. Inquiries from the local credit union led to a short course on stress management for their managerial staff. In general we made a concerted effort to be a part of the community in all its facets in order to listen to all concerns, and we attempted to aid in their resolutions. We visited most chambers of commerce in the vicinity and were highly active in two of them. We participated in service clubs and spoke to school boards, community associations, library boards, and Women's Institutes. We were invited to explain community adult education to various branches of local and provincial government. We came to know our constituency very well, and in the process we made ourselves known and made a difference.

Adult education *in* the community centres on the notion of outreach work to support learning wherever it might occur. In our program, community adult education at Westerra was designed for the people of Stony Plain, Spruce Grove, and the towns, villages and farms in Parkland County, delivered when possible right in these communities. Learners in our Water and Wastewater program visited nearby water systems to work solving problems in real life settings. On several occasions, while actively involved with a group of volunteers in determining the feasibility of establishing a Family and Community Support Service (FCSS) in Stony Plain, we transformed meetings into a liberatory education setting. Similar opportunities were found during meetings of the Rural Life Committee and the Spruce Grove Chamber of Commerce.

More ambitiously, I took it upon myself to introduce the Westerra constituency to the possibilities and opportunities of lifelong learning. This was the final piece of Brookfield's (1983) model: adult education *of* the community. When the time seemed right, at meetings of the FCSS group of other special interest groups, we facilitated processes involving everyone as we could, helping to clarify value positions, emphasizing each individual as a valuable community member while placing the issue at hand into local community context. Hospital administrators were encouraged during a two-day retreat to discuss all aspects of health care, including the differences between physical and mental health and spiritual wellbeing, before even considering goals and objectives. Directors of a local chamber of commerce were directed to reflect on their community in its entirety, all of the facets that make the community function as a whole, prior to selecting targets for the business community. None of this was easy since few people seemed routinely to reflect about issues outside their immediate concern. We all need help in reaching beyond our grasp and connecting with similar interests elsewhere. There is something liberating in the notion of being part of several communities. Perhaps being a part of many frees us from the domination of one while continuously refreshing ourselves with divergent influences.

Lessons from my Westerra experience in community adult education resonate with rural social work practice experienced by my professorial colleague in the Faculty of Social Work, Kim Zapf.

Exhibit 4.1: Rural Regions (Zapf, 2009)

Most of the literature on social work with groups assumes an urban context where the worker and group participants do not know each other prior to the beginning of the group and do not encounter each other outside of scheduled group sessions. These assumptions do not hold in rural regions where group work presents specific challenges that have largely been neglected in the mainstream urban-based literature.

Throughout the developing literature on rural social work, issues of visibility and confidentiality have been highlighted as major challenges to conventional group work principles and practices (Ginter, 2005). Urban assumptions of non-contact outside of the group do not fit well with the community-embedded practice of rural social workers and their clients (Simon, 1999). These issues of visibility and confidentiality influence activities throughout the group work process in rural regions.

A social worker attempting to form a group in a rural area will likely have to alter conventional recruitment processes. In an urban center, the social worker will probably approach or invite potential members individually; a group member does not know the identity of the other members prior to the first session. Such an approach may not be fair in a rural area. A group member should not be surprised at the first session to discover Uncle Harry is also there, or their mechanic, or a parent of their child's best friend, or their employer. Each potential member of a rural group has the right to know who else will be there (and an opportunity to refuse participation), although this could take several rounds for the worker before composition is finalized.

Scheduling of groups in rural areas must take into account important seasonal and local social rhythms of the community (harvest periods, game patterns, fish migration cycles). Single-industry resource towns can pose special scheduling problems with the long hours and shift work required of residents. Regular celebrations or special events in rural regions (sports tournaments, harvest festivals, rodeos, etc.) can interfere with availability of group members, as can unexpected but significant communal events such as severe weather, natural disasters, or funerals.

Once the group is running, the existence of the group and the identity of participants will likely be known throughout the rural community. Members may well be visible traveling to, entering, and leaving the host facility. Community residents will recognize neighbours' trucks and cars in the parking lot during group time. Similar to the group members, the rural group worker also experiences the transparency of a fishbowl lifestyle where his or her actions outside of group will be visible to group members and the entire community. The social worker leading a rural group for convicted impaired drivers had better not retreat to the bar after group then drive home (everyone will be

counting drinks!). Group members and the larger community monitor the worker for integrity and behaviour consistent with the purposes of the group.

A crucial consideration for any rural group will be how to handle contacts outside of the group. Group members and the worker can be expected to come into regular contact and interaction with each other in their various roles in the rural community. Protocols for such contact must be anticipated and discussed in the first session. Specific instances of community contact may be de-briefed in later sessions – a process which can take up a good bit of time.

Confidentiality concerns in rural groups extend beyond the immediate members of the group. Members sharing personal issues are likely to discuss partners, children, friends, co-workers, employers, etc. who may well be known to other group members. There is a responsibility to protect the rights of these third parties in group discussion. Conventional solutions such as changing names to disguise identity may not be adequate in rural settings where everyone knows whom you are talking about anyway.

Many agencies have a standard policy for social workers of not accepting gifts from clients because accepting a gift from a group member could open the door for dual relationships and potential misunderstandings. In a rural area, however, gifts (food, crafts, services) are often offered as a way of restoring balance. The worker may be a resident member of the rural community engaged with group members in relationships before the group starts and after it ends. Acceptance of a gift can represent a commitment to the larger goal of balance in the community, recognition that everyone has something valuable to offer. Of course, there are limits to be negotiated in the local context, but a blanket refusal of all gifts could distance the worker unnecessarily from the community.

Food can be an important component of any event in a rural community, and the group is no

exception. An urban group might have a small budget for coffee and possibly treats, but any thought of a more elaborate meal provided by members could be considered inappropriate, counterproductive, and a waste of valuable time. In a rural setting, however, the social worker might do well to allocate some group time for food (and a schedule of responsibilities) because the offerings may arrive even if not solicited.

By the time food is shared and concerns around out-of-group contact have been addressed, there may be little time left in any given session of a rural treatment group for work on the declared purpose. One might wonder if treatment groups are even practical for rural social workers. The literature identifies group work as the least used modality of rural generalist practitioners (Gumpert & Saltman, 1998). Of those rural social workers who use groups, most are involved with existing community concern groups or natural groups rather than formed treatment groups. Rural practice is community-oriented and community-embedded, directed at community development or change. There is clear direction in the literature for rural social workers to work with groups already in existence rather than forming new groups (Templeman & Mitchell, 2004; Collier, 2006). Developing partnerships with existing groups (such as interagency committees, recreation groups, congregations, school or adult education classes, etc.) or connecting with the local "Hardly Worth Mentioning Groups" (Banks, 2004) allows the rural social worker to avoid many common concerns around formation and scheduling. Collaborative partnerships in rural regions also recognize existing community strengths and decrease the worker's status as expert or leader, a development more in keeping with rural notions of balance and mutuality.

The social worker who considers using group work in a rural area that includes a Native American population will likely encounter a strong local tradition of using circles (healing circles, sharing circles, learning circles) for

both individual and community growth. Native American circles have their own protocols and philosophies which can be quite different from the assumptions of mainstream social work with groups. In a conventional group, the social worker attempts to create the necessary conditions of trust and sharing that allow a process of mutual aid to emerge in the middle phase of overall group development. Many Native American traditions, on the other hand, assume a positive flow of energy or spirit that gives direction to the circle from the outset (and before). Circle participants have only to connect with this pre-existing direction or flow rather than creating it anew each time through a worker's skills. Levels of sharing, intimacy, and commitment can be observed in the first minutes of a circle that might not be expected until later sessions of a conventional social work group. Rather than attempting to organize or run healing circles, the non-Native rural social worker would do well to participate and share in circles when invited, to learn of this approach and its power. The rural social worker must also realize that Native American members recruited to a conventional group may have very different expectations of the process and potential outcomes.

References

Banks, K. (2004). "Hardly Worth Mentioning Groups" and the informal community. *Rural Social Work, 9*(1), 34-41.

Collier, K. (2006). *Social work with rural peoples (3rd ed.).* Vancouver: New Star.

Ginter, C. (2005). Client confidentiality, anonymity, facilitator credibility, and contamination in rural family violence self-help groups. In K. Brownlee & J.R. Graham (Eds.), *Violence in the family: Social work readings and research from northern and rural Canada* (pp. 90-104). Toronto: Canadian Scholars' Press.

Gumpert, J., & Saltman, J.E. (1998). Social group work practice in rural areas: The practitioners speak. *Social Work with Groups, 21*(3), 19-31.

Simon, R.I. (1999). Maintaining treatment boundaries in small communities and rural areas. *Psychiatric Services, 50*(1), 11.

Templeman, S.B., & Mitchell, L. (2004). Utilizing an asset-building framework to improve policies for rural communities. In T.L. Scales & C. L. Streeter (Eds.), *Rural social work: Building and sustaining community assets* (pp. 196-205). Belmont: Brooks/Cole (Thomson Learning).

Lessons Learned
Exhibit 4.5

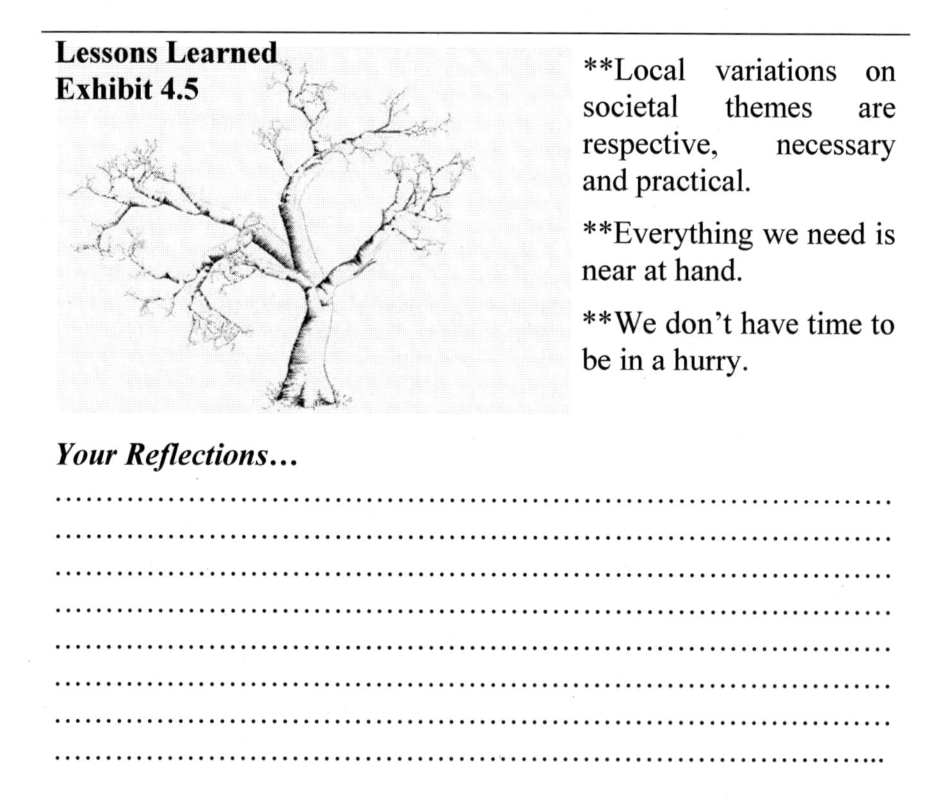

**Local variations on societal themes are respective, necessary and practical.

**Everything we need is near at hand.

**We don't have time to be in a hurry.

Your Reflections…

....

....

....

....

....

....

....

....

When I moved into university continuing education at the University of Calgary in 1987, I was challenged by a conservative climate while functioning as director of programming in the area of environmental studies from a critical perspective. At the time, commodification was settling in on the academy, and seemingly overnight liberal studies, women's studies, peace education, program for seniors, and so on were fading and ultimately disappeared from continuing education, and they were suddenly re-located to some extent in other guises elsewhere on campus. Yet as the academy remains encouraging of "entrepreneurial" flare, I found some in myself, perhaps because I knew I was part of the liberatory tradition and needed to be doing something about it. Knowing one's traditions, what they mean, and want they demand of us guides us to our moral responsibilities and opportunities.

One example of my liberatory education work resulted directly from the Calgary PAR Congress in 1989. The Congress earned us a reputation as competent exponents of participatory development, and this led to substantial funding from the Canadian International Development Agency (CIDA) for a six-year project uniting colleagues in Canada, the Philippines, and Thailand in the Canada-Asia-Partnership. The Partnership created several courses about participatory development, and I was part of a team that designed and managed a course on community-based environmental protection. My experience in this course relates directly to the "slash-and-burn" story told earlier. We used the course to help Albertans organize long-term resistance to environmentally exploitive government policies. In response to the environmentally deleterious "slash-and-burn" policies, creative and energetic community-based protest movements have been launched throughout Alberta. In the northern part of the province, many years of in-depth scientific research combined with elements of PAR failed to prevent construction of a huge kraft pulp mill near the town of Athabasca, despite occurring at a time when the world markets for pulp was depressed. The work of the Friends of the

Athabasca Environmental Association, an organization led by local people including staff from Athabasca University, is well-documented and published as a case study in community-based environmental protection (Richardson, Sherman and Gismondi, 1993). In the southern part of the province, years of similar action by the Friends of the Oldman River failed to block the "taming" of three wild rivers by construction of a dam ostensibly for irrigation purposes in a land fast losing any agricultural value. We recruited these two "Friends" to tell their stories as a major component of the Canada-Asia Partnership course on community-based environmental protection. The Friends of the Athabasca convinced us—with well-substantiated research—that the Government of Alberta manipulated the Environmental Impact Assessment procedure to essentially force the mill upon a hesitant, uncertain community. The Friends of the Oldman River convinced us that the same government built the irrigation dam with little or no public consultation. The government responsible for the mill and dam had enormous resources to draw upon. In the case of the dam, even the judicial system's findings in support of the anti-dam position did not prevent the arrogant abuse of power by government. When one branch of government fails to prevent another from damaging the earth, who else could?

PAR
is about power

Case study organizers made space for proponents of the mill and dam. However, spokespeople for the proponents were little interested in sharing information and regarded us with suspicion. Perhaps we were not "important" enough as a group to be treated respectfully. Considering the government's record of avoiding contact with the people, we may have been ignored simply as a matter of routine, a way of keeping with long-standing traditions. We learned from this. We came to understand the profound sense of powerlessness in people living on the farms near the mill and on the ranches near the dam. It was crippling to feel so helpless, so unimportant. Mostly we are alienated from our democratic responsibilities which demand participation, critical inquiry, and a healthy questioning of authority. If a playing field is level, it is fair to allow equal time for all users. If the field is not level, we may have to intervene to support the weaker end if we value equity and justice as we do in the liberatory education movement. The environment course clearly was biased in favour of the efforts of community groups to express themselves in a world dominated by the control of knowledge by experts and officials. Working for community empowerment is not neutral.

We understood the necessity of supporting the countervailing power of local environmental groups. We did this in two ways: with money and with encouragement. We hired the groups and individuals who created the case studies, and we paid them reasonable fees for their service. In this way, the Friends of the two rivers earned several thousand dollars to defray the huge legal debts they incurred on behalf of those rivers, being incapable of standing up for themselves. The Friends did so through teaching fees and billeting income. This was one time when public funds were directly available to the public. In terms of encouragement, as a result of course experiences, we were able to share an enormous amount of advice and direction with local groups while learning from and acknowledging their experience. A Ganma variation seems appropriate here as our work with the two Friends of Rivers combined with expert research into environmental issues to produce meaningful new knowledge, new foam, for local communities. The course itself was an expression of countervailing power. It taught us the importance of working together in an interdisciplinary way, enabling local people to gain the confidence and act for themselves. Through self-confidence and self-awareness, communities regain control of their environment, of our lives. What remains unclear is the knowledge-making experience of those hundreds of participants in the resistance to corporate and government hegemony.

The Friends of the Oldman included a wide range of presentations and experiences in convincing us of their resolve. Aboriginal perspectives included a visit to a local elder on reserve as well as hearing arguments from the Lonefighter National Communications Network. The Lonefighters resembled the warriors of old. Sharon Big Plume (2007) recently wrote in depth and at length about the warrior concept in Aboriginal communities as a hopeful guide to social justice work wherever it is practised.

Exhibit 4.2: The Warrior Concept (Big Plume, 2007). The following words in her dissertation are taken from Chapter Nine: Possibilities. Words in **bold type** and *italics* appear as such in the dissertation.

The first research question identified for this study asked for the tribal concept of a Warrior. Findings revealed that the significance of the Warrior concept has endured among Aboriginal community members. Warriors have played and still play a very important and meaningful role in many Aboriginal cultures. Warrior roles and duties are essentially the same today as in times past and remain basically unchanged except in application.

...not a physical battle, because in today's society, that face to face combat stuff, that's a part of the practice that changed, it's not the role that changed, it's the implementation of it, the practice of it. (From the Talking Circle)

Warriors are leaders of ideal character who have a central core of strength, honesty, responsibility and service to the community arising from their relationship with Spirit. Warriors do not just talk – they take action.

You have to find it within yourself to be there, to teach other people. (From the Talking Circle)

Far from being simply individuals who are aggressive and make war, Warriors figuratively and practically function in such a way as to keep the community safe, strong and moving forward. Warriors are inspirational to the community; they stand out and are easily recognizable by others for their leadership qualities. The Warrior's courage, honour and valour pull others forward while serving to strengthen and motivate individuals, as well as the community.

It's like he was a Warrior, and in this battle, I needed his assistance because I was looking at my loyalty and my responsibility being to my tribe, to my people. (From the Talking Circle)

Warriors have a profound connection to Spirit and as a result they seek to be honourable human beings who can act as powerful, moral examples for youth and other community members. Communities need, desire and seek someone like a Warrior who can lead the way. Anyone, whether man, woman or child can be a Warrior and most likely, everyone must assume a Warrior role at some point in their lives, or perhaps at many times in their lives.

Perhaps those children are those Warriors that we look for, and I kind of looked at that, because from my understanding about something that you don't want to do, being in the position where you don't want to be in, but you know the stuff that we talked about, persevering, doing what you need to do to make a better thing for yourself and your siblings, your family. I'm thinking we're describing these youths and these children we're working for, because guaranteed none of them want to be in that foster home, none of them want to be apprehended. (From the Talking Circle)

Warriors do not avoid the truth; rather, they seek the truth, and then once having found it, they speak the truth anywhere and everywhere.

Yes, they are speaking the telling of the truth. That's a true Warrior. (From the Talking Circle)

Warriors are courageous and they fight for what is right. They are very sure of themselves, they come to know who they are and what they should be doing, and they do it deliberately and willingly. They develop and demonstrate remarkable strength, and they stand before fear, hurt or any other reality with bravery. Warriors are extremely persistent and do not quit; they defy the odds and persevere through challenging or trying times.

...but you still get up and say, yup, because he got up and she got up and they kept walking this way, they kept in that direction, oh and they fell down many times. (From the Talking Circle)

As action takers, Warriors can see and

implement various solutions and strategies, and because they *keep trying hard*, they have the ability to inspire others to *keep trying hard to so the right thing*.

I called on my brother, who I knew was a Warrior, his job was keeping the peace. I mean battle is necessary but that's only if all other avenues of peace can't be created, and a peaceable solution, then you have to go to a different route. (From the Talking Circle)

Warriors have a tough, unyielding side of defiance and assertiveness, and as well, they have a softer side of love, gentleness and kindness.

At the same time, you know, the responsibilities that, and you know, one of the things I share about this kindness. I really agree about this kindness, about, you know. I've heard a lot from these elders that have passed, about how important kindness is, you know, how you can't be a Warrior, or you can't be who you are as a human being, a total human being, without being kind. (From the Talking Circle)

Despite the gravity, intensity, and seriousness of Warrior responsibilities, Warriors are also known for having a well developed sense of humour.

Comedy also fits in this, it was not all serious, there's a time to be serious and there's a time, but you have to find it in yourself to be there and teach other people.

Humour is a big part of who we are and there should be a chapter there on humour, right after the residential schools, because I truly believe that's our saving grace, that that's how we flourished and how we developed, because we had to have humour, 'cause like we'd be sitting around here whipping ourselves, really, you know, and crying and whining. (From the Talking Circle)

Warriors can be quite irreverent at times, but they understand how the role of humour serves the people. Warriors can use humour as a survival strategy, and as a way to lead, reassure and inspire. Humour is essential in keeping perspective. Being able to laugh in the face of difficulty or trouble can give a sense of power over adversity. As Deloria (1969) stated:

Humour, all Indians will agree, is the cement by which the coming Indian movement is held together. When a people can laugh at themselves, and laugh at others, and hold all aspects of life together without letting anybody drive them to extremes, then it seems to me that that people can survive. (168)

Warriors assume a set of roles and responsibilities as individuals and as members of society. The duty of a Warrior is centered on service to the Creator and the community. Warriors fight for a better life for the children and they fight for the betterment of society. They stand up for each other, they defend the community from harm, and they strive to promote and protect the well being of others.

...honour the Creation, being called into being, to being part of this, and to share that honour. When you see someone dishonouring a brother or a sister, then I think that's when a Warrior steps in, not in a harmful, offending way, but to say hey, that's my brother you just treated that way, that's my sister, or that's my son, that was by daughter that you just treated that way. (From the Talking Circle)

Warriors are defenders who are unafraid, strong, brave, committed individuals who live with certainty.

If you walk into the room and it lights up, there's a Warrior, someone who knows. (From the Talking Circle)

They learn and practice exemplary demeanour and conduct. Warriorship is a solemn and respected way of life, and is seen as a serious choice about how to live and be in the world…

Social workers, both Aboriginal and non-Aboriginal, are in a position to support and assist modern Warriors and Warrior societies. By supporting the re-emergence of the Warrior identity, social workers can provide opportunities for communities to re-affirm their common social visions. Social workers can support the extended family system, encourage the use of tribal languages, and encourage a strong connection to nature, land and animals. Supporting and encouraging re-connection to traditional spiritual foundations can redefine sources of authority for communities and can keep standards very high. Encouraging the development of many natural authorities can provide opportunities to develop and practice power… (p. 266-72)

Lessons Learned

Exhibit 4.2

**Acting knowledgably is empowering.

**Disciplined, thoughtful hope is the key to success.

**Direct experience provides the foundation for human learning.

Your Reflections…

…………………………………………………………………………

…………………………………………………………………………

…………………………………………………………………………

…………………………………………………………………………

…………………………………………………………………………

Sharon's words recall the meaning of the five enemies and five friends of ancient Aztec wisdom noted in Exhibit 2.1. Warriors are thoughtful activists committed to the common good and remain untiring, unrelenting champions of social justice. Oftentimes they might be quietly working in their local communities. Occasionally they might even become a head of state.

Renewed call to action. A fresh hope is astir. All of us committed to working actively and directly to revive democracy were heartened by the possibility of the impossible—an African-American US President devoted to dignity for all humankind. His call to action—a new, progressive revival for American democracy—gave us all a lift, albeit fleetingly in face of overwhelming realities of American politics. Like so many social justice workers, he had learned a lot from grassroots work in Chicago—right around the corner from Jane Addams at Hull House and in neighbourhoods organized by Saul Alinsky. Obama himself urged Americans to return to their roots to locate and revive democratic practices seemingly forgotten in the overwhelming rush of manic capitalism. If he dared to be audaciously hopeful, so too can we. Of course, he is not the first person to focus on hope as a practical strategy as we learned from another Chicago force, Studs Terkel. In face of corrosive forces silencing Americans, Sennett (1998) ends his critique with hope for a re-emerging sense of community based upon small scale human relationships.

> If change occurs it happens on the ground, between persons speaking out of inner need, rather than through mass uprisings. What political programs follow from these inner needs, I simply don't know. But I do know a regime which provides human beings no deep reasons to care about one another cannot long preserve its legitimacy. (p. 148)

These words were written during the Presidency of Bill Clinton. Instead of conditions improving, the corrosion of character analysed by Sennett deepened during the Presidency of George W. Bush, especially when the culture of fear was created after 9/11. Barack Obama was elected President of the US in 2008 with a platform in keeping with the hope imagined by Sennett. How is Obama doing? His call for change combines a solid understanding of American traditions with a personal commitment based upon his own grass-roots organizing experience in Chicago. Yet apparently that alone was not enough to change the negative forces of manic capitalism. In our Canadian context, we must recover our own grass-roots traditions if we are to find our own way out of deepening global economic and financial chaos.

What does courage look like and how can it be acquired? Looking for guidance, Faculty of Social Work learners are locating role models in the literature and in local practice. The next exhibit contains one learner's investigation into the nature of social activism in order to find a suitable entry point for herself. Cari Gulbrandsen wrote the following unpublished paper for the PAR course I taught in 2009, offering helpful insight into the world of activism.

Exhibit 4.3: Invitation to Activism (Gulbrandsen, 2009).

Introduction

I developed my final project around my need to reflect on the "action" component of participatory action research. Although I struggled with the initial writing assignment for the course, the challenge of becoming familiar with Orlando Fals Borda's original conceptualization of PAR as a methodology, the research and reflective exercise

introduced me to the challenge ahead. That challenge was to make the learning journey ahead personally meaningful, to the extent that my experience with PAR would continue beyond the completion of the course. Orlando Fals-Borda embodied the essence of PAR, and I can appreciate at a personal level how his life's work is something to aspire to. His commentary and "results" clearly exemplify his high standard of commitment to participants, his tenacity in bringing their voices to the forefront in a way that would benefit their daily lived reality. Fals-Borda created a legacy, a standard measure oneself against. As far as my own life exists in the present, I can't imagine activism on the scale that Fals-Borda embodied. I have enriched my understanding of what PAR is and also what it is not.

I feel an inclination towards activism at this point in my life. In learning what PAR is not, I resign myself to the reality that I have not yet experienced activism in the truest sense. I have, however, contributed to community as an individual; this can be my foundation. I consider my experience in class formative to experiencing PAR, setting the stage for my plans for a more activist future. My volunteer activities in the past, although personally satisfying, have been more isolated than collective. If I aspire to create PAR in the future, my activities will have to be less benign and more connected to collective efforts. I feel a call to activism, but I have to reconcile what activism means to me before I can move towards it and incorporate it in to my life.

At the very least, I view the potential to participate in activism as a privilege. The possibility that I have time to even fathom activism probably means that my own basic needs are met and that I can report adequate physical and mental health. In previous years, I contributed where I could to causes that were important to me, but the concept of activism was

diffuse, disconnected from the collective, and not fully integrated in my conscious living. I always had the feeling that my efforts in support of my causes could feel less isolated and more effectual. I have discussed this with like minded friends who have an urge known to us as the "desire to do something." Starting careers, raising children, assorted other challenges, and in some cases hardships have edged in to our intentions. I feel fortunate to be in a time and place that I can think of how to contribute in a more meaningful way to issues that are personally relevant to me. Poverty—particularly child and family poverty—family violence, and violence against women are issues that are closest and most tangible to me.

In completing my final project, what I really wanted was to meet a real life activist. I anticipated meeting Joan Farkas, a community social worker with the City of Calgary who works in the Forest Lawn office. I hoped to find out how Joan experienced her own call to activism; how she found herself at that personal juncture and what the experience is like. I hoped to find out what forms activism assumes for Joan and how she incorporates activism in to her personal and professional life. I wondered what obstacles she has encountered in the course of her journey and how she has dealt with them. I intended to remain reflexive so that I could interpret activism on Joan's terms; I didn't want my questions and pre-conceived impressions of activism to define or limit my portrayal of her experience. I hope that the forthcoming summary accurately portrays Joan's experience, and that in sharing my interpretation, my experience of meeting Joan and hearing about her experiences might also allow my colleagues to deepen their understanding of what activism means. The following interpretation incorporates my own reflections. As I chronicled my conversation with Joan shortly after the interview, I created a commentary of personal reflection, which is represented in italics. What was initially interesting to me is how I had my pen poised above my notebook at the beginning of the interview

ready to take notes. I became so engrossed in hearing Joan's story that I made note only of the references she provided me with. I became intently focused on listening without realizing it.

A day later, as I reflected on the interview and jotted down notes, I realized that Joan's commentary was still vivid in my memory. Her convictions and recollections were engaging and heartfelt, and as a powerful result, my experience as a listener was felt at a similar level. The depth of experience followed through to my reflection and writing. Meeting with Joan and learning about her activism participation was truly a meaningful interaction and writing enterprise for me. I embrace the opportunity to share my learning with my colleagues.

In true academic tradition, I conducted a literature search on activism—an integral part of the academic writing experience that I have become accustomed to. It happens that there is scant literature available on the personal experience of activism and what it means to the activist. There is much more documentation on specific, collective activist efforts and subsequent outcomes. This literature does not tend to narrow the focus to include the personal experience of the individual activist. Fortunately, there is a growing body of research that represents the spirit of PAR advocated by Orlando Fals Borda. Imperialistic, objectivist scientific traditions would insist on a wide range of background literature being presented first, to set the stage and to somehow render what follows "authentic." In preparing my reflection I decided, deliberately, to place a sample of the literature at the end of the paper so that Joan's story would be the clear focal point. I did this resolutely; I decided Joan's story did not need to be legitimized by providing a foundation of academic literature.

When I first met Joan, her reception was warm and friendly, which put me at ease immediately. Joan's passion for activism is evident, and from the start I felt that her sharing conveyed the message that activism is accessible to me. I appreciated her gesture of

inclusion, and this has remained with me as a kind and inspiring impression.

Joan chose social work as a career in her late teens. Joan described formative experiences working with Native clients in Northern Alberta. In one of her first roles, Joan was faced with the challenge of being the only white counsellor on staff of the agency employing her. As she worked with her clients and truly listened to their stories, she became much more aware of the complexity of the experiences of the First Nations People that lived in Peace River and the surrounding area. Most striking to Joan was the pervasive impact of the residential schools on the people. Joan described herself as naïve when she first started her professional training. She emphasized the importance of the clients' stories and the awareness that everyone has a valid story, regardless of the choices they have made or the turns their lives have taken. In building trust and listening respectfully, Joan found that community members would share their stories with her. One example that she recalled vividly was meeting a Native man that lived under a bridge in Peace River. Joan looked beyond his addictions and got to know the gentleman. Eventually, she discovered that he had served in the war. On his return many years earlier, he found that he was alienated from the reserve and also from the prevailing white culture; he was alone.

Joan explained the personal impact of the stories she heard from her clients in the course of her work. Throughout her years of social work, she found it increasingly difficult to disconnect who she was at work from who she was when she left work. Joan spoke to the importance of having balance and having activities in your life that you enjoy; however this wasn't the issue. She emphasized that her value system is very tied to her work, which in turn is tied to who she is as a person, whether she is at work, home, or in another setting. Although Joan had never felt particularly comfortable in the company of social acquaintances who made racist and sexist jokes,

she became increasingly sickened by such "humour." Joan proceeded to describe a disconnect between her own value system and her social life outside of work. For one thing, there weren't other social workers in that circle of acquaintances. Joan explained that she and her spouse had an active social life and numerous social acquaintances. Conversations tended to be far removed from the version of reality that Joan experienced in her work. Over several years, she integrated what she learned from her work as a social worker in to her personal value system. Joan was aware of her emotional responses to her professional work, in response to her professional work and in response to her clients' situations and realities. She felt troubled and a sense of discontent without an outlet for her experiences, reactions, and learning. Joan recalls social occasions outside of work, how she was acutely aware that the topics of discussion were completely meaningless to her. What was more troubling on a personal level was how she often felt marginalized because of her work. She realized that she was doing important work and was making a meaningful contribution to society, but Joan felt marginalized right along with the clients she worked with. Too often, Joan felt that her life's work was responded to with disdain or disinterest. Acquaintances would elaborate lavishly on their professional accomplishments. Joan's interest in their endeavours was simply not reciprocated.

This theme struck a personal chord with me. I feel lucky to have friends who appreciate discussing social issues in detail, who have a compassionate, holistic perspective and an understanding of oppression with a desire to learn more. There were many years when I settled for "less than" in relationships and friendships and felt the inevitable discomfort of compromising myself and my own values. Fortunately, those precarious relationships have slipped from my grasp, or I have chosen to let them go. I suppose that I have become more discriminating in deciding who to spend

personal time with. I have long since realized that not everyone appreciates discussing pressing social issues and the ambiguities therein. On occasion, I have been criticized for having "depressing" interests and for being too intense in discussing them. I have learned from the non-verbal cues that present themselves, cues that suggest that it is not worth pursuing this line of conversation in social settings. The blank stare is most familiar, followed by silence, or awkward shuffling of the feet, crossing of arms. These cues are often followed by a dismissive statement of some sort. I have realized that not everyone has an inclination to discuss issues such as prostitution, homelessness, or family violence. I am on the same wavelength as Joan in this respect. When I have the choice, I choose to enjoy the company of people with whom I can discuss activism and social issues. Although true activism hasn't been integrated in to who I am—at least not yet—the interest and the inclination are present and ready. I so appreciate the support of friends who mentor, encourage, and listen; the support has allowed me to evolve my interest in activism.

Over the past 15 years, I have been "looking for" activism and don't feel that I have encountered genuine opportunities until recently. I feel that the PAR course I am currently taking is a gift, one that has allowed me to construct a philosophy, building on the foundation I have already established.

My first volunteer experience, fifteen years ago, involved facilitating a peer mediation program at an elementary school. As I understood it at the time, I was doing "research on" the program. It would seem that I was missing the mark as far as PAR standards go, although I was doing some of the right things; I was collaborating "with" the participants in terms of working through the training and implementing the program in the school playground. I actually did infuse my research report with some of the comments shared by nine-year-old participants, many of whom were very articulate for their

young age. In retrospect, their comments were the strength of the research "findings." Since I was confirming the interviewees' responses to Kohlberg's model of moral development, I am sure that any representation of their real, lived experience was stifled and muted in the process. I always wondered why, ultimately, writing about the experience felt forced and why I never felt compelled to revisit the work. I recall the experiences working with staff and students in the elementary school with fondness, but the writing was laborious and not nearly as rewarding as I had hoped. Somehow, writing about activism, lived experience, and lending voice feels more fluid to me than conforming participant "responses" to a template of stages. At the time, I was inclined to believe that was what is required to create scientifically valid research.

Over the years, I have fulfilled a handful of volunteer positions. They were fulfilling in many ways, but there was always a background feeling of disconnect from other volunteers, the organization, from agency staff, and certainly from the big picture. In each case, the meaningful interaction was with the clients, which was in the moment and satisfying in itself, but the meaning did not transcend the immediate time and place. Busy with other aspects of life during those years, such as raising a small child and full time work, I decided to be satisfied with the way things were, to let the volunteer experiences simply be as they were. At the time, I decided one thing I could do was to enhance my understanding of the issues affecting clients I interacted with in my volunteer roles. I empowered myself with knowledge by reading widely about the issues. This type of learning was attainable and within my reach at the time. That familiar vague feeling of discontent lingered in the background; I always had the feeling that I could be doing "something more" or that the experience could be more meaningful.

The next step along the activism continuum, or so I thought, was to become involved in board activities.

My hope and intention was to get a sense of the rest of the big picture, a taste of political involvement, and to hopefully feel a greater sense of camaraderie and connection in the process. I quickly realized that "important" people on the board in question were handpicked from positions of perceived importance and that those chosen individuals got to do most of the talking. What was most striking was that the activity was largely removed from community; there was little if any contact with the people that experienced the issues with which the organization was supposed to be concerned. A board member could be involved for years without ever coming face to face with any of the clients. I am hoping that my board experience is not representative of board experiences in general. I was taken aback by my board experience and retreated to my more solitary volunteer activities thereafter. I was through with working in boardrooms.

Joan's activism activities

Joan's career as a community social worker includes activism. Her involvement in activism, though, extends beyond her work role. Joan comments that she felt a sense of relief when she moved in to activism that it felt better once she began the "doing" part involved in activism. Joan cites the early influence of mentors, colleagues who were involved in activism and encouraged her to begin with tangible activities such as writing letters.

Joan's activist activities have evolved to advocacy and working with community members to bring about social change. Her involvement in the Fair Fares initiative, working with marginalized clients to secure a reduced cost transit pass for those that need it the most, is a genuine accomplishment of social change. I was interested in what action was involved for Joan in participating in this initiative. One of the most powerful ideas Joan left me with is the way she connects activism with oppression. Joan equates oppression with not having a voice. She feels that you are truly oppressed if you do not have a voice. The efforts that Joan contributed

to Fair Fares involved supporting clients in expressing their voices and bringing their stories and experiences to the forefront so they could be heard. Joan worked with participants directly throughout the project, providing coaching and mentoring. She trained participants who needed the transit pass and wanted to be part of the advocacy work to present their voice to City Council. The training was intended to prepare the participants so they could feel confident and articulate in that situation. The span of the project represents the tenacity and patience involved in activism. Social change is a process that takes time to evolve. The Fair Fares initiative took place over a period of ten years. The fact sheet featured by Vibrant Communities Calgary chronicles the history of the initiative. The achievement of the 50% reduction in cost for Calgarians living on low incomes was a milestone, but there was still advocacy needed beyond that to ensure that the reduced cost pass became accessible to those who needed it and to ensure the initiative and social change was sustained. Joan recalls that there was work to be done around the eligibility guidelines after the reduced cost pass became available.

Initially, the one year residency requirement excluded many individuals who needed the pass. The willingness of Joan and her fellow activists to stay with the initiative ultimately meant that more Calgarians were afforded the opportunity for community participation. The original premise was that residents of Calgary could not fully participate in their community unless they had a way to get around. The fact sheet on the website provides the facts; answering the "what" and the "how." Joan's story encouraged me to "read between the lines" of the fact sheet. The fact sheet is a highly one dimensional representation of history. Joan's story is a richer, more substantial account. Each stage described on the fact sheet represents the collective efforts of committed individuals. Activists such as Joan assumed a leadership role in the process of the initiative. It is evident that at some point in Joan's activist journey, she began

empowering others in their activism, thereby fulfilling a leadership role. An inspiring aspect of the Fair Fares project is that it involved the efforts of many; activists worked side by side with community members and concerned citizens. Within the collective effort, leadership was required to navigate direction, discuss strategy, and to organize. This is an area I would like to follow up on. I would be interested in the process of if and how leadership was negotiated in moving the initiative forward. Joan kindly referred me to a resource where I could find documented commentary on the initiative. I investigated the resources.

According to the Caledon Institute of Social Policy, the Fair's Fare initiative began as a true grassroots effort in 1998. It gathered strength when it secured the support of Vibrant Communities Calgary, an interest group that unites anti poverty groups across Canada in sharing resources and strategies for reducing poverty. Within Vibrant Communities Calgary, those involved in the Fair Fares initiative began advocacy based on the premise that affordable transportation is critical to community participation for individuals and families. Fair Fares lobbied local and provincial governments, and in 2005 a pilot program was established. This was the beginning. The tenacity of the people involved moved it along to 2008, when it was finally established as a permanent program. This is a very general description, lacking the depth and breadth of the human elements of change. Activists such as Joan would have been involved for the duration, generating the collective energy to move the initiative forward. I am keenly interested in the concept of resilience and to what extent it is integral to the personal experience within collective activism. I suspect it wasn't always gratifying to be involved in the Fair Fares initiative; it must have reached the point where it was not always novel or exciting from the inside. I wonder how activists maintain their momentum and see social change through to tangible results.

The Caledon Institute created a document that clearly emphasized the difference this initiative has made, and continues to make to community members. The document created by the Calendon Institute presents the factual history and emphasizes the outcomes. This initiative has meant that 5000 more people a month can afford to use transit. As a result, this means that these same people can maintain employment, secure better or more stable employment, and get to important destinations, such as medical appointments and voting polls. Thanks to the advocacy and efforts of those committed to the sustainability of the initiative, more people that need it can meet the eligibility requirements and secure the pass. I applaud Joan, her activist colleagues, and the community members who decided to participate and make transportation more accessible for themselves and others who needed it. I wonder how Joan and her colleagues would chronicle the journey in retrospect, what learning they took forward with them to further activist activities.

The process of activism behind the initiative is only accessible through participants: the activists and the community members. The initiative was collaborative; some of the other activists involved were community members who would be eligible for the transit pass. Experienced activists and community partners such as Joan provided the momentum, organizing to keep the initiative moving forward. Joan's story gave me much more of an appreciation for the process of activism; the individual situated within the collective. What is presented as a holistic initiative actually represents a multitude of activities and interactions and efforts of many, each of whom have their own experience of their involvement.

Creating PAR

Joan worked collaboratively with the University of Calgary

departments of Sociology and Community Health Sciences to create a Photovoice project about women living in poverty in Calgary. The words and pictures form powerful representations of the women's daily, lived reality and vividly depict how poverty impacts their experience. The Photovoice creation is central to the final project. The voices of the women are placed at the forefront, significantly increasing the chance that their voices will be heard clearly, in their entirety. The Photovoice project was situated within a larger initiative entitled "Women and a Fair Income." The voice of the participants and the images lend voice to the experience of the women who contributed. The description of how the research was conducted represents PAR methodology; the participants were partners in creating the project; the goal was to empower them in the process and to legitimize their experience. The images and words have a direct, human quality. It is not difficult to imagine how a researcher's description would have lessened the impact by somehow separating the women from their experiences with poverty. I found the commentary of the women featured in the Photovoice project personally touching and endearing; the women felt compelled to rise above the experience of being scrutinized and controlled by sharing their stories in words and images. In keeping with this, the discussion of the women's experience within the report was straightforward and respectful of the participants' perspectives. In this instance, Photovoice genuinely speaks from a collective voice

Resilience and activism

More recently, Joan has taken a personal leap and has learned to perform as a stand up comedian, a creative extension of activism. Stand up comedy has become an outlet for Joan, a way to express her experiences as an activist. She has performed for audiences of up to 300 and is now anticipating learning impromptu comedy. Joan reminisces about how the prospect of stand up comedy terrified her as well as appealed to her when she first considered it. Joan feels that it is critical to take risks: to do things that scare you. I can't help but wonder if her activist experiences have encouraged her to be a risk taker. In this instance, embracing risk benefits and inspires others; it allows Joan to share her experiences with activism beyond her participation in the initiatives. The themes that Joan shares through her stand up comedy routines will reach the audience at a much more emotional level than a report on outcomes would. Through humour, she will enlighten the audience on the realities involved in social activism. Although I have not been part of the audience, I can only imagine that this genre of knowledge would create camaraderie and shared understanding. I would imagine that comedy and laughter would introduce an element of hope.

Literature on activism

I found that there was scant qualitative research literature available on the "experience" of activism at the individual and collective level. There were numerous descriptions of activist experience situated within initiatives; this literature typically elaborates on the initiative or the research process. I was looking for the voice of the activist and how that relates to the collective action, which is usually portrayed as its own intact entity. This corresponds to the values that many activists would understand; I was looking for the voice of the participant. This was my reason for contacting Joan Farkas. Joan's account of her personal experience was of course much more compelling to me than any journal article. I found the experience of hearing Joan's story beneficial and inspiring. I do wonder how much informal sharing takes place amongst experienced activists, new activists, and aspiring activists. Joan mentioned that she socializes with women that are involved in activism; I would imagine these women are a source of strength and support to each other. In following up to clarify a few points with Joan, she remarked that indeed, the group of activists she associates with connect on the common ground of activism. I was delighted to find out that during the course of their social justice activities they connect on a human level, as women, individuals, every

day human beings, discussing their lives, their kids, even favourite television shows. They are committed to activism and draw support and friendship from within those circles. I was inspired to find out that Joan volunteers for the Calgary Women's Centre, with the hope of building an inclusive brand of feminism; one that is more inclusive of "regular" women that are interested in issues of concern to them (rather than the more "hardcore" tradition).

What has always intimidated me about hardcore feminism is the exclusivity and elitism that can exist within the movements. There is the implication that if you aren't engaged in certain activities, that you are not serious or authentic. This is definitely feminism on elitist terms. Or if you are not well versed theoretically or academically, if you cannot yet articulate what brand of feminism you espouse in "academic" terms, that you are somehow an inferior sort of feminist and therefore not worthy of full participation. I have a feeling that I am not alone in my trepidation. As I evolve as a feminist and a humanist, I am adamant about not judging what others have to contribute and how they choose to offer their contributions. I truly believe that women and people in general will have varying degrees to give at different times in their lives. You never know what people are dealing with and what their personal resources are at any given time. I have noticed that there can be judgment within feminist movements; I want to personally reconcile that and move forward.

Fortunately, women such as Joan are setting the standard as role models, guiding inclusive collective action movements. One aspect of activism that I would like to further understand is to what extent support and interaction occurs in the course of activism; are activists solely focused on alleviating oppression and on improving conditions for participants? Is there significant peer teaching, coaching, guidance, and support in relation to activism itself that is happening in the midst of action initiatives? Joan has described the camaraderie that is possible. I suppose the

way I will learn more is to become more involved myself.

The following is a sample of the literature I located on the experience of activism. I wanted to provide this as a background for my reflections on my conversation with Joan. Joan's account was instrumental in illustrating that personal activism is situated in the context of a person's life, that it is integrated in to who they are, their value system and what they do. Only a story can begin to capture the dynamism and richness of personal activism. The articles that I will feature are certainly insightful and useful, but they provide more of a snapshot account of activism at the level of the individual. I didn't want to lose sight of the intention of activism for Joan; it is clearly about working with others to make conditions better for other people. I am writing on the premise that what makes the experience more meaningful and worthwhile for the activist ultimately impacts the experience of those for whom they advocate.

I located an article entitled "Women's Ways of Organizing; Strengths and Struggles of Women Activists over Time," in which Terry Mazhri (2007) interviewed a diverse group of forty-eight "organizers," women who organized social action as part of their jobs and in their communities. Her goal was to identify strengths and obstacles that stood out in and across the women's experiences. The term inclusion was used by many women, but its meaning went beyond the important yet traditional ways of viewing diversity in terms of race, ethnicity, age, or sexual orientation. It also meant bringing the whole self in to the professional activity. One study participant commented, "I bring a real appreciation of process, a real understanding that how you reach the goal is equally important to reaching it" (Mizrahi, 2007). Perceived obstacles of the activists in this study included grappling with the enormity and complexity of issues such as women and children living in poverty, working around the challenges of organizing within communities that have very little resources and limited time to join them in working on issues. The participants emphasized the

need to ensure the interaction between development of the self and development of the collective. A collective theme across participants was the realization that social change was going to be a long process that would require "continuity and connections." Within a collective voice, the participants emphasized diversity and multiplicity of voice, assuming that all women do not speak with the same voice within an activist movement. Mizrahi (2007) agreed with some of her participants that some extent of alienation exists within activist feminist movements and that mentoring would be one way to address the issue. In discussing experiences of activism with participants, Mizrahi discovered that a larger body of literature on activist experiences exists, accounts of "organizers" or activists is held within agencies or by individuals and not readily shared with the outside world. Undoubtedly, the collective and individual commentary and knowledge that exists or existed within social action movements would benefit individuals and groups with similar values and goals. What I found endearing and useful about this research was that it portrayed the holistic nature of activism, and discussed the relation of the whole, or the collective to the individual. At this point, for me, what exists at the level of the individual is of interest, I want to know more about how the individual approaches, joins and participates in activism and also, how and why they choose an activist approach to issues of importance to them in the first place.

Another article, entitled "The Form and Meaning of Young People's Involvement in Community and Political Work" (Queniart, 2008), sought to conceptualize activism as it was experienced by participants between eighteen and thirty years old. The noteworthy aspect of the article was that it addressed the individual within activism, without losing sight of the collective. The concept of activism was placed in a broader context of citizenship. "...the young activists encountered over the course of the study all hold an active concept of citizenship. This concept is composed of rights and

obligations, but also based on action" (Queniart, 2008). Some general findings significant to understanding an individual experience of activism are that the coming generation of activists emphasize the cause more than the collective, although they acknowledge that collective action is the synergy that brings about tangible results. The participants emphasized practical concrete action, actual activities involved in activism and report that they are motivated by tangible immediate action.

These themes suggest that activists such as Joan have much to offer aspiring activists in terms of mentoring. Less experienced activists will eventually have to delay gratification in order to nurture more enduring social change. This is illustrated by the time trajectory of the Fair Fares initiative. Solidarity amongst activists within initiatives will depend on the willingness of individuals to learn from each other and to respect diverse perspectives. This will be true of people of differing ages and generations. Another finding that I found endearing was the group of participants, thought to be representative of the coming generation of activists, value authenticity; they view activism as a philosophy of life. I am inspired by the personal commitment that implies. I don't think my peer group of "Gen X'ers" felt the extent of responsibility; alienation and withdrawal seemed to more mainstream to my age cohort. I was also touched by the finding that youth activists who reported the highest engagement in activism reported that they were socialized in to it; significant adults had modeled activism, citizenship or political involvement. That did not mean, however, that the paths of the youth necessarily followed the same paths as their parents. The youth were self aware and reflective in terms of choosing paths of activism according to issues that were of personal importance to them. I consider myself, although not a young activist, to be an aspiring activist. I can relate to choosing issues of personal importance to take "action" on. Naturally, I wish that I developed a sense

of activism earlier. I like to believe, though, that now is the right time for me to pursue it. This article emphasized the importance of inclusion. Both upcoming and experienced activists and everyone in between have the potential to make a valuable contribution to a collective effort. People within a collective initiative will have varying degrees to give, depending on where they are in their activism journey, their personal and financial resources, and other factors. I am interested in pursuing further inquiry on how differing perspectives, values, and goals are worked out in the process of collective action, and in the process of PAR.

From what I understand so far, there is a developmental trajectory of activism that is very individual. A common theme I have come to understand is that there is often an impetus that triggers an interest in activism and brings it in to the realm of conscious awareness. Some may be socialized towards an interest in activism; some may discover it later in response to a significant personal or collective experience. Interest and emotional reactions eventually transcend one's inner experience to translate into action or connection to others with similar concerns. At some point, the individual makes a conscious choice about what form "action" will take in their experience. Activism may be an occasional presence or an enduring one over one's life, depending on personal choice and circumstances. Recently, I have become much more aware of where I am developmentally in terms of activism. I am now experiencing the awareness, the need to take action. The question marks for me are who to join forces with and what form "action" will take for me. It may be awareness raising, it may be participating in research, it may be lending voice to those impacted by issues I am concerned about. I believe that time and space to think it through activism is essential to my activism journey. I will soon be ready to pursue the next step. I find the prospect of joining forces with existing activist movements promising; this will probably be the best fit

for me. I hope that what I can "give" by becoming involved surpasses what I will need to "take" in terms of learning about activism and moving towards social justice. Reflective writing and discussion will be a means of integrating my experience along the way. Okay, off I go. I'll keep myself posted!

Conclusion and a tribute

I feel fortunate to have my own spirit of activism nurtured. I think this is particularly important for my age cohort. We are not the experienced activists of the 1960s and 1970s that witnessed history in the making, nor are we the savvy upcoming activists born in the '80s and '90s. I was fortunate though in terms of having family influences that encouraged community involvement. When I read Quentain's article, I felt an appreciation for how I was socialized, where I have come from, for my own "critical history."

I would like to take a brief opportunity to remember my grandmother's contribution to where I have evolved in my journey towards activism. My grandmother (and my immediate family) believed in me and have contributed to my education and to my life in general. This has been a life force during difficult times. My grandmother was always genuinely interested in hearing about my learning and community experiences. She passed away last year, and I have given a lot of thought as to how I can honour her life and the relationship I had with her. She lived through the Depression and thereafter, lived a simple, modest life in Calgary with my grandfather, raising a family, and working as an accountant. I treasure memories of shared days baking, shopping, discussing books, visiting, and playing cards with her in my childhood, and, more recently, time spent visiting with her and sharing stories about "critical history." I so appreciate what I learned from my grandmother about giving, about generosity, and about how to treat other people. I didn't realize until I was well into adulthood the true extent of the generosity my grandmother extended to her family, friends, and

community. She always said that the essence of her life was the people in it.

My favourite and most endearing example of her capacity for giving is how she knit countless articles of clothing and blankets and donated her work anonymously to local shelters. During the last couple of years, my grandmother, alone after the death of my grandfather, remained in the comfort of her own home. She ventured out less over time, but she continued to knit the sweaters and blankets. I suspect this was a source of solace for her. The day she died, peacefully in her own home, she had set aside one of her knitting project to rest. She delighted in giving to her family, her community and to friends; and remarked towards the end of her life that she had no regrets. I will be sure to think of her as I pursue my journey towards activism in to the future.

References

Website references

Women and Fair Income project. http://www.fp.ucalgary.ca/wafi/report.htm A collaborative project (Department of Community Health Sciences and Sociology, University of Calgary.)

Looking Out/Looking In: Women, Poverty and Public Policy. A Photovoice Project, Saskatoon, Sask. http://www.pwhce.ca/photovoice/saskatoon_intro.html, Prairie Womens' Health Centre of Excellence website.

Fair Fares fact sheet, Vibrant Communities Calgary http://www.vibrantcalgary.com/http://www.vibrantcalgary.com/media/Fair%20Fares%20November%202007.pdf

Articles

Queniart, A. (2008). The Form and Meaning of Young People's Involvement in Community and Political Work. Sage Publications. http: //yas.sage.pub.com

Mizrahi, T. (2007). Womens' Ways of Organizing: Strengths and Struggles of Women Activists over time. Journal of Women and Social Work. (22) 1.

Lessons Learned
Exhibit 4.3

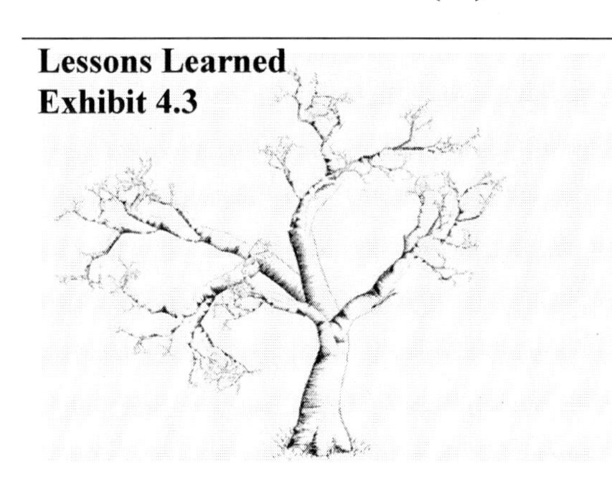

**We are a part of communities we might not even recognize.

**Exemplary stories of community activism abound in our cities, towns and neighbourhoods.

**Everything we need is near at hand.

Your Reflections…

……………………………………………………………………

……………………………………………………………………

……………………………………………………………………

……………………………………………………………………

……………………………………………………………………

Jonathan Lear (2006) created "radical hope" by combining the ancient Greek wisdom of Aristotle with traditional knowledge of the Crow nation in the person of Chief Plenty Coups. Sharon Big Plume already told us of the courage of Warriors:

> Warriors are inspirational to the community; they stand out and are easily recognizable by others for their leadership qualities. The Warrior's courage, honour, and valour pull others forward while serving to strengthen and motivate individuals, as well as the community. (See Exhibit 4.2)

Like the tree of life exercise, we draw from the depths of our past to prepare us for the present while imagining a future. For purposes of this guide, we have been drawing from liberatory adult education traditions to prepare the ground for a disciplined PAR practice that is open and welcoming of all peoples of the commonwealth. To be apathetic in our terrible times is dangerous. We must identify contemporary emancipatory impulses and figure out how liberatory educators can contribute to social change processes. If we don't figure out what's going on and how to join in, are we socially irrelevant? Are we professionally moribund? Fortunately, we have traditions to draw from. The following section reveals further evidence of our liberatory tradition.

A fresh hope is astir. From many quarters comes the call to a new kind of education with its initial assumption affirming that *education is life*—not a mere preparation for an unknown kind of future living (Lindeman, 1926).

Reviving traditions. Let's start with one of Canada's oldest adult education stories: the foundation of the Antigonish Movement that began in the town of Antigonish in northern Nova Scotia and spread throughout the world. In 1921, Father Jimmy Tompkins published "Knowledge for the People: A call to St. Francis Xavier's College." He picked up the post-Great War sense of possibility—recalling Exhibit 1.1—for a peaceful and just world in which adults, especially returning veterans and the women who made the country function well in the absence of the men, learned how to learn to keep up with rapidly changing economies and technologies. Pivotal for Tompkins were the traditions of cooperation and mutuality that he found in all provinces. In particular, he referred to La Caisse Populaire, a people's bank with an initial capital of $26.40, underway in Quebec since 1890 and now a massive institution. Through Extension services at St. Francis Xavier College (St. FX) over the years, the concept of economic cooperation was to thrive, especially in the poor fishing and agricultural communities in Cape Breton and then throughout the Maritimes. St. FX Extension became known as the Antigonish Movement. It became so successful in rousing and organizing the poor into self-supporting cooperatives that the so-called "establishment" grew to oppose it, and actually withdrew financial support from the Extension Service. A literate and questioning people posed a threat to those enjoying "power over" privileges. One Nova Scotia fishing company used to controlling the fishery reportedly

> ...didn't want their fishermen to know how to read. They were against education. "An educated fisherman is a dangerous man." So, they must be kept in debt, and they must be kept illiterate. (Welton, 2001, p. 89)

The Antigonish Movement thought otherwise and was heralded around the world as a model of adult education for collective, co-operative economic development based on organized labour and credit unions. Yet an historian of the Movement cautioned that community development without personal transformation was superficial, and he warned that, ultimately, communities could not be transformed without structural changes in regional and national political economies. Canadian historian Michael Welton (1987a) challenged us with these words, "As children of this terrible age, we must ask ourselves how we can maintain our predecessor's faith in the liberating power of knowledge and human reason" (p. 31). Structural changes did not result from the Antigonish experience in the Maritimes; although it was clear that educating the poor and oppressed, even by the priests of St. FX, was bound to have political implications in the longer term. With the Great Depression, Canadians and Americans alike looked to the Antigonish model as an alternative to the radical political ideas polarizing from Left and Right, from Communists and Fascists.

The liberatory tradition in the English-speaking world has always had a collective understanding and a political sensitivity. British adult educator John Field (1989) writes,

> We always have been mixed up in politics. Since its nineteenth century birth pangs, British adult education has a long tradition of supporting social change…In the residential adult colleges and WEA [Workers Educational Association], for example, there is a long and deep-rooted association—now perhaps grown rather brittle in the bones—with the widening definition of citizenship of the first two decades of the twentieth century. (p. 24)

During the Great Depression and war years, being political—adults learning to reflect and act—made us critical of the social order while we were creating the adult education enterprise as we know it today. The various co-operative movements had a critical social edge. Field is supported by British historian J. F. C. Harrison's (1961) interpretation of adult education as an important part of the growth of English democracy. "Central to this development has been the idea of emancipation.... The removal of old restraints and the opening up of new opportunities, both social and individual, have been basic to the movement in all its phases" (p.356).

Extending the citizenship idea, an idea that includes active participation in democracy, we ask: is adult education "dangerous" because it aims to change behaviours at a very minimum of those who govern and lead, the adults? "My argument is this: adult learning is more central to societal reproduction, resistance, and transformation than that of the children" (Welton, 1987, p. 7). For this reason, the State will not support adult education other than for immediately instrumental reasons based on job preparation. As servants of the State, educational institutions implement the instrumental agenda. Adults run the world, not children. If our energies are directed to changing adults, changing the status quo in effect, changing those who run the world, we are tampering with the social order and are liable to be marginalised as a result. Is this a root cause of adult education's sense of marginality? Adult educators throughout the 1950s and 1960s were worried about their marginality and as a profession strove to become mainstream, and they succeeded. By turning most of their energies to instrumental support of the economy through various forms of job training, they abandoned their radical roots and joined the educational establishment. The "radical" element, those interested in social change and active democracy, took on the name "popular educators." If we are not on the margins of society, perhaps we are not doing our real work, too focused on our jobs. As Brigette Krieg (2007) taught us, there is much wisdom to be found on the margins. Additionally, she learned about this wisdom while engaging authentically with the women on the margins rather than "studying" them like laboratory experiments. If we are content to "study" those on the margins of society, are we doing our work? Are we clear about what our "work" is? We will see in Part Six of this guide how to rediscover our work and thereby finding something better than merely a job. While recovering our liberatory work we need to be clear about the risks we have faced in past in so doing.

PAR
builds self-
awareness

The potential dangers of an informed and radical public in Britain are well documented by the historian R. K. Webb (1955) whose main concern is the "challenge which a literate working class presented to its betters" (vii). He studied the impact of radical thought emanating from the French Revolution commencing in 1789 and the growth of social unrest in face of the industrial revolution. Thomas Paine's *The Rights of Man* in 1792 was one of the more influential publications. This publication fits well the notion of a liberatory moment in the adult education tradition. Similar ideas were recorded and spread in a series of pamphlets and books made available cheaply to a fairly literate working class by social and political commentators of all sorts during the first half of the nineteenth century. The British establishment responded by supporting the growth of schools where people could be introduced to readings deemed as "right," at least in their eyes. Radical educators like William Godwin understood the controlling potential of education and wrote about it during the latter part of the eighteenth century (Spring, 1975). His radical critique of schooling has been taken up by many others ever since and exemplified by Ivan Illich (1970) in *Deschooling Society* and various anarchists in the nineteenth and twentieth century. A recent interpretation of the "Rise of the Anglo-World" during the nineteenth century credits British innovations in literacy and publication as a key to the "Settler Revolution" that established the Anglo-American hegemony (Belich, 2009).

Staying on the subject of Britain for a moment, from where we have drawn many Canadian values, there was an incident in the Elizabethan sixteenth century when a liberatory impulse was nipped in the bud as a threat to the vulnerable queen and fledgling Anglican Church. In 1577, Elizabeth I issued a letter suppressing "prophesying" (Elton, 1962).

> We hear to our great grief that in sundry parts of our realm there are no small number of persons, presuming to be teachers and preachers of the Church though neither lawfully thereunto called nor yet fit for the same...do daily devise, imagine, propound...by their preaching, reading and ministering the sacraments, as well by procuring unlawful assemblies of a great number of our people...especially the vulgar sort, meet to be otherwise occupied with honest labour for their living, are brought

> to idleness and seduced and in a manner schismatically divided amongst themselves into a variety of dangerous opinions . . . if any shall attempt, or continue, or renew the same, we will you...commit them unto prison as maintainers of disorders...(pp. 443-4)

These gatherings brought together people to read the Bible and discuss its meanings. Elizabeth's instincts were sound. This practice was an early sign of the Puritan Movement that became a factor in the radical ideas advanced during the English Revolution of the 1640s. This is an example of adult education helping a social movement move in a big way. Yet radical ideas have a way of excluding others once they become mainstream. These same Puritans, once establishing their authority in New England, forbade women from engaging in religious circles because of their "inferiority" (Carroll, 2011).

Similar sorts of gatherings are visible today in the study circles of Antigonish and Highlander and the literacy circles of Freire. These gatherings are people coming together in solidarity, drawing from their lived experience, to investigate reality in order to transform it into a better, more equitable form. British historian Christopher Hill's life work was documenting the powerful "plain blunt common sense" visible during the English Revolution of the 1640s. A lesson for us from those distant times shows how important it is to take action, "The radicals assumed that acting was more important than speaking" (Hill, 1972, p. 386). This assumption is to be found in the work of Jimmy Tompkins, Myles Horton, Jane Addams, and Saul Alinsky. As recorded by Cari Gulbrandsen and mentioned earlier, Joan Farkas is continuing this tradition in Calgary. She is not alone. One wonders if countries like contemporary Egypt have similar influences deeply at work democratizing knowledge-making, organizations that might lie at the root of the people's revolution. A great challenge for them, and for us in the liberatory tradition, is to keep the circles open and inclusive, welcoming and tolerant.

The liberatory tradition commits us to action. If we do not act, we are not free, writes British philosopher and activist George Monbiot (2003).

> Freedom is the ability to act upon our beliefs. It expands, therefore, with the scope of the action we are prepared to contemplate. If we know that we will never act, we have no freedom: we will, for the rest of our lives, do as we are told. Almost everyone has some sense that other people should be treated as she or he would wish to be. Almost everyone, in other words, has a notion of justice, and for most people this notion, however formulated, sits somewhere close to the heart of their system of beliefs. If we do not act upon this sense of justice, we do not act upon one of our primary beliefs, and our freedom is restricted accordingly. To be truly free, in other words, we must be prepared to contemplate revolution. (pp. 16-7)

How is the Faculty of Social Work preparing us for revolution? Are we encouraged to practice freedom? British historian E. H. Carr wrote, "The primary function of reason is no longer merely to investigate, but to transform" (p. 142). In our current global economic, financial, and political crisis, is simply re-structuring the University of Calgary transformative? Recalling Lindeman, "Adult education will become an agency of progress if its short-time goal of self-improvement can be made compatible with a long-time, experimental but resolute policy of changing the social order" (p. 105). The concept of education for social action was a key component of the community development concept that was emerging in the literature as economic and financial collapse followed the Crash in 1929 (Pyrch, 1983). It is not that we determine the nature of social change. Rather, it is up to us to facilitate the learning processes, making social change processes intelligent and disciplined. Liberatory education demands action oriented processes and outcomes in the practice of freedom.

To imagine a tradition in order to live it. How can we direct and transform our liberatory education practice to inculcate Albertans with a sense of undying hope? How can we change the image of us as lemmings blindly following the one-party rule similar to totalitarian regimes and not bothering to vote at all? First we need to remind ourselves of the radical political practices we enjoyed until the late 1940s (Barrie, 2006). Canadian political scientist Doreen Barrie writes about "the other Alberta," a colourful, politically creative time when we rallied to break free of central Canadian control. We rallied behind the United Farmers of Alberta and Social Credit to resist eastern colonialism. She concluded,

> The province's first three decades were turbulent, challenging and also exciting when Albertans, along with other prairie residents, fought hard against the elements, discriminatory treatment and unjust policies. The early grievances seem to be permanently etched only on the collective memory of Albertans. Dissatisfaction persists in Alberta despite vast wealth and this is mystifying. Perhaps readers will be less baffled now that they understand how skilfully the sense of grievance has been fostered by political elites. (p. 129)

Barrie shows how a political elite formed itself to control provincial politics. This elite has been strategically relying on fear tactics based on imagined eastern Canadian desire to reap the benefits of the oil and gas industry for themselves. This manufactured fear, less spectacular than post-9/11 American fear-mongering but just as controlling, effectively keeps most Albertans locked out of responsible citizenship. Look at the experience of Faculty of Social Work learners noted in Exhibit 2.1. Do you recall how startled I was when I discovered fear within my home province? Barrie challenged us to celebrate the entry into our second century as a province by replacing manufactured fear with the natural and organic hope she sees brooding within all of us.

As noted at the beginning of Part One of this guide, the adult education movement makes social movements move. This is the key to understanding how liberatory education practice is to function well in the Faculty and in our constituency throughout Alberta and beyond. Long time activist in several Australian social movements, adult educator Griff Foley councils us to be smarter and become more efficient organizers (Foley, 2001). The Antigonish Movement was founded by smart organizers of study clubs (Welton, 2001). The Highlander Centre has spent 75 years teaching people to organize themselves and become self-reliant. In stressing effective organization, we can foster a self-sustaining movement. Reflecting on adult education at British universities, Paul Fordham (1984) told the Rutgers University conference to revive the radical tradition in adult education that we need to be much more political. He explained, "I do not mean in a Party sense, but campaigning in all the political media, in all the ways at our disposal for a socially relevant adult education" (29). Fals Borda made a similar plea to us at the Calgary Congress in 1989 when he told us not to be afraid of being political. British radical feminist Jane Thompson (2007) reminds us again and again about the potential power of the working class if revived, and she reminded the world of its historical roots and commitment to lifelong learning and not merely better wages. Can organized labour survive the current global crisis if solely focused on material benefits for itself—or material benefits for anyone for that matter? When are we going to move beyond preoccupation with commodities? More importantly, how are we in the Faculty of Social Work going to organize study circles to search for answers to our current crises? These study circles must extend simple participation into critical liberatory educational settings.

There is room and opportunity in the Faculty to encourage each and every one of us to delve into our unique backgrounds in an effort to locate our own traditions and, in doing so, deepen the collective reservoir. In keeping with a major theme in *Breaking Free*, we start with our own stories, with our families, with our cultures. MSW learner Kulwant Neote approached an assignment in my PAR course from her own Sikh spirituality. This unique approach offered potent insight into her worldview.

Exhibit 4.4: Critical recovery of identity (Neote, 2009).

PAR and the Critical Recovery of History

Participatory Action Research (PAR) defines the people involved as organic intellectuals with the ability to articulate and organize their own knowledge so that they may take a leading role in the defence of their class and the advancement of their society (Peet & Hartwick, 1999). Orlando Fals Borda (1988) lists the four techniques in PAR as collective research, the critical recovery of history, valuing and applying folk culture, and the production and diffusion of new knowledge. Collective research involves the use of objective knowledge as data which is collected in groups. The critical recovery of history uses collective knowledge to discover or rediscover parts of the past which aid in the defence of current struggles. Valuing and applying folk culture places an importance on cultural and ethnic elements which are not recognized in regular political practice. Finally, production and diffusion of new knowledge incorporates different ways of distributing new data, information and knowledge depending on ability of the co-researchers and public in general to understand written, oral or visual messages.

Critical recovery of history is an effort to discover elements of the past which increased awareness through collective memory by using oral tradition in the form of interviews and witness accounts by members of the community. Some of the techniques used to stimulate the collective memory are data columns, popular stories, stories of the past kept in family coffers, ideological projection, imputation, and personification. By stimulating the collective memory folk heroes, data and facts can be discovered and corrected, complemented or clarified since many official or academic accounts are written with other class interests and/or biases in mind. Through this process, history can gain a new meaning from these glimpses of truth. The people involved in the critical recovery of history find that not only can facts be

remembered, but they can also play a role in improving the conditions which they live in (Dagron & Tufte, 2006).

Brandão (2005) adds that the historical dimension is always and inevitably present in PAR. This is due to the fact that PAR is not a matter of knowing how to promote or develop 'something' but it is to transform the whole in which this 'something' is a part of, including its history.

Critical recovery of history can provide the Sikh religion with some much needed answers, but in doing so those that ask questions are met with resistance. As Sikhs quickly lose their identity, it is up to those who are courageous enough to seek answers by looking back into our history and recover information that has been hidden from us for centuries. In my quest to find answers to my own Sikh identity, I look at two stories which provide me not only with an example of a critical recovery of history, but a sense of hope that my questions can be answered.

Silenced Voices

We see the light of hope in those that speak up and step forward with the truth. They are ridiculed, critiqued, and threatened, but they keep pushing to find the truth and share it with others. Sometimes it is hard to know what is true and what is false because we grow up believing in something for so long, that when we get to a stage where we ask questions and seek answers to find *our* truth, it directly conflicts with the deeply ingrained beliefs that we have been programmed with from childhood. It is common in our quest for knowledge and the truth, to encounter resistance, but how is anyone supposed to find hope when their questions go unanswered? This is when true warriors raise their minds and ideas as a sword to fight on the side of truth and justice, making their way through those who stand in their way with courage.

This courage and the fight for truth and justice are some of the defining qualities that make up a Sikh warrior, which is a concept that is central to the Sikh religion. We are told stories about Sikhism in our temples, through our elders, and peers. Stories about the bravery, courage and strength that embodied a Sikh warrior are retold from generation to

generation. Unfortunately these stories change from storyteller to storyteller with many irreconcilable inconsistencies. To question the storyteller can be a sign of disrespect as it can be viewed as a personal attack and/or religious attack and considered insulting to our elders. So as youth, we quietly listen to these stories voiding our minds of all questions, but listening for the connections between stories. We are guided by these connections into the centre of our truth by the use of the critical recovery of our history.

An example of an inconsistency in Sikhi is the Adi Granth, a holy scripture which is considered to be the holiest item in Sikhism because it is the current Sikh Guru. The scripture is recited by temple leaders and our elders, but the meaning that is taken from those words change from person to person.

There is a well known researcher of Sikhism, Dr. Pashaura Singh, who encountered much difficulty in exploring the Adi Granth. His story is unique because he researched Sikhism with the hopes of finding the truth, but was expected to follow the religion blindly, without finding answers to the questions that many people ask in their quest to understand their religion. It is an example of how the findings of academic research can be used for discussion so that we learn about ourselves by recovering a piece of history that would have otherwise been lost forever. It also speaks to us about the power and authority we may encounter when seeking the truth by showing us how this individual chose to defy the power and authority that stood in his way.

A Voice of Hope

Dr. Pashaura Singh moved to Calgary from India with an MA in religious studies. His occupation in Calgary was a priest in the local temple. During his stay in Calgary, he obtained his MA in religious studies from the University of Calgary and continued his education at the University of Toronto completing his PhD in religious studies, encountering much hardship when writing his dissertation. Dr. Pashaura Singh's dissertation was written on "The Text and Meaning of the Adi Granth" where he explored the origins of the Adi Granth and

its evolution, which was highly controversial since it challenged the current mainstream beliefs about the Adi Granth.

Unfortunately for him, he was called to Amritsar, India, to stand before the Akal Takht, a panel of five high priests in the headquarters of Sikhism, the Golden Temple. He was charged with 5 counts of Blasphemy because the priests claimed that he made 'baseless observations' in order to please his thesis supervisor who was a supposed adversary of Sikhism. They claimed that he attacked the authenticity of the Adi Granth because a Sikh scholar is, "expected to produce literature to promote the welfare of all, with commitment to Sri Guru Granth Sahib...But what happened was exactly the opposite of this" (from the Akal Thakt's judgement read to Dr. Pashaura Singh on June 27, 1994).

Following this, Dr. Pashaura Singh was given a religious punishment of chores such as cleaning shoes, prayers, and a verbal apology to the temple in his home state in order to be granted forgiveness. In addition, he was to revise his thesis and all his previous publications and submit a confessional statement in which he pleaded guilty to all charges. His confession was as follows, "Under orders from Sri Akal Takht Sahib, appearing at the Takht Sahib, this humble servant pleads guilty to the five charges in respect of my thesis (The Text and Meaning of the Adi Granth), read out as well as given to me in writing. I hereby reject in thought, word and deed all such objectionable formulations that occur in my thesis. I beg forgiveness of the Panth [All Sikhs] for whatever hurt the conclusions drawn by me in my thesis have caused to the Panth. In future I pledge to serve the Panth as a humble servant of the Panth. I also willingly accept whatever decision is announced by the Singh Sahiban". He was ordered to never publish any other objectionable material such as his thesis, which is why he has recently been in the centre of controversy yet again.

In 2000, Dr. Pashaura Singh defiantly published the findings of his thesis in his book, *The Guru Granth Sahib: Canon, Meaning, and Authority*, which alerted the coalition of Sikh temples in California, who demanded that Dr. Pashaura Singh be relived at his position as a professor at the University

of California Riverside. In their letter the coalition stated in its allegations that, "Professor Singh is wrong in his conclusions, but the Coalition asserts its own beliefs in matters must be accepted on faith, and not on scholarship".

UCR fully supported Dr. Pashaura Singh as they promptly rejected the Coalitions concerns on the bases that, "The University's policies promote the toleration of ideas. University policies do not provide a framework for assigning guilt for "wrong" ideas, nor procedures for apologizing to people whose authority has been "defied." The focus of this complaint is on limiting toleration of ideas, and the remedies requested are not within the authority of the University."

Speak Freely and Inspire

This next story is one close to my heart. It is the story of Gyani (Scholar) Teja Singh Neote, my grandfather (Babaji) who, like Dr. Pashaura Singh, sought to find the truth about Sikhism by filling in the missing pieces of our history. Also just like Dr. Pashaura Singh, Babaji's journey also started with him being a priest at a Sikh temple but in Nairobi, Kenya, and subsequently devoted his life to studying Sikh philosophy and history.

As a priest Babaji was an Akali Sikh, who are described as the most aggressive Sikhs because they are seen as the 'immortal ones' whose first duty is to be good soldiers. Although Sikhism forbids Sikhs to eat meat, Babaji's sect allowed Sikhs to eat meat provided that it is prepared according to the 'chatka' ritual. In this ritual, the animal is killed in a humane fashion by being butchered quickly so that it doesn't suffer. The animal has to be sacrificed to appease the warrior spirit which is seen as good practice for war because if a person cannot even kill a goat, how can they take the life of another human (Frontline Punjabi Youth, 2007).

One day, while Babaji was slaughtering a chicken, it flew away but its head still remained in his hand. The blood of the flying chicken got sprayed on his clothes and at that instant, he remembered the following quote from the Adi Granth, "If one's clothes are stained with blood, the garment becomes polluted. Those who drink the blood of other beings – how can

their consciousness be pure." This one incident made Babaji reflect on his beliefs as an Akali Sikh.

This incident set him in a path to find the truth and to find a living Guru, which he knew in his heart, existed. He was one of few people who found a copy of the original Adi Granth in the British Museum and firmly established that the text has been manipulated causing ambiguity in some of its verses. This makes many people who read the Adi Granth to interpret the text to their liking, thus the numerous sects in Sikhism. Other verses in the two copies of the Adi Granth were clearly different. One verse in the original Adi Granth states that there will always be a living guru, and in the copy we have today in our temples it says that the living guru is the Adi Granth, which confirmed to Babaji that he must seek out this living guru.

He found a sect of Sikhism called Namdharism, which believes that there was a continuation of the Sikh Gurus after the 10th Guru and they are now at the 15th Guru. Namdhari's were the Sikhs who fought the British without the sword but with peaceful protest. They believe that the era of fighting with the sword has passed and we must now use our minds to fight.

The 12th Namdhari Guru was the revolutionary who started the boycott of the British products such as clothing, transport, postal service, road system, schools, and courts which threatened the British rule without the use of armoury. This peaceful protest influenced future revolutionaries such as Ghandi. He was so powerful that the British had to exile him and keep the Namdhari movement under control by forbidding them to congregate in numbers greater than five. Prayers were broken up and people were not allowed to practice religious rituals or customs or they would be imprisoned in conditions that were unfit for living.

But this did not deter the Namdhari's, when then British strategically placed butcher shops near temples, Sikhs and Hindus became angered by the slaughtering of cows near their places of worship. The Namdhari's broke into the shops and released all the livestock until the butcher shops were shut down. Following this, they courageously turned themselves in and lost their lives. Namdhari's were known for giving their

lives voluntarily and with courage in order to give Indians the freedom and rights to keep their religion and identity, earning their reputation as 'freedom fighters'.

Babaji found his path in life and he tirelessly shared his findings with others around him. He never thought about the scrutiny around his work but instead focused on his passion to educate others around him even though he only earned enough money to support his family and research. He was a highly respected scholar of Namdhari history and well known for his research, writings, and lectures of Sikhism all over the world. His most notable contribution and now a legacy is the distribution of over 150, 000 religious cassettes all over the world where is devoted his retired life in making and recording the religious cassettes and actively distributing them without monetary gains. When he passed away, the funeral hall was full of people who respected his life's work and a library was donated in his name where all of his writings and recordings are stored.

Babaji never published his work but instead, he shared his research with everyone and anyone who was willing to listen because he loved the discussion that followed. His sole interest was to help others understand the Sikh religion and no matter what their questions were, he always answered them to the best of his knowledge.

This is what I have found to be the truth behind spirituality, it is the need to share, enlighten, and listen deeply to those around you so that our spirits continue to grow and beam the light of truth all around us.

References

Brandão, C. (2005). Participatory research and participation in research. A look between times and spaces from Latin America. *International Journal of Action Research*, *1*(1), 43-68.

Dagron, A.G. & Tufte, T. (2006). *Communication for Social Change Anthology:*

***Historical and Contemporary Readings.* South Orange, NJ: CFSC Consortium, Inc.**

Orlando Fals Borda (1988). *Knowledge and People's Power* New Delhi: Indian Social Institute.

Peet, R. & Hartwick, E.R. (1999). *Theories of Development.* New York, NY: Guildford Press.

The Sikh Times (n.d.). *Akal Takht Indicts Pashaura Singh.* Retrieved March 22, 2009.

***University of California Riverside Chancellor Clears Prof. Pashaura Singh of All Allegations of 'Wrongdoing'.* (2009). Retrieved March 22, 2009.**

Lessons Learned
Exhibit 4.5

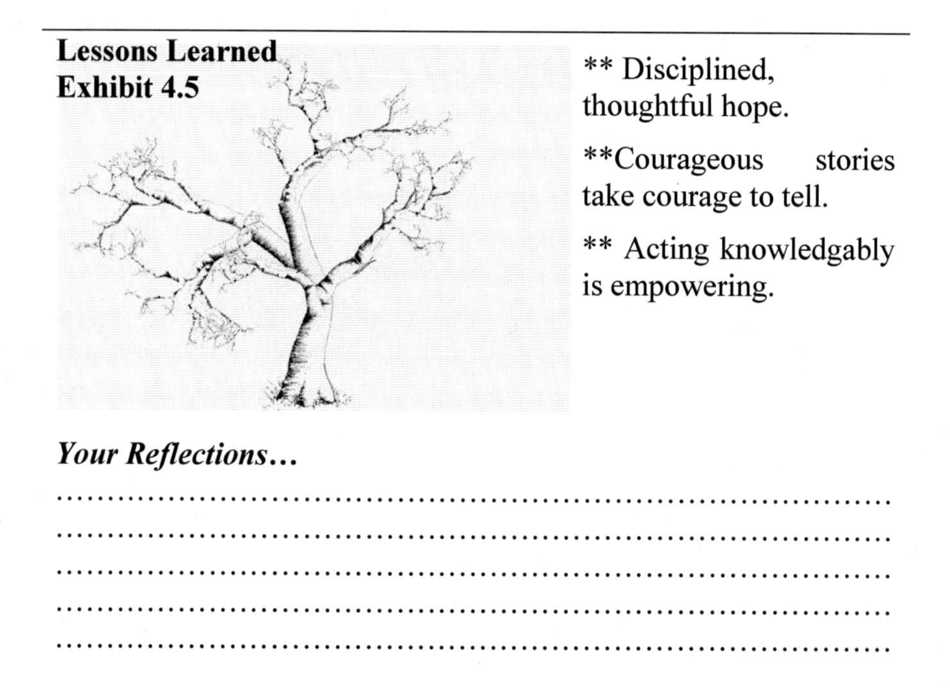

** Disciplined, thoughtful hope.

**Courageous stories take courage to tell.

** Acting knowledgably is empowering.

Your Reflections…

....

....

....

....

....

Kulwant Neote joins Michael Newman in linking social justice, and social relevance to learning:

> We can learn, and help others learn, to use benign forms of social control; and we can learn, and help others learn, to resist malign forms. If we use learning in this way, then learning becomes a tool in the struggle for social justice. (Newman, 1999, p. 79)

The trouble is: socially relevant groups and individuals in Newman's sense form a small minority in society. Not to worry; American anthropologist Margaret Mead taught us long ago, "Never doubt that a small group of thoughtful, committed citizens can change the world; indeed, it's the only thing that ever does." What is to be done? For a start, we can devote our energies to acting creatively and vigorously in keeping with our work as liberatory education practitioners. Up to now, we have found our collective voice in Faculty of Social Work experiences and in historical background traditions from many cultures and disciplines, urging us to restore grassroots democracy. To strengthen our emerging confidence in ourselves, we need to attend to another obstacle in a path to changing our realities. We need to break free of ancient forces in the academy claiming science and science-making exclusively for themselves or for those who fund them. We will do this together in Part Five of *Breaking Free.*

Lessons learned in part four. It would be too easy to simply write Albertans off as apathetic, uncaring, and lazy. It would also be far from the truth. Faculty of Social Work classrooms are alive with energetic, creative, and caring individuals who react with energy when challenged to respond to democratic responsibility. The history of the province and of the broader world is full of imaginative resistance to all forms of hegemony. This resistance is timeless with ancient signs throughout English-speaking cultures and beyond. Equally as important, English-speaking peoples, the people I know best have always been resilient under pressure and reactive to political control by elites. How can we as liberatory education practitioners facilitate and champion this resiliency? What constitutes our own resiliency? Once comfortable with our resiliency and confidence, we can address another major challenge to our social justice work.

Part Five

Breaking free of imperial science

Up to now in this guide we, as liberatory educators committed to processes of social justice, have been breaking free of constraints facing our practice. This process of breaking free is, contrary to what may be expected or assumed, a highly constructive experience. Removing the constraints of isolation into self, imposed silence, and citizen lethargy is a celebration of the hopeful things going on in the Faculty of Social Work. This destruction could not be more liberating, more constructive. One more constraint needs attention, perhaps the most formidable one to us trying to learn together at the academy. In some ways, the academy is archaic in its claim to sole ownership of the science of knowledge-making. This claim led to the creation of disciplines housed in academic departments and faculties, locked into languages with the effect of excluding as much as they include. Much of this language is ordered into dichotomies, into either/or arrangements encouraging aggressive competition and debate for short term gain. Such narrow mindedness has its critiques and its critics. These critics are notable scientists like palaeontologist Stephen Jay Gould who, while explaining the origins of the notion of dichotomy in human evolution, devoted much of his career to mediating the gap between science and the humanities (Gould, 2003). In trying to reintegrate the sciences with the humanities, he suggested,

> An understanding of the social embeddedness of all aspects of science can forge an essential tie with humanistic studies and greatly aid the technical work of scientists as well (p. 116)...A sympathetic application

> and understanding of "user friendly" themes in humanistic study will aid the approbation and acceptance of science by a suspicious general public. The breaking down of artificial barriers between the sciences and humanities will help even more. (p. 138)

Clear language free of the jargon that we acquire in the academy is prerequisite to communication between the many and diverse forms of inquiry. This brings to mind Fals Borda's (1988)

> ...shared code of communication between internal elements and external agents of change which leads to a common and mutually understandable conceptualisation and categorisation. The resulting plain and understandable language should be based on daily intentional expressions and be accessible to all, avoiding the airs of arrogance and the technical jargon that spring from usual academic and political practices, including ideological elements from the current developmentalist discourse. (p. 97)

For him, competent PAR researchers must convey the same clear message in all four levels of communication, ranging from pre-literate peoples all the way "up" to scholars. Competent Social Work liberatory education practitioners are good communicators in all settings and facilitate processes so those settings are comprehensible to everyone present.

The stimulus for the title of this part of *Breaking Free* comes from James Scott's (1998) book *Seeing Like a State*, which is a

> ...case against the imperialism of high-modernist, planned social order. [Scott stresses] the word "imperialism" here because [he is] emphatically not making a blanket case against either bureaucratic planning or high-modernist ideology. [He is], however, making a case against an imperial or hegemonic planning mentality that excludes the necessary role of local knowledge and know-how. (p. 6)

He makes a case for the indispensable role of practical knowledge, informal processes, and improvisation in the face of unpredictability. We might recall the Aristotelian notion of *phronēsis*, practical wisdom. Scott's advice is welcome in these revolutionary times. He borrows an ancient Greek term to capture this practical knowledge—*Metis*, or common sense. Scott writes about "the art of the locality," settings that are indeterminant—some facts are unknown—and particular. Practical knowledge is captured in narratives, storytelling as an approach to sharing experience and knowledge-making at the heart of *Breaking Free*. This position in no way devalues the power of official and expert knowledge located within academic curricula. Indeed, acknowledging people's knowledge in narrative form expands and deepens our inquiry into the human condition at a time when we are facing enormous changes to our way of life. Rejecting any form of knowledge is wasteful.

Coincidentally in Canada, the same spelling of ancient Greek wisdom identifies one part of the Aboriginal community, the Métis, and a real strength in the Faculty of Social Work. Also coincidentally, a significant contribution to our understanding of the power of people's knowledge was recently made by one of our Métis doctoral graduates Brigette Krieg (See Exhibit 3.3). In a practical way, her research shows how we can break free of constraining silence by celebrating the practical knowledge of Aboriginal women discounted in a maze of statistics and categories. Krieg's FSW's learning journey gave us a local instance of Scott's global inquiry into practical knowledge-making in local communities. Similar Faculty research is on-going globally. Professorial colleague John Graham has been engaged for several years with a Bedouin-Arab colleague Alean Al-Krenawi while locating and documenting knowledge-making traditions in the Middle East. In their words,

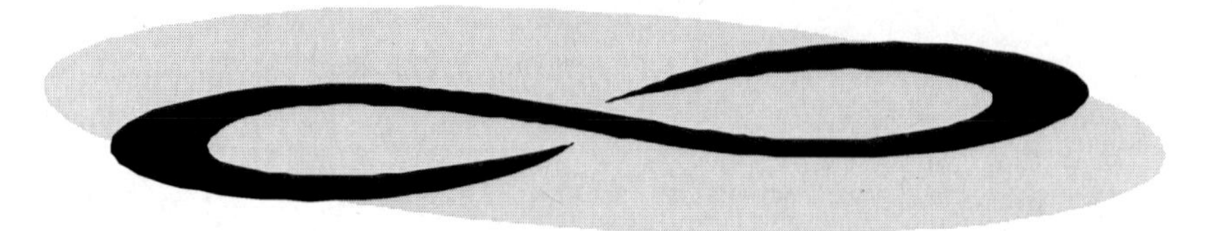

> Members of any helping profession—their practitioners, students and scholars—are custodians of their profession's knowledge base. Each research study, each intervention, each publication, contributes further to the development of that knowledge base. It is never static, never linear; it evolves over time, and its members take responsibility to play a role in that enterprise in a way that maximizes communities' social justice and authentic cultural expression. Helping professionals allow a dialogue between local cultures and professional intervention; in this process, new knowledge is being continuously created. The local (community) and global (social work) co-exist and coalesce towards a new dynamic that is unique. (Al-Krenawi & Graham, 2008, p. 7)

The PAR process is organic

The dynamic, fluid and creative nature of knowledge-making in Bedouin-Arab communities closely resembles the liberatory education practices we are celebrating in *Breaking Free*, most clearly in Aboriginal experiences. The dynamic relationship between the local and global scales at the heart of Al-Krenawi and Graham's research recalls the Ganma rivers flowing from ancient knowledge-making traditions. Coincidentally, these images have recently come alive in the Arab world.

The trans-disciplinary bi-monthly magazine *Resurgence*, published by Schumacher College in England, celebrated its 250th issue with the title "Indigenous Intelligence: Diverse solutions for the 21st century." Magazine editor, Satish Kumar, welcomed readers to a "dance of diversity" with his sentiments,

> Traditional cultures which do not fit within the paradigm of economic growth, commercial expansion, consumerism, globalisation and mass production are labelled at best as idealist dreams, lacking realism. Traditional cultures are condemned as underdeveloped and backward. The systems of industrialisation, globalisation, and centralisation are proclaimed as symbols of progress and development…
>
> In the view of our contributors, the way forward is in the harmonious relationship between ecology and economy; between idealism and realism; between Nature and culture between environment and development; between tradition and progress; between unity and diversity; and, above all, we need to embrace the paramount importance of pursuing noble ends with noble means (Kumar, 2008, p. 2).

Recalling Aristole's virtues, Kumar's words are about balancing diverging impulses guided by noble values. How is the reader balancing these impulses in your daily routine? A growing interest in narratives accompanies this "dance of diversity".

> A narrative is not merely a transmission of information. In the very act of telling a story the position of the storyteller and the listener, and their place in the social order, is constituted; the story creates and maintains social bonds. The narratives of a community contribute to uphold the values and the social order of that community (Kvale, 1995, p. 21).

PAR
is inclusive of
all forms of
knowledge

"Tacit" knowledge, those ideas lying at the very depths of our being yet protected from those wanting to control and package for profit, lies within these narratives by being impossible to describe clearly. Al-Krenawi and Graham (2009) introduce the Arabic word *Ta'seel*, "meaning to go back to the roots to seek direction, to restore originality, or to become genuine" (p. 6). Collecting and understanding our narratives, our stories, is crucial to PAR with one of Fals Borda's (1988) four techniques emerging from PAR being the creation and dissemination of new knowledge. How can we clarify that which is unclear? Lilli Heinrichs (See Exhibit 2.5) reflected at length about knowledge-making in her MSW case study completed in 2007, and she ultimately decided to share her field work notes in Indonesia as a narrative, despite her nervousness by so doing.

Exhibit 5.1: The narrative struggle. Heinrichs (2007)

We, as individual social work practitioners, need to be aware of the dynamic involved in the social construction of knowledge and use this awareness to further the goals of social justice, the fundamental value underlying all social work intervention. Social justice means transforming the way resources and relationships are produced and distributed so that all people can live dignified lives in a way that is ecologically sustainable (Potts & Brown, 2005, 224). In striving for social justice, Fals Borda (1988) contends that we need to learn to know and recognize ourselves as a means of creating people's power and the internal and external mechanisms of countervailing power (101). In that regard, an attitude that is accepting of ambivalence and uncertainty enables us to question that which appears 'normal' and taken for granted and to negotiate processes and create spaces for ourselves and others who are commonly excluded from the creation of knowledge (Potts & Brown, 2005). The co-creation of knowledge, resulting from the PAR process, also requires an open spirit of humility. "Humility helps us to grow, to listen, to share and to know how to give and how to receive. It teaches us how to create a knowledge that is 'ours,' not 'yours' or 'mine'—to create not only a

'you' or 'me,' but a 'we'" (Pyrch & Castillo, 2001, p. 381). Social justice can only be realized through the genuine participation of all people and the right of everyone to be heard and respected.

My experience in Aceh has brought a great self-awareness to my feelings, thoughts, and reactions. It has challenged me to reflect upon my sense of self, my history, and my actions with others. It has highlighted the need for skills in listening deeply, critical thinking, and analyzing relations in order to unpack assumptions, unearth patterns of thinking and acting, and recognize their effects. Realizing my personal limitations and the value of alternative perceptions is a humbling experience, a constant reminder to be reflective of both my work and myself. I have learned that we are all deeply interconnected and reliance on each other strengthens community and fosters social justice…

Through a process of collaborative dialogue, PAR can serve as humanizing force, building bridges between people, strengthening community, and increasing our reliance on each other, thereby inspiring hope.

PAR goes beyond the positivism of Western science by incorporating other ways of knowing and gives a voice to people who are oppressed and marginalized, promoting empowerment, inclusivity, and respect. Instead of demanding a separation of mind, body, and spirit, these are viewed as legitimate ways of gathering information and creating knowledge. Despite our cynicism and that all of this goes against the grain of how our society is currently structured, the principles appeal to what is human in us. The recovery of personal and social histories, reexamination of realities, and regaining of power through deliberate actions lead to the creation of knowledge that can nurture, empower, and liberate us to act in ways that make for justice and a more equitable and humane world (Smith, 1997, 8). As Australian Aboriginal educator Lilly Watson observes, "If you are coming to help me, you are wasting your time. But if you are coming because your liberation is bound with mine, then let us work together" (Wadsworth, 2001, 430).

PAR and Appreciative Inquiry offer challenges for the field of social work education, where we appear to grasp the rhetoric of interconnectedness but are still struggling to "walk our talk." Our knowledge base seems to privilege Western traditions, limiting our awareness and inclusion of other knowledge-making traditions. How we foster learning, engage in research, and develop interventions provides another opportunity to practice democracy and thereby manifest our beliefs about power relations and social justice. If we regard meaning as emerging from a complex process of mutual inquiry, then we can create an interdependent community. According to Parker Palmer (1998), "Our assumptions about knowing can open up, or shut down, the capacity for connectedness…" (51).

Our Faculty of Social Work should model the discourse of interconnectivity and social justice by exploring options that capture alternative ways of knowing. Embracing the knowledge-making traditions of First Nations here in Canada, as well as those of Indigenous people around the world, has the potential to orient social work education, interventions, and policy initiatives in new and exciting directions. This includes openness to various styles of writing such as narratives, subjective text, and storytelling, which better reflect reality than academic prose. I have found it a particularly challenging process to present this case study in a way that gives the context of my journey and my findings. Writing in the first person and placing myself in the picture in order to speak about PAR as a lived experience has been a demanding task. This struggle was compounded by the relatively limited amount of academic literature available that reflects this approach. Challenging dominant and/or unjust modes of thinking and organization involves risks. However, it is in having the courage to become vulnerable and share of ourselves that we connect with each other, blending our voices and regaining commitment to a meaningful way of life.

Lessons Learned

Exhibit 5.1

**Relating our experience in the academy through narratives is demanding and stressful.

**Knowledge-making traditions are deep and broad.

**Writing me into my academic work is risky business.

Your Reflections

....

....

....

....

The myth of objectivity has it that knowledge-making requires us to remove our personal, subjective self from scientific inquiry. Yet even in seventeenth century England during the early years of the "scientific revolution," magic remained part of reasoned inquiry (Hill, 1972). Intuition is at the root of all disciplined inquiry. Historians willing to acknowledge the idea of "history from below" (Hobsbawm, 1997) will often find humankind far richer, far less orderly than seen by those interests wanting to generate a mechanical world easier to manipulate. Schools of history, like schools everywhere, have strong walls keeping certain things in and certain things out. Who decides?

Liberatory education is not about discounting official knowledge, representing the state, and expert knowledge, representing the professions. It is about enriching them with people's knowledge (*la sagesse populaire*). Has there ever been a time when people's knowledge had its day? Yes, during the chaotic revolutionary 1640s in England.

> For a short time, ordinary people were freer from the authority of church and social superiors than they had ever been before, or were for a long time to be again…the eloquence, the power of the simple artisans who took part in these discussions is staggering (Hill, 1972, pp. 361-2).

Once we uncover the power of our own voice and find our connections with many other voices, we come to appreciate what we already have. Recalling the words of one learner recorded in Exhibit 2.1, "I feel affirmed and excited to discover that my own experience has a name and a language that others can relate to. I'm overwhelmed by the realization that there really is a community of seekers in the world who are dreaming in the same images of peace, justice and creativity."

Including me in my writing. American anthropologist Mary Bateson (1994) finds it extraordinary

> ...that in a society where we regard the self as central, we are so often engaged in silencing its expression or putting confidence at risk. Volumes have been written about the miracle represented by learning to use the word *I*, yet that capacity is under constant attack. (pp. 67-8)

We claim the right to speak our minds yet we seem to distance ourselves from being direct about so doing. We need to be clear about what we mean by personal agency. She continues,

> I am in defiance of scientific convention and much of literary history when I claim the freedom to begin many of my sentences with the word *I*. Yet it rescues me from the temptation to be categorical. The word I want is *we*, but there are limits to the assumption of agreement, so I 'personalize' as a more honest way to be inclusive. Impersonal writing often claims a timeless authority: this is so. Personal writing affirms relationship, for it includes these implied warnings: this is what I think at the moment, this is what I remember now, continuing to grow and change. (pp. 75-6)

As I explained in the Preface to *Breaking Free*, I am now comfortable being me, although it took many years to overcome the conditioning that had me hidden away. At the same time, unlike Bateson I am comfortable using the collective *we* because this guide is facilitating the basic collective value in PAR—Fals Borda's concept of "collective research." We are seeking general agreement about *our* responsibilities.

Looking to reconcile approaches to knowledge-making, Gould (2003) strives for an understanding of mutuality amongst humanists and scientists. To advance his point, he reflects on the ancient Greek proverb of the fox and the hedgehog; the one representing agility and guile in pursuit, and the other the steadfast adherence to one strategy. Both strategies are valuable, yet "foxes generally do very well indeed, but when the chips go down in extremis, look inside yourself, and follow the singular way that emerges from the heart and soul of your ineluctable being and construction, whatever the natural limits—for nothing beats an unswerving moral compass in moments of greatest peril" (p. 7). What lies within us and/or what we can access in our timeless quest for social justice provides direction and comfort for our liberatory education practice.

Brenna Atnikov, MSW, (2008) realized it was her adherence to PAR principles that made her an authentic "catalyst agent." In her case study based on several months working with youth at an NGO in Ghana, she showed many signs of the agility of the fox as she worked to strengthen the confidence of her young charges. Ultimately, her basic values saw her through. As she writes in the following exhibit, "in looking back, I realize that by maintaining my commitment to the values and principles of participatory research, I can be proud of being an authentic 'catalyst agent,' and am certain this is a role I would take on again in my practice." This was Brenna the hedgehog.

Exhibit 5.2. Realizing One's Worth: The importance of participation in active community building (Atnikov, 2008).

Reflections

Without question, writing this document is the toughest assignment I have had to date in my academic career. The difficulty did not arise from the required length of the paper, the topic (per se), or even in the very act of writing. This is the first time I have ever been so emotionally connected to what it is I am required to produce and have found it challenging to represent through words alone what it is I have learned. My work in Ghana was both the most personally and professionally challenging experience I have encountered and it has taken months to not only be able to think about it, but to reflect and write about it as well. And yet, as much as I have struggled with my work and its outcomes, it has been a steep and meaningful learning curve.

I went to Ghana expecting to do participatory research, which is well documented as a conscious effort to inquire about practice (Conle, 2000; Pryor, 1998). Initially, my intention was to inquire about how participation in a community based action group mitigates the psychosocial impacts of living in poverty. In other words I was curious to learn how contributing to social change in one's community could also stimulate meaningful individual change. I only recently figured out that what I was really doing was inquiring about *my own* practice as a facilitator of Popular Education and how one challenges their co-researchers self perceptions of value and worth to the point where individuals come to know, fundamentally, that they deserve better. In other words, how can I help to build critical awareness and make people angry enough that they cannot help but be stimulated to action?

My inquiry fuelled learning and created knowledge I had not expected – perhaps the sign of good participatory research – but it has overwhelmed me and I feel as though I have been

at a loss for what to do with my new awareness. I see development work entirely different now; I see the individual trees in the forest, rather than the forest as a whole, and am certain that each one needs to be individually tended to and nurtured for significant change to occur. This thought, in and of itself, continues to overwhelm me to no end and perhaps is yet another source of the emotional difficultly I have experienced since my return from Ghana. There is so much to do, so many individual saplings to cultivate and encourage.

I then read Margaret Wheatley's (2006) reflections on the fall of the Berlin Wall and small change:

> **I know of no better theory to explain the sudden fall of the Berlin Wall. Before that event, there were many small changes going on throughout East Germany, most of which were not visible to anyone beyond their immediate neighbourhood. But each small act of defiance or new way of behaving occurred within a whole fabric. Each small act was connected invisibly to all others. The global impact suddenly became visible in those few days when people tore the Wall down. The fall of the Berlin Wall demonstrates the power of 'think globally, act locally'. It proves that local actions can have enormous influence on a monstrous system that had resisted all other political attempts to change it... It was local actions within the system, combined with many other influences globally, that coalesced into a moment of profound change. (44)**

It is these thoughts that keep me motivated; that it is often the small, sometimes undocumented actions of grassroots people that contribute to magnificent transformations of society. If this truly is the case, then my work with twenty-one young people in Ghana might mean something. Without these small reassurances I think I would constantly be worried about how to create the "profound change" Wheatley speaks of. I know now that simply being involved is crucial, as it is the incremental changes to our society's fabric which will eventually lead to the immense change we desire.

These ideas began to take root soon after my return from Ghana. I wrote in my journal:

Up until this moment, I misunderstood the nature of social action, assuming that it had to be big, grand, and get a lot of attention. But in reality, it happens daily, can be small, but still have large and significant impacts on the people's lives that are touched by that action.

To be honest, I cannot specifically remember what was happening at the time I had this thought—what prompted it—but it did help me escape from the anxiety my thoughts of failure were wreaking on me. I began to understand what Wheatley was referring to in her passage above, and recognized that my goal of changing the whole education system in Ghana was foolish. Rather, awakening the students to the idea that there are other ways for teachers and students to interact with one another at Newells Academy, and then seeing this possibility enter the dialogue amongst everyone involved, represents the small meaningful change which actually constitutes deep, meaningful transformation.

In fact, during the participatory evaluation piece of my work I believe I witnessed the personal change and healing I had initially inquired about, thus observing small changes which will eventually compound into great ones. During one of our final sessions, one of my co-researchers stood up on behalf of the rest of the group and proclaimed their wish to not return to Link Social Youth Club. Their reasons were simple – they had experienced an alternative way of working and being, and did not want to go back to a place where they and their ideas were treated without respect. I relate this often to a scene in the movie *The Matrix* where 'Neo' is told there is no way that the experience of the matrix can be explained. It can only be encountered. I liken this to the Photovoice group my co-researchers and I went through – that there was no way to explain what it would be like and now that they knew what it felt like to be treated with respect, dignity, and inclusion there was no going back.

I captured my thoughts on our exchange in my journal:

> ***At first I wanted to throw my hands up in victory and scream "Ha, you see!" to the teachers... I wanted to express my solidarity with [the students]... Tell them, "Ya, don't go! Boycott!" But then I calmed myself down and tried to think about what such a response would accomplish. Not much. I suppose. So rather, I argued that what needs to happen is for all 21 youth to return to Link and teach the teachers about the way the group interacted with me – that part of the work we are dong together requires other people benefit and learn what they have learned.***

By the time of my departure a week later, the youth had not decided how they were going to proceed. I suspect several did not return to Link Social Youth Club, but that others understood my message of the obligations and responsibilities they now had as a result of having completed this experience with me.

Looking back now, I am even more moved by this demonstration of resistance and what it represents in regards to the changes the youth experienced in only a few short months of work with me. As Studs Terkel (2003) writes in regards to those who fight injustice, defiance exposes a confidence that cannot be reckoned with; that in saying *'no'* to the official word one reveals self-esteem and affirms oneself as important – someone who must be counted. After I read Terkel's words, I myself wrote:

> ***Saying no to the official word is exactly what these kids were doing at the end of our time together. Had they ever said 'no' to authority before? Where were they finding the courage to do so, especially in an environment so full of control, obedience and fear? How had this experience contributed to them finding that courage?***

Perhaps it is because, just as I had thought, the outcome of participation in social action is self confidence (Fernandes & Tandon, 1981).

In mid-June though – not yet even a month since my arrival to Oyarifa – I was still struggling with understanding the barriers to a collective self esteem which, if cultivated, could help to inspire change. Conversations with my host brother revealed that many people in the village were in a state

of "mental slavery" (Harry Martey, personal communication) and felt both unavoidably tied to the White person as well as a deep desire to be free of their seemingly constant grasp. This conversation forced me to reflect on Lear's *Radical Hope*, of which I mention in my journal:

> ***I wonder how this all relates to Radical Hope and the idea put forward in the book about the collapse of a civilization. Is Ghana – and all of Africa – still suffering from centuries of oppression, and at the same time struggling to build a new culture within the context of capitalism, Western influences - education and religion… In other words, are the children I am going to be working with living in a world where their collective, cultural identity is uncertain? Where the cultural concepts they use to define 'the good life' are not yet fully formed? And is this the struggle that is playing out before me?***

In other words, it became clear to me that part of the challenge I was facing was that both the youth and the community had yet to develop a collective sense of what idyllic future they were working towards. They had yet to articulate what 'the good life' looked like, and thus, had nothing for which to mobilize around and spur them into action.

According to Lear (2006) this vision of the future is essential for personal well-being. He expresses this importance when he writes,

> **A crucial aspect of psychological health depends on the internalization of vibrant ideals – the formation of a culturally enriched ego-ideal – in relation to which one can strive to live a rewarding life. Without such ideals, it is difficult to see what there is to live for… there is also the psychological devastation for young teenagers when they cannot find ideals worthy of internalizing and making their own. (140)**

Thus, it became clear for me that a critical piece of our work during the Photovoice experience would be to either recover or create a new vibrant ideal. The envisioning of such a *utopia* – as Freire (1992) refers to – would spur our work on further.

I recognized this as a major piece of my work with my co-researchers and write about this in my journal:

> ***I feel as though I am starting from the very beginning of the road here. The utopia, the dream that Freire refers so much to, has not been collectively recovered here; therefore, not collectively expressed or envisioned. The community has not mobilized itself yet and therefore it cannot begin to transform its reality until utopia is verbalized and shared. So perhaps this is another function of the group – and another tangible result – that together the group will collectively create – or rather draw out each person's utopia and collectively create a vibrant ideal that the entire community can mobilize around.***

Thus, the formulation of *utopia* (Freire, 1992) is a critical piece of the work in participatory research. It is an element which has an important, tangible function within a community based action group as it is the movement through this process which can lead to the establishment of the hopeful world people want to collectively articulate and struggle for.

Beyond learning to think smaller, another significant source of distress was figuring out how to facilitate the Photovoice experience within the realities of the children's social context, which included a significant source of oppression and silencing. Clearly development work cannot be done in a vacuum where one works with just one group of people. Yet, it felt as though so many of the other stakeholders' worldviews needed to be altered before they could be safely included into the process and work respectfully with the youth without interfering with the their ability to genuinely participate themselves. I found myself contemplating:

> ***How do you go about changing the values and attitudes which lead to one's beliefs about what is right and wrong, good and bad, and the best way to go about making change? Nothing can happen in isolation, but something's got to give.***

How does one create a new normal for a child, school, family, community, etc? When does one normal become unwanted, outdated, and another the preferred way of living? How does the colonial legacy left in the education system here dissipate into nothing? ... I'm working in a culture, environment, and context that I do not entirely understand and which, I'm learning, has a major influence on this project. People arriving late or not at all, parental interference, teacher interference, community/individual attitudes towards children... These all serve as challenges.

Finally, my last significant struggle in Ghana relates to the question—*what is my role here?*—which I constantly asked myself. With the village as immobilized as I found it, and with the resistance I felt from so many sources, I questioned whether it was my responsibility to initiate change for this community. I wrote in my journal:

How much responsibility do I take for another community's development? And I guess the more important question is: How does or where does "an outsider" fit into the process when the community has not initiated change by themselves? Is it an outsider's responsibility to come in, say "oh change needs to happen here", and if so, then how do they proceed? I've been wondering this for so long and still have no answers.

Even more, beyond the question of responsibility was the notion of respect, and whether it was even considerate of me to come in and initiate the inquiry and question asking that I did.

It was only after I returned home when I began to find some of the answers I was looking for in regards to what I envision as my role in community development work. Fernandes and Tandon (1981) describe the idea of the "catalyst agent" as an appropriate role for an outsider to take on. This is a person who injects new ideas into an old system by asking thought provoking questions and stimulating new ideas. Fernandes and Tandon (1981) are clear about the fact that the people themselves are the "doers" as they are the ones with the knowledge to create change. Hence, looking back I can say

with confidence that the role I designed for myself was done respectfully. I attempted to ask tough questions that would require individuals to probe everything they had previously taken for granted, but knew it was them—and only them—who could answer the questions and thereby recover and create the knowledge that was needed to transform their community.

In addition, during my time in Ghana I made a concerted effort to broaden the horizons of my co-researchers worlds by encouraging them to think beyond their village and community. Interestingly enough, in reading Oscar Lewis' work after arriving home, I found that he believes an element of the culture of poverty is an orientation to only looking inward on one's home society. Lewis (1998) claims, people with a culture of poverty are those "who know only their own troubles, their own local conditions, their own neighbourhood, their own way of life" (pg. 7) and that they do not see the similarities between their problems and those of others like themselves elsewhere in the world. I too had an inherent belief about this and found it important to expose the youth to news stories beyond their country and to be aware of the plight of others. In doing so, it was my hope to counter false consciousness and the belief that "we are the only ones who are suffering" and to connect their struggle with oppression and marginalization with others. Thus while I had uncertainties about my role in Ghana, in looking back now, I realize that by maintaining my commitment to the values and principles of participatory research I can be proud of being an authentic "catalyst agent" and am certain this is a role I would take on again in my practice.

Lessons Learned
Exhibit 5.2

**Learning journals are able to capture deep learning as it is happening.

**Critical questioning our experience creates a wide range of answers.

**The final arbiter of our inquiring mind is our essential value base.

**Disciplined, thoughtful hope.

Your Reflections…

……………………………………………………………………

……………………………………………………………………

……………………………………………………………………

……………………………………………………………………

The head and the heart. Orlando Fals Borda commented on the division in Cartesian science between the head and the heart. He envisaged a balance between the two approaches, "the clinical cold approach of the head with the warm feeling from the heart" (Pyrch, Morris & Rusted, 1990). In this way, "not only do you achieve more knowledge but you enjoy obtaining that knowledge" Fals Borda shared this wisdom during the PAR Congress in Calgary in 1989. He invited me to pursue this line of inquiry into knowledge and knowledge-making in preparation for the eighth World Congress on PAR, held in Cartagena, Colombia, in 1997. He asked me to facilitate a discussion between twelve committed and experienced action researchers from around the world and to encourage them to venture to Cartagena to share their wisdom in the "Panel on Schools and Methods: Convergence and Divergence." I wrote a paper titled "Mapmakers on Mapmaking" about my experience as the facilitator trying to capture the struggles of those who have created "the literature," those who I call "mapmakers" (Pyrch, 1998). The following exhibit extracts from that article the words most closely reflecting the "warm feeling from the heart."

> Remember Pascal's dictum that the heart has reasons that the reason doesn't know (Fals Borda in Pyrch, Morris & Rusted, 1990).

Exhibit 5.3: Mapmakers on Mapmaking (Pyrch, 1998).

I propose to explore what motivates the twelve members of the Panel – find out the personal reasons for their commitment to our work. I do this to humanize – make open, honest and accessible—the perpetual uncertainties of those writing on our behalf, those who have earned the right to speak yet struggle with the best way to do so. The context is the lengthy

preparatory work put in by the twelve. The actual Panel presentation is described elsewhere (Pyrch, 1997)...(p. 652) ...

The notion of a "family of action research approaches" at the very least suggests a formal family relationship in that we sensed kinship in our approach to knowledge-making which is democratic, action-oriented and inclusive of all forms of knowing. Yet I/we wanted something more as we responded more or less openly and deeply with our personal stories – sharing from the heart as well as the head. An alternate view of family is one formed out of affection, mutual support, and a desire to be with people who understand us and with whom we can learn deeply. For me, this relationship is that of community... (p. 653) ...

Early on, I sensed a willingness to share deeply. Robert Chambers sent me a copy of the final chapter of his book published later in 1997 in which he is reflecting on personal values and beliefs. I shared his words with the rest of the Panel:

> **Perhaps the most neglected aspect of development is the personal psychology of what powerful professionals believe and do. Personal change is a minefield...It is value laden. It concerns what sort of people we are and become: closed or open, fearful or secure, callous or caring, hating or tolerant, violent or peacemaking . . . The bottom line is to be nice to people. This is close to 'love thy neighbour as thyself'. Courtesy, respect, patience, consideration, generosity, reflecting on and being sensitive to others' realities...such virtues seem the core of personal and interpersonal well-being. (Chambers, 1997, p. 232-3)...**

These sentiments recall economist E. F. Schumacher's (1977) celebration of the time when "such forces as love and compassion, understanding and empathy, become available...as a regular and reliable resource." Skolimowski's (1994) vision of participatory research comes to mind – "the experience of loving and being loved; from the experience of pain which enables us to understand the pain of others." Reflecting on learning and spirituality, Parker Palmer (1993) advises:

> **The mind motivated by compassion reaches out to know as the heart reaches out to love. Here, the act of knowing is an act of love, the act of entering and embracing the reality of the other, of allowing the other to enter and embrace our own. (p. 659)...**

I was beginning to be comfortable with what I intuitively knew from the beginning of my discovery of PAR—*a legitimate way to love, to feel close to people, to participate, but within the safety of a system.* I was becoming confident my fear of appearing weak in the paternalist hierarchy of the academy and in the de-humanizing culture of economised society need not prevent me from reaching out passionately. (p. 660)...During the Panel presentation in Cartagena, each of us had the opportunity to share with the seven hundred people in attendance something of the fear even the most experienced of us has...

I must confess to some nervousness as we arrived in Cartagena. Would everyone actually turn up? Rumour had it that several well-known people from the North either were personally afraid to come to Colombia or had been advised not to by their governments. Yes, all present—although even this proved difficult to establish in the havoc created as 1800 people arrived instead of the expected 500. The twelve Panel members agreed to make a personal statement about their attraction to action research, and although there were one or two reservations about this no one suggested an alternative at this late date. One Panel member was prepared to refer to the experience of a student rather than self. In this case, it was clear the experience was personal but it was easier to relate through someone else. Another member confessed to staying up very late at night puzzling over what to say despite lengthy notes prepared for the occasion. Another prepared a personal statement, had it written out and on the podium, but did not read it because – *"I lost my confidence."*

This experience is unique in his life as he is used to attending conferences directly related to his expertise where the personal does not appear. He said he was disappointed with himself for missing an opportunity to do something unusual—and perhaps needed. I said something about his impressive publication record and he said he was confident in this area but felt 'fear' in this new

area. I wondered how he came to be so open with me an almost stranger. He said he felt there is something important in the PAR celebration of the holistic/spiritual/sacred. I think this must be it—a longing in someone strong in the critical/abstract/rational to find/recover the other aspects of his being.

He was pleased with how receptive people at the Congress were with his ideas. He had thought his approach might not have been appreciated by the PAR humanism/passion. Seems to me we need him as much as he needs us (p. 666)…

My students enjoy hearing these personal comments about the mapmakers as much as they value the maps themselves—the literature produced by members of the action research family. Our work is more approachable when we share some of our human foibles—introducing lightness into a serious world. (p. 668)

Lessons Learned
Exhibit 5.3

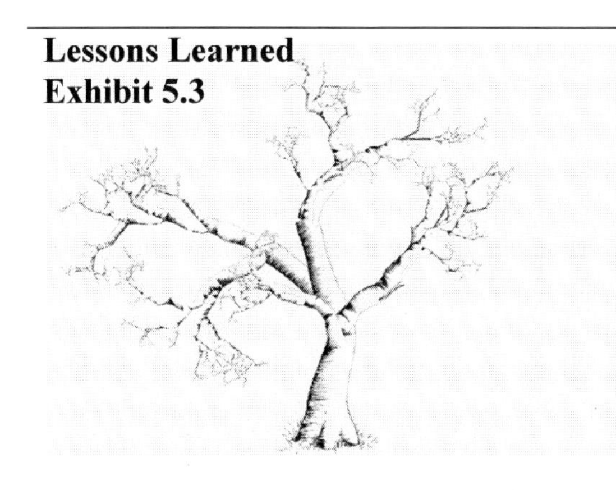

**Direct experience provides the foundation for human learning.

**Love lies at the root of action researchers and drives their scientific inquiry.

**Even the most famous amongst us fear revealing our uncertainties in public.

**Every discipline can learn from and contribute to other disciplines. This constitutes interdisciplinary inquiry.

Your Reflections…

……………………………………………………………………

……………………………………………………………………

……………………………………………………………………

....
....
....

Orlando had encouraged me throughout the preparations for the Panel presentation to get the mapmakers to share deeply, to reveal human uncertainties existing even within the intellectual leadership of the PAR movement, to show the human aspects of the scientific community. He knew full well that the hundreds assembled in Cartagena—many still tied to positivist social science—could not easily discount "warmth from the heart" if it came from international leaders. Yet he has been reluctant to do so himself. I wrote about this reluctance elsewhere (Pyrch, 1996), where I was able to record some of the amazing stories he and wife Mariá Cristina Salazar tell about their scholarly work on behalf of the oppressed peoples of Colombia. He was educated in European intellectual traditions, Marxism in particular, and mainstream American sociology as a doctoral student in Florida. Although he was reluctant to tell his own personal story, as a PAR pioneer he championed the stories and knowledge of *campesinos*. In one of his last publications, co-authored by a biologist, he argued the need for endogenesis, a biological term meaning "growth from within" (Fals Borda & Mora-Osejo, 2003), by writing,

> From the scientist's point of view, the knowledge of local realities turns out to be as rich and useful as made possible by his/her personal involvement, that is, through life experience or *vivencia.* Scientific insight and authority come from this involvement with real life. We have learned that endogenesis of this kind opens the way for useful discoveries and initiatives apt to alleviate social problems within the local world. (p. 33)

We might recall the Ganma rivers and Orlando's adoption into the Yolngu world when reading this endogenetic argument. As he entered his twilight years, Fals Borda's personal acknowledgement of the power of his own soulful inquiry driving local knowledge-making seems a fitting legacy for one of the PAR pioneers.

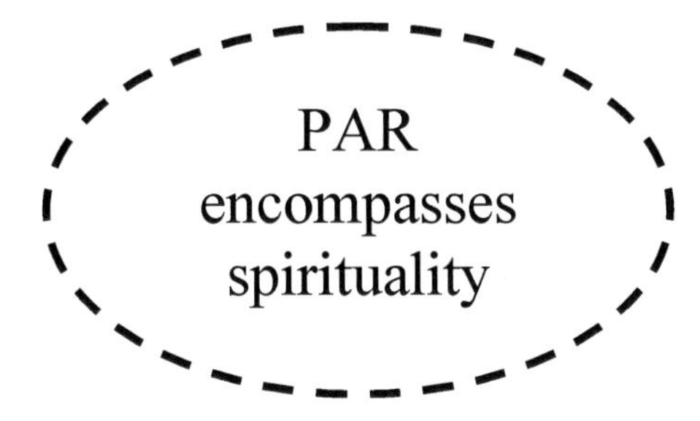

The burgeoning world of qualitative research is opening wide the doors of acceptable inquiry in graduate research. Social Work research is rich, diverse, and courageous. Robert Brown (2005) wrote a Testimonio for his MSW thesis, an act of courage in itself because of the newness of this approach in qualitative research.

Exhibit 5.4: Testimonio (Brown, 2005).

My testimonio is a statement, my statement of the experiences, struggles, visions and perspective of the world in which we live. It is my personal narrative about who I am, what I have gone through, and how I see the world. As a social worker and as a human being, this statement is about resistance. As a social worker, I see the world through a critical lens, one which reflects upon the injustices of the world. As a human being, I see the world with heart and wonder. As both, I see the world through a lens that regards the most vulnerable people of our world as victims of social stigma, discrimination, social exclusion, physical attack, poverty, hunger and displacement. I see the world through a lens that regards the few powerful elite as people who victimize those vulnerable for the purpose of profit…

This testimonio is also my time to write in a manner that is traditionally viewed as unacceptable. My writing is from my heart, and is most certainly biased. This testimonio is my way of resisting not only an oppressive and unjust society but also the dominant culture which controls the means of acceptable learning and knowledge sharing, excluding all the minorities that use different means as wonderful and highly successful ways of sharing and passing on knowledge…

John Beverley (2000) states that a "testimonio is a first-person political text told by a narrator who is the protagonist or the witness to the events reported. These tellings report on torture, imprisonment, social upheaval, colonization processes, and struggles for survival. These works are intended to record and produce social change"...

Testimonio shares values with Robert Mulally's (1993) Structural Social Work theory. This theory examines the power inequities between social and political structures and how they impact those among us that are most vulnerable...

I am a 33 year old white male struggling to finish my Master's degree in social work. I have had several years of professional social work experience in a variety of complex capacities. I am currently recovering from a car accident that caused me great pain and a long rehabilitation that I am still undergoing over three years later. Throughout my recovery I have suffered greatly and I have had many losses. I went through a difficult separation and divorce from my wife. My financial independence and my ability to reason and make sound judgements were also severely affected, since part of my injuries are related to a suspected brain injury as well as very serious depression. During this time of recovery, I have had a unique ability to reflect on the nature of social work critically from both a clients' perspective as well as from a professional perspective...

After my car accident, I was faced with many difficult challenges, one of them being a client of the social welfare system...I struggled each and every day to make sense of my pain to find myself feeling more frustrated as time went on. At one point, my life became one where I was wholly dependent on the social system for care, yet I still felt alone and misunderstood. I would go to all of my appointments feeling as if I was playing a game and not really getting anywhere with my healing. Slowly, I began to identify

and understand the struggles of the clients that I had worked with so many times and for so many years. During my recovery, within my heart, I was searching for a social worker who could empathize with my pain, my loss and my struggles while also managing my care. I was searching for somebody to care for me and help me in the way I was trained to do as a social work professional. The medical model in which I had become dependent did not acknowledge the emotional suffering that I needed support for and the confusion that I felt regarding the direction they were taking me on with my healing. I felt isolated and social workers weren't available to help me make sense of this, empathize with my losses and manage my care so that I could heal in a way that was purposeful and meaningful to me. All of that work I did on my own and I still have further healing that I need to do…

Mulally (1993) states, "even though the neo-conservative ideology of welfare offends the traditional social work commitment to compassion, to social justice and to preserving the dignity and autonomy of individuals, social work to date has been ineffective in challenging the crisis confronting it". As a social worker, I have often felt we just accept the political demise that is placed on us. I have often felt powerless to fight back against the cutbacks and the position of continued control that's been placed upon me…

It is easy for me to identify with the experiences I have encountered for I feel I am now one of those among us that are vulnerable, whose life has been damaged. I have felt and continue to feel powerless, silenced and isolated. I have been dependent on the system for help. I have felt the shame that comes with being different and losing one's ability to be seen as an active and productive member of the consumer based society in which we live. I can feel compassion and express my love to many people. I can be a loving member of my

family. I can help all people I encounter who are in need, in the small ways that I can. I can raise awareness regarding issues of social justice. I can live up to the values and ethics found within the Social Work Code of Ethics and try my best to defend those among us who are powerless, voiceless and suffering. In light of all this, I am not perceived as a valued member of society by the powerful majority. I have trouble working, therefore, I am dependent and thus expendable and forgotten, just like all of the people and experiences I have discussed. It would seem our society does not value and credit the soulful emotions and goodness of heart as worthy. Many people I have encountered have been touched by the lives of social workers and helped to find peace and meaning in their lives. Unfortunately, it does not take long for me to see so many of us have not. Time will tell what happens to me; however, I will always do my best, no matter what condition I am in, or where I am, to defend the rights of the people who are silenced…

Lessons Learned
Exhibit 5.4

**Combing academic rigour with passionate compassion produces powerful learning.

**Painful experience can be tempered with critical analysis.

**Disciplined, thoughtful hope.

Your Reflections…

…………………………………………………………………………

…………………………………………………………………………

…………………………………………………………………………

…………………………………………………………………………

Our students are uncovering empowering moments in their research even when it causes some pain, as Robert Brown explains. Brenna Atnikov exhibited the liberating impact of PAR on individual empowerment; including the concepts of self-awareness and self interpretation. One of the lessons in Part Five of *Breaking Free* might be a returning to the self as the ultimate arbiter of practice, this after spending so much effort in the earlier parts of the guide on the power of the collective. Does this acknowledge the strength of the hedgehog? In other words, have we recognized the power of the ethical standards of the Faculty of Social Work to keep us firm in our belief? And, for that matter, what are those standards?

On spirituality. I return to the beginning part of this guide to re-join Vandana Shiva in "breaking free of the mental prison of separation and exclusion and see the world in its interconnectedness and non-separability, allowing new alternatives to emerge" (Shiva, 2002). We are free to travel where our spirit leads. As I said earlier, for me spirit is my relationship with similar forms of energy past, present, and future for the purpose of acting together to transform our realities. My work is to create spaces for my spirituality. In so doing, I facilitate processes for learners to do likewise, to celebrate their own spirituality. Spaces of spirit are thereby co-created. There is evidence in our Faculty of a deep sense of the spiritual, despite being difficult to locate in quantitative inquiry. Wilda Listener, MSW, (2004) reflected on her own spirituality in her unpublished case study of on-reserve family violence. She said I could share this excerpt from her paper with you.

Exhibit 5.5: Aboriginal Storytelling & Social Work (Listener, 2004).

PAR is inclusive of all forms of knowledge

The aboriginal social work perspective has been ingrained into me. My background is in Blackfoot and Cree ways of knowing. My maternal grandmother and mother were my first teachers. I was told the stories of the old ways and the knowing of the spirit of my ancestors. I recall something that I told my mother about the way I was feeling. I told her, "Mom, sometimes I get the feeling that I do not feel I am from this world; like I am from another time." Her response calmed me as she spoke, "When you were a baby, something occurred, and your grandmother told me that your

spirit was from a long time ago." This memory has stayed with me, and I write it here to illustrate the power of the story and of its intention. It's not that on this earth at this time I felt out of place; it is that I could feel across time that things were different and that the ancestor family was still with me. I could feel within me the values and knowledge learned, as if from another time, that were not even told to me, but I knew and listened. The reason I told my mother about how I was feeling was that it seemed those around me did not share my values and behaviours. I felt they forgot what the old ways were like and what it meant to be human.

Even though I mainly speak the English language, I feel I think a different way, a way which I did not learn in university and which cannot be taught in an academic setting. I see the world and my social work practice in different ways than my non-aboriginal peers. I learned several aspects that are important when dealing with people. The first one is relationship. Family is very important to me but not just the nuclear family—the extended family and others considered family, such as close friends and peers. Anyone who relates to a person adds value. Relationships could also mean interactions with objects or animals. This means everything in the universe is special and has connections to everything else. Another aspect is interdependence, meaning that an individual not only has relationships with other people and things but that people and things have a place in the universe, and all are needed.

Lessons Learned
Exhibit 5.5

**Spirit directs us to relationships—perhaps invisible—with all forms of life.

**Language represents only one part of our experience.

**Indigenous languages cannot be heard in languages of colonization.

Your Reflections…

....

....

....

....

Within the spaces of spirit, we seek, and often find, the satisfiers of the fundamental human need for transcendence (Max-Neef, 1991). Trans-disciplinary inquiry may be this satisfier within the world of research. According to Max-Neef (1991),

> Trans-disciplinarity is an approach that, in an attempt to gain greater understanding, reaches beyond the fields outlined by strict disciplines. While the language on one discipline may suffice to *describe* something (an isolated element, for instance), an interdisciplinary effort may be necessary to *explain* something (a relation between elements). By the same token, to *understand* something (a system as interpreted from another system of higher complexity) requires a personal involvement that surpasses disciplinary frontiers, thus making it a trans-disciplinary experience. (p. 15)

This trans-disciplinary experience is facilitated within the spaces of spirit wherein we practise our personal spirituality. What is required is the strength of the exploring pioneer. James Carse (1986) moves us beyond mere explanation as follows:

> Explanations establish islands, even continents, of order and predictability. But these regions were first chartered by adventurers whose lives are narratives of exploration and risk. They found them only by mythic journeys into the wayless open. When the less adventuresome settlers arrive later to work out the details and domesticate these spaces, they easily lose the sense that all this firm knowledge does not expunge myth, but floats on it. (p. 165)

Social justice work practice floats on the histories and myths of humankind's evolving presence in Alberta and beyond to include all influences that might bear on our practice and life. Indeed, we might be assisted in re-connecting life and work by re-connecting the fragments created by a mechanical and linear world view. Our stories enable us to re-establish these connections.

In his spiritual quest, Kim Zapf (2007), professor emeritus of social work in Calgary, draws from a long journey with Aboriginal traditions while reconnecting nature and human nature.

Exhibit 5.6: Profound connections between person and place (Zapf, 2007a)

When the environment is understood as a conscious entity, a partner, then spiritual transformation must occur *with* the environment or *as* the environment, not *in* it...I argue that most authors have presented spirituality as either one more aspect of the individual client to be assessed or as simply another resource for possible use in clinical practice. From rural social work (with particular emphasis on the world (229) view from Aboriginal social work), a much broader perspective emerges that demands a very different understanding of spirituality that does not separate person from place... (p. 230)

As a Western discipline with a focus on person-environment interaction, social work can be seen as problematic from the perspective of traditional knowledge because the person and the environment are still understood as two separate (although interacting) entities, with one (the person) commanding all the attention. In contract to this Western notion, the foundation metaphor of traditional knowledge has been characterized as a perspective of "I am I and the Environment" (Ortega y Gasset, 1985), "I'm not in the place but the place is in me" (Suopajarvi, 1998, 3), or "the earth knows us" (Spretnak, 1991, 91)... (p. 235)

There have been some encouraging signs in the literature, but they are rare and typically introduced, and then quickly dropped as undeveloped hints of what might be possible... (p. 236)

In the near future, I think it unlikely that the urban-based profession of social work, or the dominant society for that matter, will

easily embrace (p. 237) a rural perspective, an Aboriginal world view, or a deeper ecological understanding of the profound connections between person and place. Does that mean that social workers are doomed to accept a limited notion of spirituality as a disconnected client characteristic, while the land remains a passive and lifeless background for human activity? Is it possible for social work to help Western society "learn to live attentively in place" or "to re-inhabit" our world (Spretnak, 1991, p. 82)? Can we come to better understand our environment in spiritual terms, to appreciate and express and celebrate our connectedness? (p. 237).

In a simple yet profound question put forward by Haas and Nachtigal (1998), I found a possible starting point for rethinking social work's commitment to *person-in-environment.* Their question was "What does it mean to live well in this place?" I concur that wellness cannot be separated from place as easily as our limited notion of *person-in-environment* has pretended. But I am troubled by that preposition "in" because it maintains the dominance of human activity with the environment as secondary, a passive backdrop. As we saw earlier, deep ecology suggests substituting the preposition "with" for "in," thereby changing the fundamental question to "what does it mean to live well *with* this place?" This is certainly a step in the right direction, a notion of living in full partnership with a living conscious environment that sustains us and toward which we have powerful and respectful obligations for mutual survival.

Still, I wonder if we could even move beyond "with" to understand the question as "what does it mean to live well *as* this place? -- thereby rejecting the fundamental distinction between person and place in favour of a unifying spiritual connection. (p. 238)

Lessons Learned
Exhibit 5.6

**Everything we need is near at hand.

**Liberatory processes are holistic, intertwined, and mutually dependent.

**Clarity of language and purpose.

Your Reflections…

……………………………………………………………………
……………………………………………………………………
……………………………………………………………………
……………………………………………………………………
…………………………………………………………………..

To be fully present *as* this place directs us back to the ancient knowledge of the Yolngu of Arnhemland and Ganma. The waters of one river come from the land and the other from the sea, but the river as a whole is on the land and of the land (Watson with the Yolngu community at Yirrkala & Chambers, 1989). The place where the rivers meet and foam created is the place of indigenous power and tradition, the place of locality. What would practising social work *as* Alberta look like? Moreover, what is Alberta? Can we move beyond the province as a piece of property to a place of possibility? Where to start?

As we are breaking free of imperial science, we find ourselves in places in our natural world where we can create new spaces for our trans-disciplinary inquiry. Kate van Fraassen crafted such a space in our 2009 PAR course while playing a six-string guitar to help foster and develop her inner-most musing. At the time, Kate was a master's student in the Faculty of Environmental Design. A power point presentation accompanied her paper.[7]

---

[7] http://wcmprod2.ucalgary.ca/studentpar/node/8

Exhibit 5.7: Knowing in new ways (Van Fraassen, 2009).

Learning about Participatory Action Research the past three months has provoked an inner exploration. I have explored the values that ground my thinking, my motivations for going to graduate school, how I think, how I express myself, and above all else what I know. This process has been difficult and exhilarating all at once, moving me in a way no other class has. Perhaps the waves of emotion I felt during class and while reflecting outside the classroom are indicative of the fact that PAR is a way of life.

I am new to this way of life and am still orientating myself. Many times I feel overwhelmed and unsure where to step next. There are however, certain aspects of PAR that quickly spoke to me on a deep level and make sense in a way no theory or academic argument ever has. One of these aspects is the valuing of different ways of knowing. Recognizing that I in fact know in different ways was a challenge at first. I have gone through 17.5 + years of education strumming the string of my rational mind, rarely playing all 6 strings of my guitar. This paper and my "knowing in new ways" project are my attempt to uncover the different ways I know and reflect on why valuing all ways of knowing is central to PAR. The crossover between my written and visual expression is the foam created through the merging rivers of my rational and metaphoric capabilities. In light of my background and interests, I have anchored my process in navigating why I value nature and how to express that value. My intent is to uncover how human capabilities beyond our rational mind can facilitate such an expression.

Orlando Fals Borda (1988) has gifted us with the 4 Techniques of PAR: collective research, critical recovery of history, valuing and applying folk culture, and production and diffusion of new knowledge. Orlando's 4 techniques build upon all human capabilities, not merely the rational mind. This application has been illustrated to us by three of the guests who shared with us in class. Tammy and her experience with photo

voice and digital storytelling, Francis and the methods he used with women in Ghana, and Judy's work with the Indian Village at the Stampede. All three of these individuals have gracefully embraced the full 6 strings of their guitars to play the music of PAR. The initial action of recognizing and applying different ways of knowing, or folk culture is at the centre of their PAR stories. Tammy and her team used photo-voice to communicate their knowledge of life in the sex trade in Calgary. The photos, quotes, and music Tammy chose to share struck a much deeper emotional cord in all of us in that classroom then if she had only spoken to us or provided us with an analytical paper. Neither of these actions would have been less valuable, but they would not have massaged our minds as completely as her digital story did. My own reaction to her digital story and the way she told it was part of the inspiration for this exploration.

What is knowledge and who can create it? This question has been at the core of the discussion in class over the past three months and at the core of PAR as I understand it. For me, part of answering this question is pondering on what knowledge I have and in what forms? Griffin (2001) developed the analogy of the 6-string guitar as a way to describe our human capabilities. These 6 strings include emotional, relational, physical, rational, metaphoric, and spiritual capability. The author uses the analogy to engage educators to consider the under recognized capabilities, those being all but rational knowledge, for their learning potential (Griffin, 2001). The potential of the 6-string guitar inside us all, also lends itself to doing PAR, as illustrated by the many guest to our class, by the Guide, and by my exploration of how I express my value of nature.

Emotional Capability

Griffin (2001) discusses the learning potential of recognizing and accepting both positive and negative emotions. Acknowledging and understanding our emotions enables us to learn about ourselves and make change. The work of PAR can

be very emotional, as all of the guests to our class have commented on. Using our emotional capabilities to understand the personal and group processes we are going through is important to this kind of work. The challenging comments Judy received from both her PhD committee and the community she is working with are common in PAR. This is different kind of work that involves interacting with people in ways they may not have been engaged before. It is Judy's emotional capabilities that give her the strength and courage to keep doing the good work she is doing.

In exploring why I value nature my emotional connection to it emerged as very important. When I am experiencing both positive and negative emotions I turn to nature to work through the situation I am in. When I seek emotional clarity I go skiing or for a hike and return refreshed. Being in nature gives me the space to work through my emotions and identify if and how I need to make change. Nature has provided me with a classroom in which I have developed my emotional capabilities. Thus, my expression of my values of nature became an immensely emotional process and a key characteristic of this project.

Relational Capability

PAR, in contrast to conventional approaches to research is a collective activity. It involves people and working with them to achieve a collectively determined goal. Learning, according to Griffin (2001) is also not a solitary activity; it involves time alone but depends upon time with others to fully blossom. Relational capabilities are needed for and are developed in all 4 of Orlando's techniques, as all of them involve collective effort. PAR is not PAR without collective participation.

Some of the most powerful collective efforts I have been part of have taken place in Nature. I attend summer camp throughout my youth and every summer myself and 7 other campers headed out on extended trips into the backcountry on foot with our two counsellors. It was on these excursions that I discovered my capabilities to work with others. I learnt to communicate how I was feeling in the worst of weather and on the best of days, I learnt how to work with my fellow campers

to accomplish task from as routine as putting up the tent to as significant as establishing our route. Nature was not only the learning setting but also a major learning variable. I learnt to respect it and understand some of its systems. Moreover, as I developed my capabilities to relate and work with people my relationship with nature strengthened. We were not only working together but also working with nature. I value these lessons and consider these moments as foundational to establishing my value of nature.

Physical Capability

The more something appeals to our 5senses the more likely we are to understand and remember it (Griffin, 1994). Each week at class effort is taken to appeal to our senses. Music plays, food is shared and video images are shown. These gestures do not merely create a comfortable atmosphere they assist us in understanding PAR, as they are part of PAR. We exist as a whole person, nose, eyes, ears, legs and all. If PAR is about reflecting on the situations we are in and working to positively change them we must understand those situations with our full body.

When I am in nature I feel as though I am getting a full sensory massage. The smells, the sounds, the views, the feeling of the wind and the movement of my body over the landscape makes me feel alive. This feeling of reawakening my senses is one of the major things I value about nature, and a sensation I have tried to express in my project.

Rational, Intellectual Capability

Much attention is given to rational capabilities in research, in school, and in society as a whole. This attention often casts a shadow over other capabilities and ways of knowing. Griffin (2001) explores all the capabilities of the human mind in an effort to shine light on the potential and value of the other 5 strings of our mental guitars. Similarly, PAR aims to end the monopoly of rational knowledge by recognizing and empowering people's knowledge. This is not to say there is no value in rational capability. It enables us to do a multitude of

tasks including analyzing information, read and understand ideas, and convey our ideas through words and sentences (Griffin, 2001). The issue is the placing of one way of knowing, most commonly rational knowing, over all others. This action severely limits us as individuals and society as a whole. As Griffin asks, would you want to play a 1-string guitar?

While nature has never solved a math problem for me, it has provided me with a place to clear my mind so that I have the energy and clarity to work through the steps to solve a problem.

Metaphoric Capability

Griffin (2001) describes the metaphoric mind as being closely related to the rational mind but different. She describes it as "the reservoir of the intuitive simultaneous, spontaneous, diffuse, and non-linear functions of thinking" (Griffin, 2001, 119). When you hear a certain tone in someone's voice, or see a pattern in the clouds as they move through the sky, that is the workings of your metaphoric mind. I believe this way of knowing is at the centre of Orlando's (1988) second and third techniques, critical recovery of history and valuing and applying folk culture. In the videos we watched throughout the term music, images and movement was a frequent feature. From Pete Seeger and his guitar to the traditional images and songs of aboriginal women from Australia at the 1988 Calgary Congress. These sounds and images were both communicating a critical recovery of their respective histories and sharing their folk culture and ways of knowing. These moments were some of the warmest and most effective lessons for me all term.

When I began to ponder how I would express why and how I value nature I was lost. How could I ever capture all that nature is to me? My connection to it is so strong yet my ability to express that connection so weak. While some of that value has been expressed here in words, I have opted to leave much of that expression in a metaphoric form. (Please see my "Knowing in New Ways" project)

Spiritual Capability

We have discussed in class how difficult it can be to talk about spirituality in an academic setting. This difficulty may be due to a shyness to engage with something that is not only very personal but also dynamic and ever changing. In her attempt to define the un-definable Griffin offers the following (this has been shared in class already, but it is one of the best articulated descriptions of spirituality I have come across):

"Spirituality is an awareness, wonder, deep sense of awe of the present, the potential of persons or nature. It is an awareness and awe of connectedness of what is and what could be. It includes your vision of what could be foryourself – your purpose in life – for others, for nature," (Griffin, 2001, 121).

If PAR is a lifestyle, I think spirituality is at the root of the motivations to practice it. PAR is a worldview that acknowledges the capacity of all people to have and create knowledge, and a commitment to work for change that enables that creation to happen. To do this kind of work individuals must be moved by more than a commitment to a methodology, it must touch them on a deeper level. Apela Colorado brings to life the spirituality of PAR in her description of *sweet grass* and how the blades of grass are connected, hold each other up and support each other (Castillo & Pyrch, 2001). She shares that working with her colleagues on PAR fills her with the same "good thoughts, good feelings, harmony and blessings," as she receives from the sweet grass and the prairies (Castillo & Pyrch, 2001, 381). Apela Colorado is clearly deeply moved by PAR, and PAR provides her with a purpose in life, for others, and for nature.

While I was baptised and grew up Catholic, I no longer go to church. Nature is my cathedral and my inspiration. I am overcome with a sense of awe and connectedness when I am in it. For me, nature has a deep spiritual value that I hold very dear. It is essential to my being.

What does all this mean? Why is playing a 6-string guitar important for understanding and doing PAR? At a conference on Low Impact Development this past November answers to these

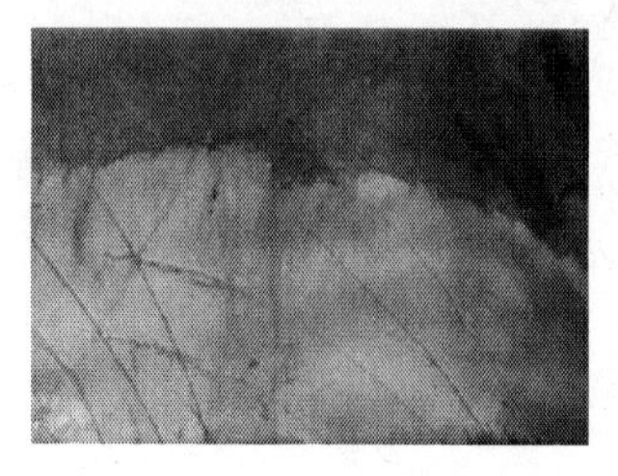

questions emerged me. The conference was for the Alberta Low Impact Development Partnership, individuals interested in and who work building things such as bioswales and constructed wetlands in Alberta. The technical aspects of the conference was not what moved me, it was a short presentation on public perceptions of the different development techniques. In a survey residents were asked to draw both their ideal urban landscape and a 'naturalized' one (City of Calgary, 2008). The pictures revealed more than 100 focus groups could have, it illustrated what resident's value about urban landscapes, how they understand it metaphorically, emotionally and so on. The ideal urban landscape was organized, manicured and had a barbeque, the naturalized landscape was a messy swirl of ugly garbage greens and puke yellows. From these illustrations City of Calgary Water Services staff recognized that *how* they communicate and design their projects must resonate with not only the values of residents, but speak to their multileveled ways of understanding.

While this example is not a PAR exercise, it taught me an important lesson about ways of knowing and communicating. I left the conference with the message that people communicate and know in numerous ways and that all the sustainable technical-speak in the world will never 'sell' an idea if it does not respect this diversity. How we conduct our research, PAR or otherwise, or do our work determines the types of knowing we are able to engage.

Liamputtong and Rumbold (2008) write extensively about arts-based research and its rich ability to access experiential and other types of knowing. These methods are particularly suited to working with individuals who do not respond well to typical verbal forms of research engagement, such as surveys or interviews. I think such approaches to research are also a way to reveal to researchers and co-researchers alike, the different ways in which they know. My experience with my

Knowing in New Ways project exposed gifts and capabilities I did not realize I had, perhaps similarly to the Calgary residents asked to draw their ideal urban landscape.

Art-based communication is already being used in Southern Alberta in the fight to protect The Castle landscape (Douglas, 2007). Artists are sharing their love for The Castle Landscape through gallery showings of their work in hopes of inspiring others to support the creation of a park in the area. They are using their metaphoric capabilities to touch the emotional, spiritual, and metaphoric capabilities in others. By appealing to more than the rational mind they are able to communicate on many levels, and perhaps appeal to individuals who may not have been persuaded by logical, rational arguments for conservation. I believe that through their collective work these artists are not only taking action but also working for change in a way that respects Orlando's 4 techniques.

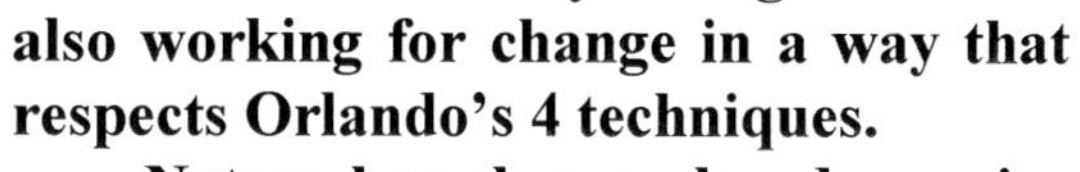

Nature has always played a major role in my life and is something I value greatly, but words have never been able to capture the deep feelings I have. Understanding its marvellous systems or writing and speaking about the importance of sustainability have never captured my underlying motivations and values as my Knowing in New Ways project has. My struggle to communicate values is not unique. Robert William Sandford (2008) writes passionately about the difficulty mountain town communities have in communicating what they value about their way of life, the landscape, and their towns. This failure to communicate opens up space for developers and decision makers to move based on values and ideas that are easily expressed, those based on economy. Sandford (2008) urges communities to work together to collectively express the futures they desire for the paces they live. This is where I believe embracing all 6 of our strings and using methods shared by Liamputtong and Rumbold can empower communities to tap into all their capabilities and press for the change they want to see. When words and rational procedures fail we need to allow ourselves to work in new ways, based on our other capabilities. Doing so can expose hidden understandings

and motivations, empowering us in unexpected ways. This has certainly been my experience.

This process of learning to play my 6-string guitar has been both exciting and nerve racking. For weeks I have imagined in my head what I would do, what colours and images could express the thoughts and feelings I want to share. In the end what I needed to do emerged from the materials in front of me as I allowed myself to play a beautiful song on my 6-string guitar.

Lessons Learned
Exhibit 5.7

** Liberatory processes are holistic, intertwined and mutually dependent.

**Nature provides appropriate settings for trans-disciplinary inquiry.

** Spirituality is about relationships with self and all forms of energy animate in inanimate.

**We have within us multitudinous forms of expression.

Your Reflections…

………………………………………………………………………………

………………………………………………………………………………

………………………………………………………………………………

………………………………………………………………………………

………………………………………………………………………………

Kate van Fraassen and Kim Zapf are "rejecting the fundamental distinction between person and place in favour of a unifying spiritual connection". What does it mean to live well *as Breaking Free*? Kate's classmate and colleague, Social Work PhD student Darlene Chalmers, might suggest "you start your research on your being," as she concluded her PAR course experience.

Exhibit 5.8: You start your research on your being (Chalmers, 2009).

"If research doesn't change you as a person, then you haven't done it right" **(Wilson, 2008, p. 135, italics in original quote).**

I have pondered this quote for a period of time in relation to both its meaning, and its significance in guiding the conceptualization of this paper. What is the nature of the change that is being referred to regarding one's personhood as a result of undertaking research—a knowledge activity? More specifically, what is the relevance of Wilson's quote to the philosophy, methodology and method of PAR in the co-creation of knowledge? Is it likened to what a number of authors cite in that the use of this methodology as both a philosophical and conceptual framework in knowledge building, results in an experience that is both transformative and spiritual (Fals Borda, 2006; Maguire, 1987; Pyrch, 2009; Reason, 1998; Smith, 1997)? It is through my ongoing learning about PAR as a research methodology and my interest in the particular aspect of personal transformation as a result of engaging in a PAR process, that I set out to develop this paper.

The following pages will be presented in journal format and, in part, provide bits of syntheses of my personal learning journal developed over the past weeks. In this way, the paper is a continuation of a personal exploration albeit with an opportunity to focus on a specific area related to PAR. The examination of the transformative or spiritual nature of knowledge building with groups and communities, and the relationship between this experience and knowing one's self, our inside knowledge, has resonated for me throughout the course. I have also been influenced by recent readings on Indigenous and Aboriginal epistemology and in particular the

significance of "relationality" within this worldview and its philosophical congruence with PAR, and potential import for both Indigenous and non-Indigenous researchers. In this way then, my final paper presented as a final journal entry for this course, will offer an intellectual exploration and analysis of the spiritual nature of PAR while drawing on Indigenous research methods and epistemology. Practically, the journal will serve as a potential starting place for a future literature review as it relates to my own research, and finally it will comprise a chapter in my individual "textbook."

The Relationality of PAR and Spirituality

A revisiting point for me in exploring spirituality and personal transformation in relation to PAR are the words of Willms (1997) who writes "you start your research on your being" (p. 7). A fundamentally profound statement, this too was passionately put forward by Francis Boakye in a presentation on his PAR project in Ghana. I interpret the possible meanings of this statement as twofold and by no means view them as mutually exclusive. First, an ethical imperative of Indigenous, post-modern, feminist, critical, and anti-oppressive research paradigms is the location of oneself. In this manner the researcher is essentially making a statement about both her theory of being in the world and her understanding of reality. The process of self-locating allows for the research tradition that one aligns with to surface and thus makes known the assumptions and influences of the held worldview. Ladson-Billings (2000 as cited in Strega, 2005) states that "[h]ow one views the world is influenced by what knowledge one possesses, and what knowledge one is capable of possessing is influenced deeply by one's world view" (p. 201). Worldview defines how we see and understand ourselves and others, and contributes to defining life meaning in terms of our economic, political and spiritual leanings (Coates, 2003). Once again, I return to "you start your research on your being."

The second interpretation of this

statement is directly related to knowing oneself in an existential and deeply profound sense. In this way I view self knowing, in relation to being, as extending beyond the necessary paradigmatic and theoretical aligning that is required as part of sound research processes. This form of self exploration, perhaps often misinterpreted as self-analysis, is important. It requires a process that propels one toward an understanding of self through an examination of what exists at the core of our being, and is often referred to as spirit, spirituality or soul. However, this process of "self knowledge is impossible unless we go behind our surface existence" (Aurobindo, 2001 as cited in Spittles, 2008, p. 9).

The significance of location of self is discussed by Absolon and Willett (2005) in relation to Aboriginal research. Understanding oneself (deep spirit) and worldview (spirituality) cannot be disentangled. The authors write "that one of the most fundamental principles of Aboriginal research methodology is the necessity for the researcher to locate himself or herself" (p. 97). In this way, "location is about relationships to land, language, spiritual, cosmological, political, economically, environmental, and social elements in one's life" (*ibid.*). Through the process of locating and essentially authenticating oneself, undertaken by the sharing of stories between participants, produces the emerging transformative nature of research.

What is spirituality, how is it understood, and how do we transcend beyond the surface to truly know? Within western social work practice, education, and research spirituality has only recently begun to be recognized in the literature in relation to human health and wellbeing. For the most part, religion has been understood as an interchangeable term or concept with spirituality. However, Chile and Simpson (2004) clarify in stating that "religion and spirituality are not synonymous…[s]pirituality…is the inner self that defines who we are" (p. 319). The authors further write that spirituality is fundamentally premised on relationships.

In cosmological terms this includes the individual, the collective and the universe in an interconnected web of being. Coates (2003) writes that "[c]osmogenesis recognizes all life forms as having intrinsic value and celebrates human imbeddedness in nature and the interdependence of all things" (p. 63). Fals Borda (2003) echoes the importance of "harmonious reconstruction of the relationship of people and nature" and the significance of this relationship in the lives of the people of Colombia and Latin America (p. 35). The interconnected web of life is fundamental to Indigenous worldviews and in essence defines the inner self. This worldview includes relationships with place, land, nature and animals (Wilson, 2008).

How does transcendence beyond the surface happen in the quest to understand spirituality and soul in relation to "you start your research on your being?" Spirit at Work (2003 as cited in Spittle 2008) provide a useful framework for understanding the dimensions of spirituality and although related to community development, the parallels and applicability to the experiences of those engaged in PAR (which I will relate later in this paper) are numerous.

In writing about the role of the 'soul' in community development, a very clear distinction is made between what is known as codes of conduct or a spiritual moral/values framework, and what is considered as "knowing oneself"—spirituality. The spirituality framework is typified as having both a vertical and horizontal axis. The vertical axis is the inward or self, and is described as one having a conscious profound connection to the universe. The horizontal axis is the "vehicle through which the vertical soul-self acts, creates and relates in the living world" (p. 11). The horizontal axis is a dimension where fundamental relationships exist between spirituality, self and community in terms of the principle of *interconnectedness* (*ibid*, italics in original quote). What is then proposed is that the more developed the vertical axis (knowing self as soul), then the more developed the horizontal axis; specifically the more one understands the interconnection between self and others. Ultimately, "the measure of 'knowing oneself as soul' is commensurate with the measure of *knowing the other as self* (emphasis added)" (p. 12). An Indigenous perspective is further helpful for understanding and summarizes what has been stated. As referenced in a previous journal, Cajete (2001) presents that "[t]hrough community Indian people come to understand their "personhood" and their connection to the "communal soul" of their people…it is the context which the person comes to know relationship, responsibility and participation in the life of one's people" (p. 86).

The Spirit at Work framework provides one perspective for understanding the nature of spirituality, however Reason (1998) cautions that "[w]e need to beware of inflating the notion of the spiritual to some remote end state that can be attained only after immense effort" (p. 163).

The Philosophical Basis of PAR: Inner and Outer Work?

So, what does spirituality have to do with PAR? Peter Reason (1994) shares his personal reflections on the nature of his experiences as a participant in numerous co-operative inquiry undertakings and his personal life. He writes about the intentionality of his life and work (one in and of the same) as "a lifelong quest, both an inspiration and a struggle. I experience this intention as having a spiritual dimension, as providing a sense of meaning and inspiration to my life" (50). Similar ideas abound in the literature. Maguire (1987) suggests "[p]articipatory research assumes that both the researcher and researched be open to personal transformation and conscientization" (p. 39); Fals Borda (2006) writes that the "participatory philosophy could produce personal behavioural changes…" (p. 30); and Pyrch and Castillo (2001) state that "some of us involved in PAR have used words like 'spirituality' and 'transcendence' to describe not only the journey, but the impact of what we have been feeling…" (p. 381).

It is useful at this juncture to (re)examine the philosophy and the fundamental tenets of PAR in attempting to make a connection to the 'inner and outer' congruence for those who participate in this activity. PAR is fundamentally about social justice, liberation, freedom, equity, sustainability (individual, collective, and ecological), action, and participation (Fals Borda and Rahman, 1991; Maguire, 1986; Pyrch, 2009; Reason, 2006; Smith, 1997). The nature of co-operative inquiry, which includes action research, is often also associated with knowing ourselves, thus awareness of our inner work in order to undertake our outer work. Congruency seems apparent, at least in my interpretation, in understanding the nature of spirituality in the framework previously presented whereby the degree of vertical (inner) understanding is represented by horizontal (outer) expression or actions. The outer actions are played out through connections with others.

Chile and Simpson (2004) offer that "spiritual approaches emphasize interconnectedness that require a holistic framework which incorporates related issues such as social justice, economic fairness, human rights, and ecological sustainability" (p. 320). The basis of PAR, as a participatory methodology, is about interconnectedness. A fundamental aspect of interconnectedness—PAR and spirituality—is through what Park (2006) defines as relational knowledge; "knowing others both affectively and cognitively which has a distinct relational meaning" (p. 86). Moreover, "[r]elational knowledge grows out of active communal life and, conversely, it is relational knowledge that makes it possible to create and sustain a community" (p. 88).

PAR and the act of participation (contributing to social justice) can be understood as deeply personal and collective ways of being. According to Reason (1998), participation becomes both ecological and political statements such that humans are communal beings connected with the cosmos

and all living things, with agency to impact and affect the nature of decisions and the world. Additionally, the author argues "[p]articipation is a spiritual imperative. To deny participation not only offends against human justice, not only leads to errors in epistemology, not only strains the limits of the natural world, but is also troublesome for human souls" (p. 162).

What is the Meaning for Me?

The writing of this paper began with questioning and attempting to make sense of the transformative nature and essence of spirituality as experienced and described by many who have engaged in PAR. I meandered through the beginning phase of a research process by examining the action of grounding or locating (in the ontological sense) and in knowing oneself beyond the surface. My wondering included a framework for understanding spirituality presented as both inner and outer expressions (action) and how both are inextricably connected, and finally I attempted to make a connection between the philosophies of PAR and spirituality; the swirling foam is beginning to form. To summarize in PAR form, I use praxis and the spiral, and the metaphor of the circle in Indigenous science, and return to the beginning.

I interpret the congruence between PAR and spirituality based on the commonalities of self and other, social justice, and fundamentally individual and collective relationality, unfolding through action in the community. Based on these commonalities, I also interpret a fit between PAR and Indigenous epistemology. Sinclair (2003) writes that PAR is a good fit with Aboriginal epistemology in that "knowledge is a sacred object, and seeking knowledge is a spiritual quest" (p. 3). She further states that this "non-directive, holistic approach to community research and action" is highly relevant for "Indigenous communities who have experienced disempowerment by western research hegemony" (*ibid*).

Relationality is significant to PAR in the the interconnection with others in community, as well as to

definitions and understanding of spirituality; the inward (self) and outward (others as self). Relationality representing all forms of the interpersonal relationship is fundamental to Indigenous worldview and research. Colorado (1988) argued that Western science models such as collaborative and participatory methodologies are complementary with Native science and Aboriginal culture. She states that "the participation of people in participatory research, [is] similar to "relations" in Native science" (p. 63). Although philosophically complementary in a number of aspects, and offering promise for mutual exchange and understanding, challenges exist for both Indigenous and non-indigenous scholars in relation to how the research may be played out in everyday life. Sinclair (2003) concluded that "the intricacies and specifics of practically integrating and applying the practices and protocols of an Indigenous worldview with western research methodologies have yet to be synthesized into clearly articulated forms" (p. 120).

Final Words of this Finite Game

PAR is a philosophy and methodology for the co-creation of collective knowledge. Knowledge as a construction is an entity unto its own, and as such is related to power in terms of its intent and purpose. Power is also connected to individual and collective identity within which personal transformation can also be viewed. For some individuals and groups identity is spirituality which can contribute to social change. In this way, a sense of being can be a source of both personal and collective power. hooks (1993) speaks about spirituality and recovery in the lives of black women. She writes that black women's reality of living in spirit, can contribute to solidarity and the creation of community. She believes that by black women developing a collective sense of spirituality, the result can be the catalyst for action and social transformation (p. 190).

I end this journal with a quote from Paulo Freire (2001) that seems fitting at this moment: "I hold that my own unity and identity, in regard

to others and the world, constitutes my essential and irrepeatable way of experiencing myself as a cultural, historical, and unfinished being in the world, simultaneously conscious of my unfinishedness" (p. 51).

Lessons Learned
Exhibit 5.8

**Liberatory processes are holistic, intertwined and mutually dependent.

**Everything we need is near at hand.

**Knowing oneself is essential in participatory approaches to research.

**Spirituality is about relationships with self and all forms of energy animate in inanimate.

Your Reflections...

....
....
....
....

We began Part Five of *Breaking Free* by noting our habit of placing everything into dichotomies, placing concepts into either/or positions. This phenomenon was discussed at length in one small group which met to discuss the Highlander presentation at the PAR Congress in Calgary in 1989. The conversation produced a consensus statement that seemingly opposing positions can work together once mutual trust has been established. One member of that group, Om Shrivastava, invited to Calgary to represent the rich and lengthy Indian PAR tradition, wished to move the discussion a bit further. In his efforts to do so, he said,

> It's beyond trust. It's something that we understand as part of the process—that I'm really very honest with you of what I really believe. And if we are working on this

> thing, then our beliefs and values must have some kind of compatibility. I think that is how it goes beyond trust. And then about us/them: they understand me as me, mine, myself…Trust is a first basic thing…But there is a power relationship as there is in all PAR. When power relations are sorted out, there is a chance for real partnership. (Notes from my learning journal)

Searching for the right words, Shrivastava was thinking that his words—"The we/they problem is… It's… It's…It's transcended"—offered another voice in the group with sounds of agreement from others. Transcendence is Max-Neef's (1991) fundamental human need that incorporates all others. Discussion about language, meaning, and the problems created by placing concepts into opposing positions has occurred throughout this guide. Recalling Schumacher's positive sense of divergent problems: "A pair of opposites—like freedom and order—are opposites at the level of ordinary life, but they cease to be opposites at the higher level, the really *human*(emphasis in original) level, where self-awareness plays its proper role" (Schumacher, 1977, p. 126). This higher level suggests a trans-disciplinary approach where all aspects of reality might interconnect. In keeping with Zapf, van Fraassen, and Chalmers, this other level might be a natural space where everything, animate and inanimate, is in harmony.

Shrivastava did not use words like trans-disciplinary, interconnectedness, or self-awareness but hinted at these concepts in his wish to emphasize the importance of moving beyond trust when doing PAR. At the same time, trust is a pivotal prerequisite to liberatory education practice aiming to create conditions necessary for dialogue and critique in direct relationship

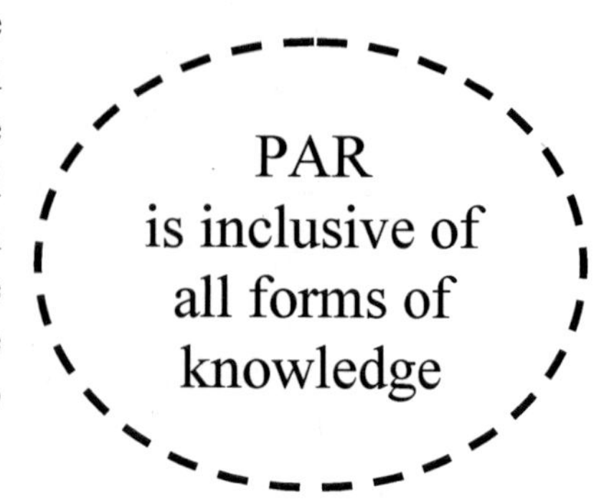

with social action—the Ganma rivers creating and relating to new knowledge in a timeless dance. Once we have achieved this kind of trust, we are ready to begin re-connecting our fragmented world while remaining inclusive of all forms of knowledge. If we add fairness to this inclusivity, we are behaving like the Canadians John Ralston Saul envisages. I assume we trust one another by this juncture in this Faculty of Social Work space—our preparatory work completed—so we can get on with the reconstructive, perhaps transformative, challenge we currently are facing as citizens of Alberta: demanding our imaginative participation to move into a culture of courageous hope and away from the detrimental "slash-and-burn" policies of the present.

Lessons learned in Part Five. The seventeenth century scientific revolution in Europe initiated marvellous inventions and conveniences to make material life easier. But not all was smooth sailing. Forces critical of the hegemony of a mechanical and linear view of the world and human interaction have been at work ever since seeking human scale alternatives. The dichotomous divide between scientific reason and humanistic faith created fragmented knowledge governed by the myth of objectivity. The divide has been narrowing in recent years, and trans-disciplinary inquiry is re-connecting the head and the heart. We are learning we have powers we never knew we had or had forgotten we had over the years—knowledge acknowledged in spaces open to all. With these powers in hand we are now ready to live the life of liberatory education practitioners working with renewed passion on behalf of justice, equity, and peace. We need to get on with our work; that is our commitment to facilitating lifelong learning in our social justice work.

Part Six

Re-connecting work and learning

Up to now we have been breaking free from powerful concepts functioning as barriers to liberatory education practice for social justice. I am crafting *Breaking Free* as a sign of hope, in order to encourage the Faculty of Social Work along a path of liberatory education practice. This hope emerges from the real experiences of our learners in concert with the literature and "conducted" by instructors. We are free to continue connecting and re-connecting concepts in preparation for the hope and courage it's going to take to live this liberatory education life. It is absolutely essential for us to be doing so in this time of global financial and economic uncertainty and national political upheavals—looming signs of a new depression and/or the collapse of global capitalism. Learning at work is one key to opening up the possibilities before us. Griff Foley (2001) and I, in our collaborative work, frequently

> …try to get people who have an interest in facilitating productive learning to think more deeply about their work. [We] find that this helps them to act more effectively and more in accordance with their deepest values. (p. 13)

If we focus on learning as a matter of routine in our social justice work, we create inquiring minds in ourselves, in our colleagues, and in our clients no matter what their circumstance or condition. These inquiring minds cannot easily be controlled unless we abandon our individuality and our interconnectedness. Moreover, focusing on our work means we can conceive of practical interventions; we possess more agency in our working lives than we might realize. So much depends on how we define work.

Re-connecting the fragmenting ways we seem to have been functioning with for far too long is part of a current global and national imperative to heal societal ills. "E. P. Thompson, in his classic article on time and work discipline in industrial capitalism (1967), documents the lengthy and difficult transformation from pre-industrial work rhythms to industrial discipline, a process he pithily summarizes as resulting in the separation of work and life" (Apffel-Marglin, 1996, p. 147). Re-connecting work and life is another emerging imperative in the twenty-first century, especially for those of us committed to holistic approaches to local healing of our troubled societies.

Canadian sociologist David Livingstone (1999) interprets the shift between work and life as follows:

> In pre-industrial societies, most people *worked to live*...Only with the emergence of industrial capitalism did most people begin to *live for their productive work.* (p. 227)

In contemporary capitalist societies, Livingstone (1999) sees work divided into three spheres of life: paid work in the sphere of commodity exchange, domestic labour, and community volunteer work. Three colleagues and I composed a variation on the Livingstone theme. In our critical introduction to workplace learning, we (Bratton, Helms Mills, Pyrch & Sawchuk, 2003) classify work as paid work, "motherwork," and voluntary work. There are other variations on the theme. Studs Terkel (1972) discovered a similar threefold distinction in his massive collection of working Americans talking about their work. He cites Ralph Helstein, the president of the United Packinghouse Workers of America, as saying,

> "Learning is work. Caring for children is work. Community action is work. Once we accept the concept of work as something meaningful—not just as the source of a buck – you don't have to worry about finding enough jobs. There's no excuse for mules any more. Society does not need them. There's no question about our ability to feed and clothe and house everybody. The problem is going to come in finding enough ways for man to keep occupied, so he's in touch with reality." (as cited in Terkel, 1972, p. xxviii)

"Our imaginations have obviously not yet been challenged", Terkel concluded (*ibid.*). Opening up the concept of work to include more than the job obviates the negative meaning of "unemployment" and frees us to ascribe proper value to the rich work we do that is unpaid. We should also attempt to redefine "payment" to include more than salary and to honour the multitudinous, noneconomic ways in which we contribute to the general well-being of society. The challenge has been taken up in a burgeoning literature searching for new connections between work and learning. Why is this challenge important to liberatory education practice? If we value work in a more broadly defined sense than just as a commodity, we might find "work" more satisfying when not limited to our social welfare job with its inevitable stress and strain. As a result, our work world could transform into a holistic blending of equally worthwhile elements. This personal discovery might make us better counsellors for those who are jobless at the moment but still engaging in their work; if only they knew it. If we help the jobless understand their valuable contributions to life, life replaces work in its fullest sense, allowing us to fully enjoy both.

Livingstone shows the labour force growing better educated in a formal way but with limited opportunities to use this education in the job-place. Is there some potential in transferring that education into motherwork and the needs of civil society so that it is not wasted? In his exhaustive study of underemployment in contemporary capitalist societies, he (Livingstone, 1999) argues that the education-jobs gap can be reduced by economic strategies including broadening ownership of work organizations, facilitating workplace democratization, shortening the workweek, and acknowledging and valuing new forms of work.

> Overall, there is serious public support for democratizing measures such as cooperative forms of ownership, workplace participation, shorter workweeks and gender equity in unpaid labour. People in general are giving these progressive economic alternatives more serious consideration than the writings of professional economists. The elements of viable solutions to the education-jobs gap exist in the tacit foreknowledge of

> the general public. Where are "the serious leaders who are for the people?" (pp. 273-4)

Dare we hope President Obama is a "serious leader" committed to democracy? Is anything he is proposing similar to Livingstone's suggestions for democratizing work? What about the political leadership in Alberta and Canada? Perhaps one way of judging their performance is to use Livingstone's progressive thoughts about economic democracy as a lens. Through this lens, how are our leaders doing? They shout out their commitment to "jobs, jobs, jobs," but what do they really mean? Matthew Fox, American founder of the creation spirituality movement, argues that superficial statements advocating for more jobs are a way to simply dumb down citizenry. While "reinventing work," he suggests (Fox, 1994),

> We should not allow ourselves to be deceived that today's crisis in jobs is just about more jobs; it is not. The job crisis is a symptom of something much deeper; a crisis in our relationship to work and the challenge put to our species today to reinvent it. We must learn to speak of the differences between a job and work. (p. 5)

Perhaps our narrow understanding of the concept of work is a direct consequence of the hegemonic focus on jobs as the answer to any and all societal ills.

South African adult educator Astrid von Kotze (2002) re-connects working with living by focusing on the exclusion of poor people from "work" by associating it only within the rigid terms of employment. She argues, that "employment" describes a relation of production rather than something which poor people do in order to support themselves and their households. She rejects the deficit notion of "unemployment" as synonymous with "not working", and hence the suggestion that only employment-type work. Von Kotze continues,

> Such work is concerned with supporting and sustaining the basic conditions of life. It is work like teaching youth and caring for the sick, rebuilding neighbourhoods and harvesting and preparing food, maintaining a safe and healthy environment and creating artefacts and stories that build hope for the future. Learning how to do such work

> happens in the process of doing it rather than through structured and planned educational interventions. (p. 234)

This resembles motherwork, a lifelong process of on-the-job learning that sustains society yet is not factored into economic accounting practices in any political system at present. It is the kind of learning Brigette Krieg found alive and well on the margins of society inhabited by too many Aboriginal women. *Breaking Free* is entirely about celebrating this type of learning. It resembles the work of Social Work learners oftentimes overwhelmed by full time studies, part time jobs, and demanding families. Take a few moments and write out what you understand your work to be. Is it the same as your job description?

....

....

....

Wouldn't it serve the concept of social justice better if we valued these aspects of your work as potentially rich learning opportunities on the job? We might thereby avoid "over-working" ourselves and each other.

Von Kotze lists satisfiers of several fundamental human needs beyond mere subsistence. She focuses on various "livelihood activities" including "the numerous cultural and aesthetic activities in which individuals and communities engage in order to restore, reproduce and re-invent their identities, a sense of belonging and dignity" (p. 236). As such, she argues that the notion of livelihood includes a sense of well-being rather than mere survival. Life is more hopeful once we look beyond the economic parameters, once we put down the economic lens. As Max-Neef (1991) noted some years ago, universal human needs are satisfied by multiple factors of which the economy is only one. This in no way diminishes the economic imperative to keep us gainfully employed and healthy, but it does open up the conversation to include our rich contributions to our well-being beyond the job-place. In our current global financial and economic crisis, and the growing national and global political uncertainty, re-definition of life's fundamental concepts of work and job is urgent. Remember, everything we need is near at hand and within our traditions.

There is no exaggerating the challenges facing us. American adult educator Mechthild Hart's (1995) "radical proposal" aims to liberate work and education from the bottom line and introduces gender into our inquiry explicitly.

Exhibit 6.1: Liberating work and education from the bottom line (Hart, 1995)

Employed women (and a few men as well) who seem to hold on tenaciously to their "family orientation" are the bearers of experiences and knowledge, and of an overall orientation to work and production that needs to be acknowledged, understood, and made available. The work of raising children requires an orientation that aims to sustain and preserve life. This orientation clashes directly with the rationality of "our economy" with its built-in imperative to exploit or disregard all living things… (p. 118)

If today a revolution is in the making (or can be envisioned), calling for a fundamental restructuring of work, this revolution does not come from the introduction of new technology. I would call it revolutionary to divest work from its last vestiges of physical or bodily involvement in production and glorify the symbolic manipulation of a distilled reality into the ultimate form of progress. Rather, I would call it the culmination of century-old trends in Western culture: to control nature by banning it from our reality as much as possible. By engaging in a large-scale and cultural denial of our inescapable bond with nature, we have in the process destroyed nature. Acknowledging that we have bodies and are an integral part of nature would be truly revolutionary, calling for a radical rethinking of our cultural heritage and value hierarchies…

If we were to move "feminine qualities" up the ladder of social values, we would begin to dismantle the unhappy dichotomy between "feminine" and "masculine" qualities, as men as well as women would be associated with [raising children]. Above anything else we would demythologize the concept of "the family," and of a corresponding "family orientation" by reframing it *as living and working with children.* As such, it would be the work of mothering, or motherwork, which would become an issue for all workers and where the very term "worker" would include this reality. By making the issue of living and working with children a central one, we would give "fatherhood" a new meaning, and change it from a biological claim, or an abstract "provider role" to an achieved status. In such a way, "fatherhood" would become more like "motherhood," and the term "parenting" would for the first time be correct, no longer silencing an unequal distribution of work and responsibilities between "mothers" and "fathers." (p. 119). . .

If we focus on the politics of the economy, the issue of gender points above all to the concealment of the importance of non-market work. Without women's essential work of raising and caring for the next generation, we would have no future, and not even cheap labourers for the capitalist owners of production. Concealing the *economic* importance of the work done mostly by women also feeds into the predominant Western masculinist dichotomies, whether they are Marxist or mainstream. These are the binary oppositions between "family" and "work," (p. 120) between "private" and "public," between the "reproductive" and the "productive." (p. 121)...

what kind of pedagogies or educational processes would be appropriate? First, examining the entire political economy of motherwork is helping us break through the stifling confines of the current debate, to open up new themes, and to deepen our understanding of the many important and

complicated questions contained in the experience of work. This is also helping us to discover new links between work and education and new possibilities for educational practice, and to leave the industrialized paradigm defining "workers' education" or "workplace education." Likewise, highly effective blaming-the-victim attitudes towards "deficient" workers would be called into question. So would the emphasis on training for the behaviours, skills, and attitudes that are either fit for low-wage jobs or for the corporate megamachine as a whole…Secondly, by placing motherwork into the context of a political economy, our ideas of work-related competencies, skills, and knowledge would be greatly expanded. If we were to consider work such as mothering a model for good, productive work, how would our conceptions of these central educational categories change? How can we develop forms of knowledge based on non-market subsistence work? (p. 122)…

Current proposals for restructuring workplaces to make them more "educative" would look quite different if new organizations of work would be systematically reconciled with the work of raising children. I believe that such a reconciliation would be a prime avenue for a much needed overall humanization of work. This is the promise, rather than the threat of bringing the issue of children into the "world of work": to disrupt this world of work and its logic, to "liberate" it from its deadly bottom line, its equally deadly fixation on ever faster, ever more efficient, and ever more risky technology, and to reconnect it with issues of life and survival. (p. 124)

Lessons Learned
Exhibit 6.1

**Disciplined, thoughtful hope.

**Liberatory processes are holistic, intertwined and mutually dependent.

**Knowledge-making is a democratic collective relationship of equals.

**Dichotomies (feminine/masculine) produce conflicting values.

Your Reflections…

....
....
....
....

One is reminded of Gould's efforts to uncover the origins of dichotomous positioning of life into either/or confrontations.

Hart's strongly feminist ideas about reconciling work with the rest of life's demands fits well into the liberatory tradition which drives *Breaking Free*. My colleagues and I (Bratton *et al*, 2003) wondered if the liberatory tradition might be interpreted as a feminine phenomenon, if not a feminist one. A number of questions arise.

> There are many feminist perspectives in the adult education literature (Tisdell, 1993), but are there perspectives that interpret adult education itself as a feminine concept? If adult education is a feminine concept, could this explain why adult education has been a marginal player in educational systems, basically paternalistic cultures celebrating "power over" relationships? "Power with" relationships like interdisciplinary and trans-disciplinary inquiry are still rare in the academy. If adult education celebrates

> femininity including a nurturing interconnectedness, our influence may be hidden behind the dominant culture's focus on individuality and aggressive competitiveness – flexible capitalism. If this is true, we can understand more fully why adult educators are marginal at best and perhaps anathema to an educational establishment wanting to remain in control of the "learning business," and to the management establishment's preoccupation with the "bottom line." Can we create new metaphors to celebrate the fluid, organic and free nature of adult learning? Can these metaphors facilitate workplace learning as a democratic process? How might we combine our liberatory tradition with the burgeoning interest in action research? How can we reconnect with our work and not be overwhelmed by our job? (Bratton et. al., 2003, p. 148)

Answers to these questions could be informed by Brigette Krieg's understanding of the creative forces lying at the margins of society, forces we have discounted for too long.

Historical Note: Historian of Christianity Elaine Pagels (1995), writing about the Gnostic tradition in the early Christian era, noted second century Bishop Irenaeus' concern with the appeal of the Gnostic concept to women who were increasingly excluded from his own church (p. 170). Is this somehow connected with the possibility of linking feminine concepts with anti-authoritarian impulses within the liberatory tradition?

Does the workplace—located much more widely than ever before within our three dimensional model of work—offer a space to withstand the controlling impulse of educational institutions to control learning? Or does the workplace in the older sense of "job-place" become the site of new controlling forces like "business" searching for "intellectual capital" for commodification? Is the search for tacit knowledge a new effort to control workers (Bratton et. al., 2003)? These questions were asked at the Second International Conference on Researching Work and Learning held at the University of Calgary campus in 2001. Once more take note of the many and varied gatherings of trans-disciplinary inquirers right here, so close to home. A range of answers to their challenging questions is emerging in subsequent on-going international conferences researching work and learning.

It is heartening to see our liberatory tradition in the adult education movement re-appearing as we are finding our way out of the culture of fear and searching for radical hope. According to British adult educator Ian Martin,

> For me, the loom of my kind of adult education has always been about seeing it as part of something much bigger and more widely shared, what Juliet Merrifield calls the "public work of politics." To see adult education in this way, as "part of the road toward a democratic society," is to embrace it as a vocation—and necessarily, I think, a radical and dissenting vocation—as distinct from merely a field of practice, professional identity or academic specialism. Understood in this way, adult education is part of the work we choose to undertake as distinct from simply the job we get paid to do (Martin, 2009).

Richard Sennett (1998) focuses on reconnecting work and life as an antidote to the corrosion of character in America and, by extension, wherever American influence appears.

> One of the unintended consequences of modern capitalism is that it has strengthened the value of place, aroused a longing for community. All the emotional conditions we have explored in the workplace animate

> that desire: the uncertainties of flexibility; the absence of deeply rooted trust and commitment; the superficiality of teamwork; most of all, the spectre of failing to make something of oneself in the world, to "get a life" through one's work. All these conditions impel people to look for some other scene of attachment and depth. (p. 138)

That "other scene of attachment and depth" is the local community where "we"—Sennett's "dangerous pronoun" and the title of the last chapter of his book—reconnect with what we know and trust best. We addressed the potential superficiality of teamwork in Part Two, where we noted the authentic practice of "teams" in the Faculty of Social Work, in particular the work of Kim Zapf, Les Jerome, and Margaret Williams. We need to work together as creatively as possible in order to generate the strength to actually get on with our real work.

On working. By removing ourselves from our work, we give up some of our strength. By limiting our work to a "job," we devalue the other kinds of work we do by only focusing on a limiting view of life as "economic," as a commodity. By reflecting on the joys and pains of learning in an expanding world of work, we enter new depths of inquiry, finding new opportunities, obligations, and responsibilities. By avoiding the trap of "unemployment," family therapists in New Zealand are able to locate encouragement in a jobless family.

> The loss of dignity is compounded by the guilt of not having a job and by the contempt of others and comments about "lazy dole bludgers." The pressures of family financial needs and the lure of commercial advertising add to the problem. It is little wonder unemployed people often experience classic depression with feelings of sadness, hopelessness and self-blame. Thus many people in these situations present problems to therapists that in fact are the "symptoms of poverty." These may include psychosomatic illnesses, violence, depression, delinquency, psychotic problems, marital stress, truanting, parenting problems, and so on. However, the meaning placed on their experience of events often does not include a political analysis of poverty. On the contrary, they, and many others, consider them to be failures, individually failed. Their feelings of sadness, hopelessness, and self-blame stem from this problem-based web of meaning. (Waldegrave, 2003, p. 24)

For Sharon Big Plume, "being a social worker is a job, but being a Warrior is a commitment to a certain way of life; hence, a code of ethics and personal conduct for a Warrior may be more expansive and intricate than that required for a social worker" (2007, p. 249). Although she does not connect Warriorship and work in the same sense used in *Breaking Free*, her research does suggest re-connecting life with the three dimensions of work suggested in this guide. She concluded,

> Differences between Warriorship and social work include the contexts in which Warriors and social workers must operate. Empowerment for each occurs on different levels. Paid social workers may be constrained by their respective agencies, or may even retreat behind agency structures, policies or regulations. Social workers are taught to maintain an objective distance between themselves and their clients, which can reduce personal discomfort or risk. On the other hand, Warriorship requires an immense personal investment. Great care is needed when combining sacred Warrior principles or practices with existing social structures. (*ibid*, p. 258)

Even though our job-place might be within public and private agencies with multitudinous rules and regulations, our workplace includes other spaces perhaps more compatible to Warriorship—where we engage in motherwork and voluntary activities. We need the agility of the fox to function effectively in these spaces while emulating the confidence of a hedgehog in the power of our work. Is a Warrior agile and confident in the same way? Can these qualities be learned? Are they part of our curriculum?

We commence by celebrating the knowledge we have. James Scott (1998) emphasises "practical knowledge" as a safeguard to "imperial science." Recognising one's own knowledge encourages us to go further, to recognise the knowledge of others. Empowering experiences of learners in liberatory education spaces opens up the possibility of recognising other forms of knowledge in addition to the rational and instrumental. This possibility created the guitar metaphor and leads to a recognition of multiple forms of intelligence.

But recognising multiple forms of intelligence is not enough; we must act upon them to transform our realities. Michael Newman (1999) is our guide.

> Adult education for critical thinking is concerned with the positions we adopt, the sides we take, the alliances we form, and the solidarities we enter into. This kind of adult education is not detached and dispassionate. It helps us explain how knowledge, consciousness and power are generated and controlled; and then examines how knowledge, consciousness and power can be generated and controlled in ways that will enable us to live in equitable, peaceful, and sustainable ways on a habitable planet. Adult education for critical thinking is constructed on an ethical stance. It is a form of education by and for those wanting to understand the world in order to change it. It is education for social justice. (p. 56)

All of this sounds rather grand. How can we function in our own job-place where human scale experiences challenge us daily?

Resiliency at the job might offer a way to recovering some of our integrity. Unrau (2008) makes a useful distinction between "resistance" and "resilience." For him, to resist means to oppose. For him, resilience means dealing with energy by not engaging in it. He draws on Judo as a metaphor to explain his meaning.

> The general principle, in Judo, is to use an opponent's strength instead of resisting it, quickly adapting to changing circumstances to bring the energetic forces of the opponent back on him. If an attacker pushes against me, I step to the side, allowing the attacker's momentum to throw him forwards. This is in flow with energetic forces, instead of against. In Judo, one needs perception, awareness, and foresight to know what the attacker will do next, so that one may act accordingly. To face an opponent, one must be present

> and aware of everything that is happening in the moment. When one is aware, there is no "us" or "them." In this state, we can act accordingly to every situation that arises. (pp. 89-90)

Being aware of the strength of flexibility, fluidity, and discipline—and using this strength in our daily life—is required in liberatory education practice. It demands discipline, and this can be learned in our courses and highlighted in narratives and case studies. Nancy Davis, MSW, 2006, devoted her case study to figuring out how to remain resilient in uncertain times, drawing from her own lived experience in the social welfare system while offering sound advice to her colleagues. In itself, this blending of the personal knowledge reflected in her own practice plus the public knowledge housed in the literature, resembles a resilient practitioner.

Exhibit #6.2: Resiliency in the workplace (Davis, 2006).

I propose pro-social, protective factors themes emerging from this case study and my own professional practice.

****Healthy workplaces. Long standing issues and health concerns with staff left unsupported can be overlooked, which have detrimental effects on an organization. Kelloway & Day (2005) assert that the costs of unsafe, stressful and unhealthy workplaces are horrific in personal, economic and social terms. They state that a healthy workplace must make careful consideration of the physical, psychological and social contributing factors within an organization.**

Seeking outside support is vital for social workers, especially those engaged with participants who experience multiple levels of crisis in the everyday lives. Working for an organization who supports their employees by providing a benefits package that allows for counselling, and promotes the well being of their staff through multiple means is crucial when deciding which organization to work for…

**Personal mastery and self-directed learning. How do we remain learners in the work force? How do we promote learning organizations? Helpful to me practice was seeking feedback from co-workers and participants alike. Our team had previously created an atmosphere of mutual respect, asking for permission before offering feedback, speaking from our own truth with the understanding that we were sharing with a genuine interest in supporting and assisting each other and respecting ourselves enough to be true about our own needs in our working relationships. Feedback, unlike professional direction, was given, not in an effort to change others, but to share "our experience." The recipient was only expected to share their thankfulness for having a person care enough to share with them. Of course, if you received the same feedback from multiple individuals, chances are you need to do something about it. We mutually understood that feedback was neutral and that we were to be accountable for our role in relationship with each other. This helped us feel safe and respected. Professional relationships that involve maintaining others sense of worth, dignity, promote safety and learning must be supported.

Even though this self-exploratory case study was a painful process, the "learning" throughout made this journey valuable. Learning "through" and "with" others in a supportive non-judgmental atmosphere is beneficial to any practice. Agreement has to be reached that co-workers and supervisors alike will support each other through the learning process of making mistakes and correcting with minor adjustments in order to develop and hone our skills. Senge (1990) speaks of the learning organization and states that organizations continue to survive through individuals in the organization who continue to learn with other members…

**Communication…We learn in relationships by talking about our internal feelings, by being curious, empathetic, being specific and descriptive, by demonstrating respect, being

genuine and using immediacy. These are useful skills for practice in all our relationships. Very often I have witnessed individuals and co-workers moving into trouble spots when they mask their own self experience and instead talk about others…Asking for help is not an easy thing to do when you feel others are questioning your ability, but it is so necessary…I took the time necessary to come to terms with my experience and determine what it could teach me. O'Hanlon (2004) states that we are such a problem-solving and action-oriented society that we rarely take time for ourselves, asserting that women in particular have difficulty taking time without feeling guilty.

****Intra-dependent relationships and cultivating emotional energy…I have learned that it is extremely valuable to be accountable in the workplace, but also to have permission in order to hold up a mirror so that others may do the same. Setting boundaries and examining what you can and cannot do in a day is vital to genuinely sharing yourself in the workplace… Everyone has a certain amount of daily stress to contend with this is doubled for the social worker who expends emotional energy at work dealing with participants who experience a broad range of trauma and crisis…It becomes extremely important for social workers to have some pathway towards healthy development…**

****Clear roles and responsibilities. A realistic appraisal of the environment involves knowing what one can and cannot do, as well as knowing what one can and cannot change…**

****Developing a sense of purpose…I found it helpful to think about the following questions in my journaling process. What has been the driving force in my life? What is it that I feel I am here to share with the world? A sense of direction or mission gives a sense of purpose, such as a special talent, passion or interest that can act to strengthen resilience…**

**Humour and joy...Being joyful is a rare gift and should have its place in the work we do. Do we often consider what brings joy to our lives and do we actively seek these things out? I found the following questions helpful to find my joy again and I have reworded them so that they make some sense to you. Think of things I spend time on. Do I lose track of time when you engage in these tasks? Do these activities spark my creative side? Do I conjure up ways to do it differently or better? Do I daydream about these things when I am not doing them? Do these things energize me? Does it feel more like play than work? Answering these questions may help you find a hidden joy.

**Adaptive depersonalization. Adaptive distancing is a personality related skill that allows a person to step back from a maladaptive environment and de-personalize (Norman, 2000). Do I recognize what part of an issue is mine and what belongs to others? When an event occurs, do I go into resistance instead of telling myself the truth about what is really going on?

**Performance and personal renewal...Even though most social workers acknowledge that a holistic practice has to encompass the spiritual, emotional, physical and intellectual, we are always hard pressed to find room for these things in our own lives. As the rate of society's health in these realms deteriorate, it becomes imperative now more than ever for us social workers to take care of ourselves first and foremost...

**Managing stress... Stevanovic & Rupert (2004) conducted a survey about career-sustaining behaviours and about satisfactions and stresses licensed psychologists experience at work. Respondents indicated that the following elements assist in alleviating work stress: spending time with partner/family; maintaining a balance between personal and professional lives; maintaining a sense of humour; and, participating in personal therapy. Additionally helpful were: spending time with friends; discussing work

frustrations with colleagues; seeking case consultation; maintaining contact with referral networks; participating in continuing education programs; reflecting on positive experiences; and, engaging in quiet leisure time activities…

****Importance of leader support…Gelsema, Van der Doef, Maes, Akerboom, & Verhoeven (2005) found that three job characteristics (job demand, control and social support) are predictors of job stress. Demand refers to time pressure, work pace and physical workload; control refers to the degree of decision authority, as well as to the degree of task variety and sole discretion; and, support refers to the amount of social support received from supervisor or colleagues…**

****Summary…Through our ability to communicate genuinely and honestly about our own experiences and perception of the world, we are able to develop our ability to create supportive and nurturing relationships with those we work with as well as with important individuals in our lives who provide us with love, understanding and clear expectations of what we can accomplish. These relationships in turn, assist us with our capacity to cultivate the emotional energy we need to accomplish, not only our roles and responsibilities, but provide us with the means to engage more fully in our own lives. We gain personal renewal and manage stress more effectively if we know what we want and what our purpose is. We co-exist and engage in the dance of life together co-creating effectiveness, creativity and meaning.**

Lessons Learned Exhibit 6.2

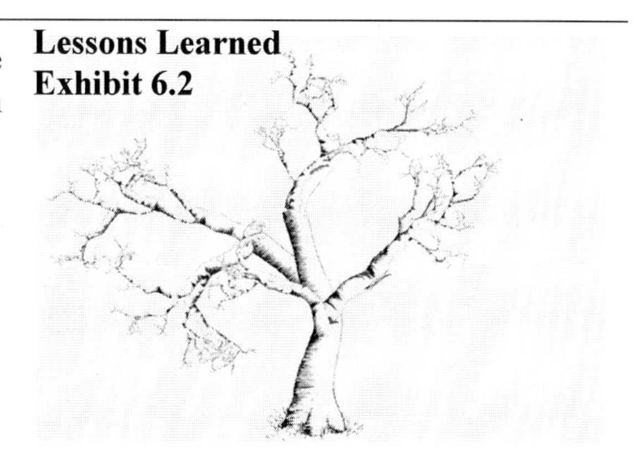

**Direct experience provides the foundation for human learning.

**Focusing on our learning, which can be painful, keeps us engaging with our experience constructively.

**Courage to reflect and be accountable for the role the professional plays in their own experience as the professional realm is always a co-creation process.

**Maintaining a learning journal facilitates working and living.
**Disciplined, thoughtful hope.

Your Reflections…

……………………………………………………………………
……………………………………………………………………
……………………………………………………………………
……………………………………………………………………

What makes this advice so helpful is the genuine and authentic sense that Nancy is speaking from what she knows best: her own life and work, both of which are presented harmoniously in her case study. Her words tell of resilience in a dynamic engagement of her paid work and her motherwork, a healthy balance of work and life becoming a unified energy. Her constant reflecting on her learning along the way exemplifies liberatory education practice while self-healing along the way. Re-connecting work and life extends our understanding of our place in the world, freeing us from those roles limiting if not lowering our expectations of ourselves and others.

On learning. Much has been said in *Breaking Free* about learning and its importance in life and work, yet we have never actually seen "learning." It is something taking place in our body, mind, and in our social environment that we often take for granted. There are plentiful learning theories, abstractions having, at their absolute best, something practical to say to guide liberatory education practice. Bratton *et al.* (2003), analyzing the burgeoning workplace learning literature, suggest six critical points for our understanding of learning theories. The six are as follows: recovering our multiple selves; embracing new forms of knowledge; living with complexity, uncertainty, accelerating change, and the possibility of chaos; understanding power; acting upon that power; and celebrating democracy. Indicators of these six points are appearing throughout the guide, and like the six string guitar introduced in Exhibit 2.1, these points require a "hand" to re-connect the fragments of our lifelong learning journey to continue to the infinite game in Part Seven, another seventh moment. Each individual hand will activate the six critical points individually, preparing a personal guide to document one's own practice of liberatory education for social justice work.

How have we responded to these six critical points until now in *Breaking Free*? First we began recovering our multiple selves by breaking free of narrow individualism and locating connections with others in our daily activities and with like-minded souls past and present in the literature. Secondly, stimulated by Aboriginal voices and by a growing trans-disciplinary inquiry bringing together diverse disciplines and practices, we are embracing new forms of knowledge. At the same time, we are coming to recognize and value knowledge within ourselves and each other, knowledge unique to each individual while shared in safe places to be absorbed and enjoyed by the community. Third, within these safe places—learning circles of timeless practice in many cultures and retained most authentically by Aboriginal customs—we withstand the confusing, deafening noise of forces of manic consumption and fear. Fourth, together with our rich knowledge shared in places of solidarity, we experience the power we have but fear to act upon because our confidence is weakened by pressures to conform to forces of globalization, professionalization, and commodification. Fifth, as we search deeply together in our places of safety, comforted by age-old traditions of human struggle for dignity, autonomy, and equality, we are recovering in our workplace the courage and hope to recreate grassroots democracy and dignity in all its meanings and possibilities. Sixth, this recovery is enabled by our resiliency to withstand yet again those hegemonies waiting in the wings—new forms of political expediency attempting to silence free expression and democratic engagement. Clearly we are engaging with creative energy and commitment to the demands and opportunities facing humankind's urgent and desperate need to survive these fearful times. How do we now proceed?

Lessons learned in Part Six. International inquiry into the nature of work and learning is re-connecting life with work. This inquiry is a part of broader trends in all disciplines to heal the fragmentations created by imperial science and the co-optation of work into the world of commodities. We are learning that we do not have time to be in a hurry.

Part Seven

Beginnings: the infinite game

Your individual guide is evidence of your knowledge-making efforts reflecting your own reality. Liberatory education practice might be imagined as an eternal search for dignity within our various realities. I did not create the liberatory education practice; it created me. It is one expression of humankind's interminable struggle to be free. It is timeless and endless. I have been drawing upon many metaphors to reflect my experience with liberatory education practice, and in my attempts to explain it; I have been drawing you, the reader, into this continuing search. As I said earlier, *Breaking Free* is a story in itself, my story. Carse tells us, "If we cannot tell a story about what happened to us, nothing happened to us" (p. 167). Being unwilling to accept that nothing happened to me, I am obliged to become a storyteller. I urge you in your reconnecting life/work to tell your stories as well. I urge you to urge others to do likewise. What better way to share our knowledge-making processes than to listen to each others' stories? As if we needed encouragement, we might recall that Aristotle's philosophy was based on the power of narrative to convey the virtues guiding the base of humankind's morality. You have not done nothing; you have a story to tell.

Stories are for learning. The "seriousness" of storytelling lies in their empowering potential to model "goodness"—in this case, good social justice work. The many stories in this guide were selected and positioned to direct your learning so that we could collectively understand our work as lifelong learners for social justice. The wisdom of the ages is to be found in the stories; they house not precise ways to behave but rather, indications of how others have lived and are living their lives in service of the commonwealth. Mary Bateson helps to create lifelong patterns of learning as we struggle to understand life's meaning and our roles within it.

Exhibit 7.1: Lifelong learning (Bateson, 2000).

The stories our children need most to hear are not the stories of daunting success, achievements so impressive and final that they are hard to identify with, but the repeatable stories of composing and improvisation, in which adaptation is more central than dazzling accomplishment. Learning occurs in stages, but the process never completely ends for the individual even as it is repeated from generation to generation. In a world of accelerating change every graduate needs to understand that much of the shiny new learning is obsolescent, while the authority of elders is contingent on their willingness to continue to learn even as they teach. When society is fluid, young and old alike need to improvise and to teach each other. Wisdom is gradually revealing a whole new meaning, traced out through the life cycle. Today we do think of wisdom as depending on the flexibility, playfulness, and willingness to learn that are sometimes lost or denied with age, the kind of intelligence that includes self-criticism and the habit of reflecting on experience.

Narratives focus on dramatic events and transitions. But within our repertoire of ways of thinking about human lives, we need ways of thinking of the plateaus between transitions,

long periods of little obvious change or learning, when maintenance and continuity are paramount, even as we remember that all such periods are temporary. We are skilled, in this culture, at talking about change and transformation, not so skilled at thinking about sustaining what follows. We deal with on-going problems with quick campaigns promising spurious victories: crash diets instead of new habits, urban renewal by bulldozer, or such a flurry of simultaneous experiments in schools that parents and children are simply bewildered. Excitement about change leads all too readily to short-term efforts that are abandoned as quickly as they begin to show results. (pp. 31-2)

Lessons Learned
Exhibit 7.1

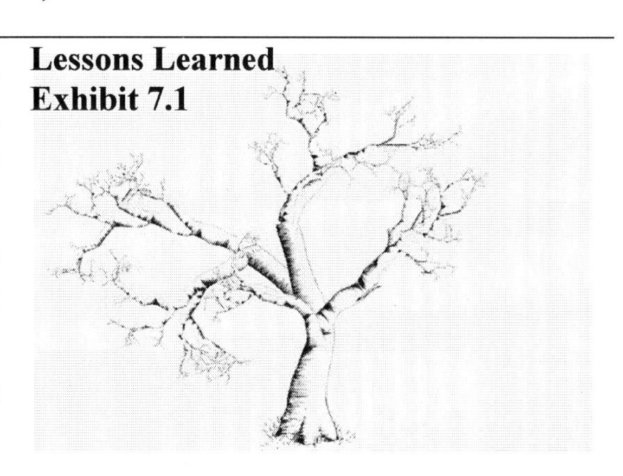

**Our stories celebrate modest, local and small-scale human relationships.

**Powerful learning is not bound by time or place.

**We don't have time to be in a hurry.

Your Reflections...

....

....

....

....

The stories collected in this guide highlight particular times and experiences notable in some fashion in the Faculty of Social Work at the University of Calgary—class assignments, theses, publications, and various events. *Breaking Free* helps us record the more routine learnings in our journey, most readily gathered in learning journals serving to maintain and sustain our social justice work for the long haul. Class assignments, theses, publications, and events are, like this very guide, "finite" games with beginnings and endings. For their part, "infinite" games can be shared in the boundless fluidity of our learning journals and sung during story time.

In my singular way, I am trying to help sustain the liberatory tradition in this collection of exhibits but without presenting the tradition in my own image. My purpose is not merely a matter of ego or immodesty; it is an obligation to give back what I have received. I do this so I can continue learning, encouraged by the Aztec elder Malaquìas who we met in Part Two, to meet old age "with grace, having met fear, seeing with clarity, sharing power, and making wisdom my friend." All the while, I acknowledge the knowledge around me—indigenous energies we often attribute to Aboriginal peoples. Returning to Wilda Listener, MSW, 2004:

Exhibit 7.2: Aboriginal storytelling for learning (Listener, 2004).

Traditional Aboriginal culture relied heavily on learning as a tool for balance, healing and personal growth. Ermine (1995) refers to Aboriginal learning in what he calls "inner space" rather than the Western culture in search of knowledge and learning in outer space. This journey toward inner space is when people self-reflect and learn about the world from within. Aboriginal people did not have to go out to make discoveries to find valuable information…

The Aboriginal approach allows for storytelling, learning and growth to be the centre. The way I used it in the case study is in the circle telling stories and by getting other people to share their personal stories, not just what they went through but what they learned…storytelling is an ancient ceremony used by many different cultures not just to transmit culture but also to help heal people and it helps the storyteller remain in balance. The process of an Aboriginal approach is to start a healing process from within and work out way out into the community. It has a ripple effect. By throwing

stories into the lake slowly and surely, the lake will feel the effect. It will not take wide spread techniques for people and communities to be in balance, and that learning must be done on an individual basis…

One of the major drawbacks to using this Aboriginal approach is not everyone is where they should be. That is, there are Aboriginal people who do not follow the traditions and culture, and will not teach their children the methods and processes. Many Aboriginal people have a colonized mind…I have heard elders say that when they have to translate what they are saying, some important meaning is lost. I do not want anyone to miss the messages they are revealing. They are the teachers. Bastien (2004) states that "language carries our breath to the ancestors," which means if we do not speak our language the ancestors will not hear us and we will not understand them…

I think one of the challenges for social workers adapting the Aboriginal approach is remaining open. This is not just the job of clients and community, but also the helpers and healers. These individuals are the keys to Aboriginal communities healing and they need to allow for being a part of a process of continuous self reflection and development. It is not enough for social workers to go through the motions but for them to take care of themselves and to be balanced. I did not find much literature about social workers continuing to remain in balance…

I think more learning needs to be done away from the academic environment. The learning individuals do on a continuous basis should be valued since it was in Aboriginal cultures. That is, the inner space discussed earlier. This learning does not earn people degrees or outer accomplishments. This learning earns pathways to true healing and knowledge from within. In the field of social work, there is significant interest to make it more professional like law or medicine. It does not have to go to these lengths because in its earliest roots, our profession started from the

heart. I do not know how to professionalize the heart so that it is taken seriously. The heart has been forgotten if we as social workers are only using the mind. It needs to be brought back into the field of social work where it belongs. Social workers need to change society's heart not just their mind. This all starts with social workers doing their own healing.

Lessons Learned
Exhibit 7.2

**Everything we need is near at hand.

**Learning commences from within.

**Learning is enhanced when the head and the heart are both in play.

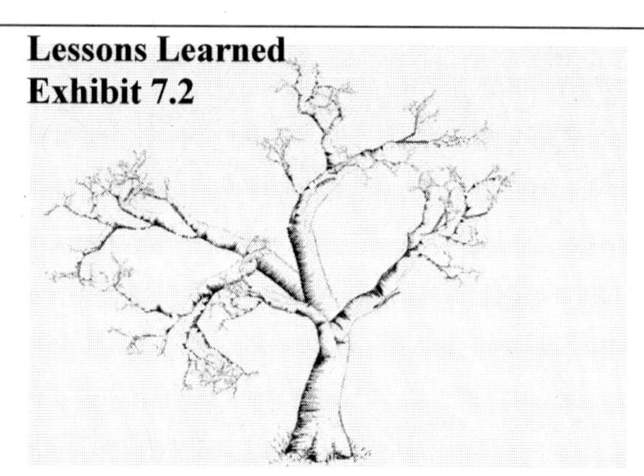

Your Reflections…

……………………………………………………………………………
……………………………………………………………………………
……………………………………………………………………………
……………………………………………………………………………

These lessons are clear in Sharon Big Plume's (2008) concept of being and becoming a "warrior." The notion of lifelong learning as an infinite game is part of warriorship as well. She wrote,

> Aboriginal culture is based on transformational teachings and practices, specifically the development of powerful and responsible wisdom, which is a <u>process</u>, (emphasis in original) but because it is much more difficult to learn and to teach a process, the temptation is to look for simpler ways to design, deliver, and test content. Therefore, this study is not asking if social workers or social work educators can do better what is already being done, adjusting content. Instead the study

> asks if there is something better we could or should be doing; a different process—warriorship. (pp. 7-8)

Warriors are in it for the long haul. This was Lear's (2006) understanding of Chief Plenty Coups' courage in making tough short term decisions with long term impact, albeit silently, as his people faced cultural disaster. What are we to learn from Chief Plenty Coups' ordeal? This question has a sense of urgency at the moment as we are facing the possibility of devastating economic, financial, and political disaster world-wide.

> We live at a time of a heightened sense that civilizations are themselves vulnerable. Events around the world—terrorist attacks, violent social upheavals, and even natural catastrophes—have left us with an uncanny sense of menace. We seem to be aware of a shared vulnerability that we cannot quite name. I suspect that this feeling has provoked the widespread intolerance that we see around us today—from all points on the political spectrum. It is, though, without our insistence that our outlook is correct, the outlook itself might collapse. Perhaps if we could give a name to our shared sense of vulnerability, we could find better ways to live with it (Lear, 2006, p. 7).

This kind of uncertainty captures the realities facing Chief Plenty Coups, a challenge he met with "radical hope," thereby forestalling despair. Unless we can successfully avoid despair, we could succumb to the circle of violence that has controlled us for too long. How can we in *Breaking Free* name our shared sense of vulnerability?

To understand stories, to grasp their full meanings, we need some encouragement. Jesse Negropontes, MSW, co-authored in 2008 a rich field report[8] of a project on behalf of the United Church of Canada to mobilize young people faithfully to engage in their communities. They drew upon arts-based approaches to learning from

[8] http://playbelongtransform.eaglewingmusic.org/Welcome.html

across the globe. One section of their book looks at "keys to unlock the story" (pp. 18-22). You might want to visit these pages for some helpful keys to unlocking meaning in stories, and the entire website features many user friendly popular education techniques and processes. Everything we need is near at hand.

It is heartening to see so many Social Work learners searching within themselves and helping others to locate the individual stories within us all. Indeed, they are being encouraged by the example of my professorial colleagues to do just that. For some time, Kim Zapf has been exploring his own voice within the context of social work education, and profound wisdom is emerging.

Exhibit 7.3: Learning to teach from my own story (Zapf, 1997).

After several years of teaching in urban campus locations, I had the opportunity to teach social work courses to classes of Aboriginal students...who wanted to know me as a person rather than as a conduit of concepts from the textbook. They were concerned with why I was there, how important or useful this material had been to me in my own life and practice, and whether I could model the processes I was talking about. Rather than achieving an intellectual grasp of the material for grading purposes, they seemed more concerned with making direct connections to the processes [p. 85] of development and healing in their own communities, family and selves. They would ask about my experiences and share their issues as we explored together the utility of the practice models.

This kind of teaching excited me. I wanted to gather and save all the stories I had learned to bring back to my classes in the city… [p. 86]

In my recent teaching in the main campus social work program, I have been making attempts to open up my imperfect thinking processes in the classroom, modest efforts to engage in this connected teaching process and to use my own voice as I am coming to understand it. I have selected three examples, chosen because I use them often and have received appreciative feedback from students. I emphasize that these

are offered only as examples, not as models (your stories are in your experiences and your attempts to make sense of them). I also acknowledge the severe constraints of writing these down. The very act of writing freezes my story in time, whereas the real story may change from telling to telling reflecting changes in myself, the context, and the students.

The first story has to do with identifying myself as a partner in the learning process by sharing a personal struggle to overcome cultural categories assumed during my early socialization.

> ***Many of my courses are centred around cross-cultural issues. In the first class, I often show an overhead projection of a black-and-white photograph taken around 1955 depicting myself, my brother, and my mother standing in front of a train station about to take a 350 mile trip across the prairies. I am pre-school and I look very serious wearing my twin pearl-handled cap revolvers and my cowboy boots. It would be my job on that trip to protect my mother from Indians as we rode the train across the prairie!***
>
> ***Now I had never met a real Aboriginal person in my life to that point. But I had a strong sense of the imminent danger, acquired from the comics, television, and movies of my day. Of course, I also had images of "good Indians" such as Tonto and L'il Beaver.***
>
> ***What impact do those powerful cultural categories still have on me today? If I am trying to work with a First Nations resource person or community leader, do I still expect Tonto, a" good Indian" who is loyal but not as smart, who looks up to me, who relied upon his or her association with me for status in the larger community, who walks close but a few feet behind me, who does not speak English as well as I do, who can be trusted with most things but not the really important decisions? If I am still bound by the categories passed on by my culture in childhood, how can I possibly learn from and enjoy a relationship of respect with my First Nations friends or co-workers today?***

When I stand at the front of the class beside that life-size photograph of me some forty years ago, students are confronted with the reality of the changes I have had to make and continue to work on. I can then share specific incidents in my struggle and the influence of people how have helped me. Overall, this sharing appears to have much greater impact on students than my standard lecture on the processes of unlearning and reframing.

The second story speaks for itself in sharing my uncertainty and self-doubt.

> ***My first social work job, in my early twenties, was a Juvenile Probation Officer in a large city. Working with young offenders (although they were "juvenile delinquents" then), I accepted the underlying assumptions of the system that hired me. The whole process of juvenile justice was based upon an "end of the line." We had a continuum of services ranging from supervision in the home to community group homes to secure group homes to training schools. As the end of the line, training schools were for those kids who were a clear threat to the community. A juvenile became a ward of the state at the time of committal to training school and the length of stay was indefinite. When deemed to be ready, the young person would be returned to the community under the supervision of another agency – the Aftercare Service.***
>
> ***This was a very rare event, and most of my work involved counselling, support, and recreation in the community. There were, however, a handful of kids on my caseload who were committed to training school, usually on my recommendation after all other alternatives had been tried and failed. I never saw any of them again because they reported to an Aftercare Officer after release. I accepted the need for training schools because a system of increasingly restrictive options requires some final place, an endpoint. I trusted that the staff there was as committed to young people and their development as***

> ***I was, and I actually believed that the secure structure of the training school would be beneficial for some kids.***
>
> ***After two or three years of this front-line work, I returned to school in a different part of the country for another degree; subsequent job opportunities kept me a considerable distance from the setting of that first job. Then one day, some 15 years later, I was 2000 miles away reading my newspaper when I came across a story reporting that male staff members at two of those training schools had been charged with multiple counts of sexual assault against residents going back over two decades.***
>
> ***I will never know if any of the kids from my caseload were victims of these abhorrent attacks. But I do know that I was part of a system that removed kids from the supervision of parents and everyone they had known, and sent them to a locked secure setting where they were completely vulnerable and without recourse. I did this with the best of intentions and with a misguided belief about the other players in our system. I cannot undo what may have happened, but I can try to accept my responsibility, learn from the experience, and share the story with students who may soon be in their first jobs and called upon to make decisions "in the best interests' of the community.***

This is not an easy story to share, but it is an important one. Students need to see me as a committed worker grappling with difficult ethical issues, not a detached academic who has all the correct answers for abstract ethical dilemmas. Maybe some will remember the kick-in-the-stomach impact on me when I read that newspaper account; maybe they will recall the despair of never really knowing and living with the possible consequences of blind assumptions and trust in the system. Perhaps they will think twice in a similar situation.

Not all stories must be negative to have impact. For the last example, I have chosen something a bit lighter, one that

serves to break down some of the distance between graduate students and instructor.

> *When I first arrived at graduate school to begin my PhD program, fresh from practice in the Yukon, I felt very out of place and inadequate. It seemed that all of my classmates had much more research knowledge and experience than I had. I was sure the school had either made an error in admitting me or had done so just because I was a novelty from the North. Either way, they would soon learn that I had no right to be there because I was incompetent.*
>
> *I found that I could continue to fool them in my course work. Course by course, I could pass and no one discovered that I had no right to be there. Then came the dissertation proposal and I fooled them once more by submitting something that was accepted. At this point, however, I knew I would be "found out." The next step was approaching members to sit on my Committee. Working so closely with me, surely they would discover my incompetence. Still, I mustered my courage and approached a favoured professor to request that he chair my Committee. I explained that I thought that I was an incompetent impostor who had fooled them all along but was certain to be found out now.*
>
> *To my surprise, he agreed that of course I was incompetent but that was irrelevant to how the game was played. He and the other Committee members would be there to act as a buffer between my incompetence and the rest of the world finding out. If they succeeded and I graduated, then I would have an obligation for the rest of my academic career to act as a buffer for other incompetents who might come along and request my help. (We worked very well together and I continue to fulfil my obligation to this day!) [pp. 91-2]*

My argument for the use of voice in teaching is not revolutionary or unique; I make no claim to having discovered narrative and voice, or their application in adult education.

Feminist authors and teachers have a long tradition of owning voice and working from experience. In some cultures, storytelling is the established norm for conveying information and vision. What I have discovered is more personal. Through studied reflection on my own experience, I am learning the value of teaching from *my* story in *my* classes. It has been my goal throughout this discussion to share my personal process of discovery and the implications that arise with the hope that I may stimulate others to reflect on their own teaching. I have attempted to write as I am learning to teach – in my own voice… [p. 95]

Direction

This personal journey does not lead to a conventional "conclusion," but I think it identifies a general direction for future work in the area of voice and social work education. There is some evidence that society in general and the professions in particular are embarking upon a process whereby individuals and groups are reclaiming their "voice," becoming the subjects rather than the objects of their life stories. As a participant in this "postmodern" movement, the social work profession appears to be clarifying a goal of collaborative partnerships between workers and clients, expanding our notion of empowerment to include helping vulnerable groups find their voice. Little has been done, however, regarding the worker finding and using his or her voice. There could be an exciting and important opportunity here for social work educators to explore and develop this assumption of voice in the classroom, to model in the teacher-student relationship the very partnership being advanced for the field.

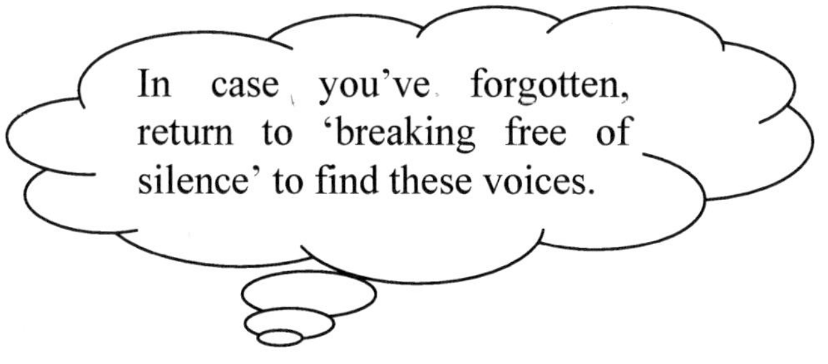

I want to finish with a poetic image from William Schneider (1995), curator of Oral History at the University of Alaska in Fairbanks:

> **As a listener, the stories don't end when the storyteller stops and the telling is over. The stories get washed along in the river of my life. At times they glisten in the sun and I take notice, at other times they are buried in the sands of experiences. (p. 82) …[p. 97]**

Lessons Learned
Exhibit 7.3

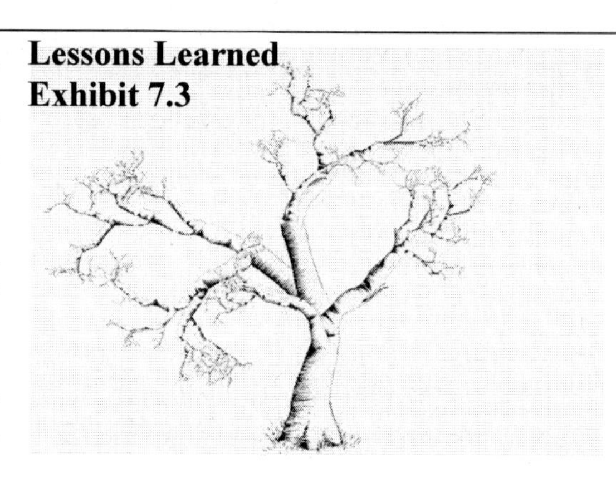

**It is OK to leave our writings with 'Direction' and thus avoiding 'conclusion'.

**Telling our personal stories enhances our teaching effectiveness.

**FSW classrooms are celebratory of multiple voices.

**Direct experience provides the foundation for human learning

**Clarity of language and purpose.

**Well paced humour enhances learning.

Your Reflections…

…………………………………………………………………………

…………………………………………………………………………

…………………………………………………………………………

…………………………………………………………………………

Some of the profound learning in these stories of indigenous experiences housed within Exhibits 7.2 and 7.3 lies at the heart of the concept of community development, largely conceived in Canada and the US during the 1920s and 1930s as an extension of rural sociologists responding to economic depression (Pyrch, 1983). For Kim Zapf, the rural setting is where Aboriginal knowledge-making has the clearest practical application. Perhaps the second decade of the twenty-first century is a time when these older traditions are reviving. As we learned earlier in this guide, the latent richness of indigenous knowledge spawned the PAR movement commencing in the 1960s. There are signs in contemporary international social work, notably in the concept of "localizing social work" (Al-Krenawi & Graham, 2009), that acknowledging indigenous energies is once again making good practical sense. Here once again lies a reminder of our connections with the Aristotelian tradition. Sometimes we simply miss the obvious things in life. The latent power of indigenous energies is being felt throughout the Arab world and surely must give us, in our relative largesse, the courage to stand up, to act, and to recover our own democracy. What can we learn from the recovering Arab passion?

Exhibit 7.4: Helping professional practice with indigenous peoples (Al-Krenawi & Graham, 2009).

How might helping professions be more locally relevant, such that they can bring out the best of the Global South communities within which they work? Within Bedouin-Arab communities, there are religious and culturally bound strategies and personnel that can be used to enhance social work practice, making it more effective. One of the authors, Alean Al-Krenawi, conveys his personal and professional story as a Bedouin-Arab who received undergraduate and advanced studies at universities in Israel and Canada. After his first

degree, he practised for eleven years. Especially early in his career, he felt a strong dissonance between his professional training and the culture of his home community: the Bedouin-Arab if the Negev, with whom he worked daily. He made mistakes and had many failures, his ability to create and sustain a helping alliance was often limited, his assessment of client problems, and clients' own understandings, were often in mutual conflict. His ability to decode client communication, and to understand what client's were intending to say, was poor. Clients expressed dissatisfaction with quality and outcome of his proposed interventions, and they terminated prematurely. Alean talked to his father about his difficulties who responded in metaphor. Pointing to the sky, Alean's father said, "You are there with the airplanes." Pointing to the ground, Alean's father continued, "The rest of us are walking on our feet." The message was immediately clear. Alean's training has placed him in a different epistemological frame of reference than that of his fellow Bedouin-Arabs, who were his clients. This was an epiphanal moment. Alean became a lot more comfortable intervening according to the principles of his own culture; the training he had received in helping professional practice, based on culturally incongruent assumptions from the North, were no longer the first frame of reference, nor the final factor in determining how, why, where, or when to intervene. Alean increasingly saw himself as the conduit through which dialogue could occur: a dialogue between local and global knowledge. His success with intervention improved, so much so that he ultimately determined he would return to school and research the changing requirements of professional practice with his community. (p. 171)

Lessons Learned
Exhibit 7.4

**Direct experience provides the foundation for human learning.

**Indigenous knowledge is profound and is there for the asking.

**Everything we need is near at hand.

**Theory and practice, in dynamic relationship, are mutually beneficial.

Your Reflections…

……………………………………………………………………………
……………………………………………………………………………
……………………………………………………………………………
……………………………………………………………………………
……………………………………………………………………………

One wonders what new demands and opportunities await Alean and the Arab world after the upheavals commencing in January 2011. Is there something we can do to help them? How might they help us? Is there something we might do together?

On the possibility of the impossible. It is comforting to know *Breaking Free* cannot end, so I needn't attempt a conclusion. As we are engaging together in an infinite game, it seems more appropriate at this point to reflect on current possibilities in light of our commitment to social justice work. James Carse (1986) continues to be helpful. While reflecting on "power," he writes,

> Although anyone who wishes can be an infinite player, and although anyone can be strong, we are not to suppose that power cannot work irremediable damage on infinite play. Infinite play cannot prevent or eliminate evil. Though infinite players are strong, they are not powerful and do not attempt to become powerful.
>
> *Evil is the termination of infinite play.* It is infinite play coming to an end in *unheard silence.* (emphasis in original)
>
> Unheard silence does not necessarily mean the death of the player. Unheard silence is not the loss of the player's voice but the loss of listeners for that voice. It is an evil when the drama of a life does not continue in others for reason of their deafness or ignorance. (pp. 39-40)

It might be that the individuals in Brigette Krieg's and Sharon Big Plume's research—Aboriginal peoples long thought silenced by the dominant society through racist laws and oppressive practices—were never silenced at all. Perhaps they have been speaking their knowledge despite these laws and practices. If Aboriginal peoples, especially the elders, have been speaking their wisdom unceasingly even after the colonization of their lands and cultures but go unheard in the broader Aboriginal community, this is an "evil" according to Carse. This evil is a consequence of the loss of Aboriginal languages. A similar consequence is evident when one language fails to translate effectively into another. We are too quick to believe that mere translation conveys meaning. We are too quick to think that translation is even literally possible. At best, we interpret what someone else says according to our own world view, in a particular time and place, and create our own meaning from there. We seldom actually listen deeply to one another in the first place, as we learned in Part Three of *Breaking Free*. Perhaps now that we are learning how to listen, encouraging each other to interpret our words together, and acting locally in practical direct ways, a more just society is imminent.

If the broader Canadian society does not value Aboriginal wisdom, it might be the dominant culture simply forgot how to listen. Is there anything we can do to change this? Carse cautions that attempting to remove one evil merely produces another evil. If it were possible to recover all Aboriginal languages in their thousands, what would happen? If we silence other languages to make room for these thousands, is another evil created? "Evil" restricts play to one or another finite game. If Brigette's co-researchers replaced women in the mainstream of society, these mainstream women might be marginalized; one kind of oppression often replaces another. Rather than replacing one with the other, can we facilitate processes whereby the two experiences can respect each other sufficiently to create dialogue—the Ganma rivers? This respectful exchange has been impossible in Canadian society until now; it seemed the one did not need the other. Do the current global economic, political, financial, and environmental crises force us into attempting the impossible—a new world of mutual trust, respect, and love; a new world valuing all forms of knowledge-making without undue judgement? Or rather than a new world, do we look more closely into our indigenous places, our immediate localities? Our immediate locality in *Breaking Free* is, quite simply, *Breaking Free*. Drawing upon Kim Zapf's wisdom, how can we live well *as Breaking Free*?

The "victory" of capitalism over communism released the tyranny of manic market economics and insatiably greedy, wealthy elites. That same tyranny is collapsing under its own weight as we speak. Can we imagine a replacement of this tyranny without succumbing to Scott's "hegemonic planning mentality?" What frameworks do we have, or might we imagine, that exist in the spaces free from the hegemonies impeding the infinite game? How are you building these frameworks into your undergraduate and graduate studies, and in practice?

It is helpful to keep things as "fluid" as possible. This simple yet eloquent concept was understood by learners in Exhibit 2.1:

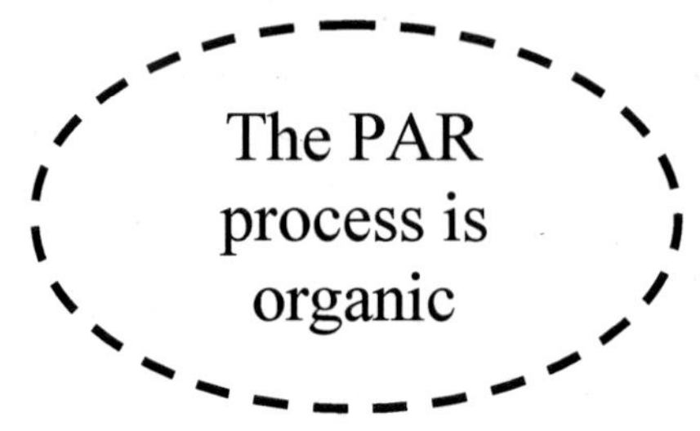

"I thought it was great (a classmate) was not sure what to do with the term 'popular education.' She just followed the flow of her ideas and linked them to what she assumed would fit with the meaning of this topic. She actually made me aware that stepping out of the box does not mean to be on the wrong path; but that there are various ways to reach a destination." Another said, "What I enjoyed the most about the sharing was making connections between my understandings and others' understandings. Now, a couple of days after the class, I have had time to reflect upon the sharings of my fellow students as well as what you had to say about the class and the class assignment. I have begun to make some connections between the course and the class assignment. So far what I have come up with is that not knowing about what the assignment will look like is an educational experience in itself. By not having a plan or a clear and definite expectation for an assignment handed to us students by a teacher, we are encouraged and challenged to direct our own learning. Instead of being the traditional students we are student teachers. In a sense, my unexpected surprise is popular education in action."

On hope. We search the world deeply, and oftentimes we find hope. This search for hope is organic; all humans will seek out hope whenever possible. The students of Exhibit 2.1 had a multitude of views on how to define and cultivate hope.

> One of us wrote, "Hope is a collective responsibility to inspire and stay positive for those who are facing a world of heartache. We need to constantly remind each other what we can become if we have hope. Hope is so important, despite being very difficult to have. But for me personally, it is what keeps me going." Another wrote, "The future is not a result of choices among alternative paths offered by the present, but a place that is created—created first in the mind and will, created next in activity. The future is not some place we are going to, but one we are creating. Paths are not to be found, but made, and the activity of making them, changes both the maker and the destination.' This has really influenced me to think differently. I think it challenges me to look at the future as something I want it to be, not just something that is going to be…I have realized this is a key ingredient in change; you need to believe it is possible, yet sometimes hard to do, but if you don't believe in it then what are we striving for?" (Extracted from Exhibit 2.1)

While reflecting on the meaning of freedom, American educator Maxine Greene (1988) declared, "When people cannot name alternatives, imagine a better state of things, share with others a project of change, they are likely to remain anchored or submerged, even as they proudly assert their autonomy" (p. 9). Murray Dobbin, one of the presenters at the Parkland Institute conference in November, 2008, said we were missing visions for a bright new future; our preoccupation with strategies and tactics seemed aimless.[9] Many presenters and participants alike at the conference were searching for new frameworks to meet impending disaster. The conference theme in 2007 was "Crisis to Hope: Building Just and Sustainable Communities." There are regular gatherings like this in Alberta, usually small scale and not reported in the popular (controlled by whom?) media. These gatherings and their exclusion from the popular media are indicators of the on-going and long-standing resistance in the province to the provincial political elite, as identified by Doreen Barrie in *The Other Alberta.* Recording these gatherings in *Breaking Free* represents the countervailing forces of grassroots democracy that social justice work is—could be or should be—about. How best to make these forces known more broadly?

One way is to hold annual conferences, in the manner of the Parkland Institute that have been on-going for the past dozen years. The PAR Congress in Calgary in 1989 brought the radical movement to Alberta as did the Founding General Assembly of the North America Alliance for Popular and Adult Education in 1994. G6B, the group of six billion counter force to the G8, met in Calgary in 2002.[10] The Faculty of Social Work hosted conferences on homelessness as well as environmental issues in 2009. Social Work students organized the Liberation-based Healing Conference in 2011. Hundreds of Albertans participated in these events directly—and thousands more, including Albertans, Canadians, and the international community alike, indirectly. We might be engaging in some semblance of democracy after all. If we shout out our stories we might blow away the apathy we seem bound up in.

If all the exhibits, individuals, courses, and resources in the Faculty are imagined as musical notes, how can we sing a song of hope by arranging these notes in our uniquely interpretive fashion? How might we sing them? Where? We need only recall the power of songs of resistance introduced by Tyler MacPherson in Exhibit 3.5 to appreciate the amazing strength of singing out our vision of what might be. Or we might sing out a vision of what actually is, if

---

[9] http://www.ualberta.ca/PARKLAND

[10] http://revcom.us/a/v24/1151-1160/1158/calgary.htm

only we dared look closely enough to see it. Let's look again. What do we see? We commenced our learning journey together, drawing from the wisdom of the Yolngu of Arnhemland, home to the rivers of foam. Their wisdom takes on many forms. Traditionally, Aboriginal Australians are *of* the land and have an intimacy with it that creates songlines as guides for their life's journey.

> In theory, at least, the whole of Australia could be read as a musical score. There was hardly a rock or creek in the country that could not or had not been sung. One should perhaps visualize the Songlines as a spaghetti of Iliads and Odysseys, writhing this way and that, in which every "episode" was readable in terms of geology (Chatwin, 1987, p. 16).

Each of us in *Breaking Free* can take all the things we've experienced, the rocks and creeks, and create our individual "guides"—songlines. As we share them together, what might happen?

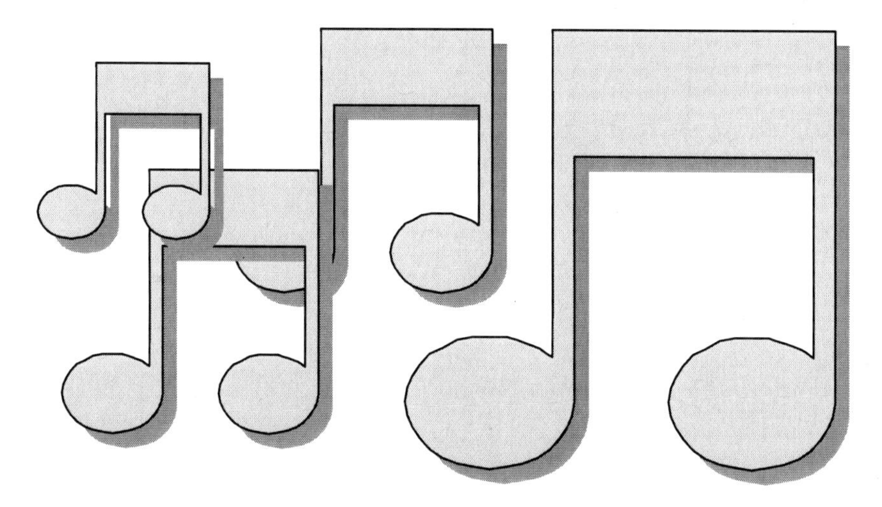

We are trying to capture as many sounds, forms, flavours, shapes, and tones as we can in order to present our learnings in all their depth and breadth. This next exhibit records the richness and potential of arts-based phenomena growingly familiar in FSW events. Ian Prinsloo (2008) wrote, as shown in Part Three of this guide, of the wondrous things we have around us if we dared listen carefully. But listening in itself is insufficient until processed into a presentation of the knowledge-making experience.

Exhibit 7.5: Expression as Presentational Knowing (Prinsloo, 2008)

The next phase of the project was to take the material and create the public expression that we would present at the Social Justice Forum. We were now moving into the presentational knowing phase of Heron and Reason (2006, p. 149). Presentational knowing is sourced directly from our experiential knowing and is our attempt to create meaning and illuminate significance. It is often expressed creatively through story, drawing movement, sculpture, music, drawing, etc. For this phase of the work we engaged two professional actors to portray the all of the voices of the story. Our method for achieving this task was to first work through the material as theatre artists, seeing what connections there were between the dialogue, poems, and other material. From the material gathered we revised its structure to create a form suited to a live performance. On this point some may find issue. For if we are making arrangements of material are we not then changing the story? I don't agree with this criticism. A story is always a set of arranged events, ordered to bring forth points that are felt to be the most meaningful or important. If someone simply writes out the events of their life the meaning and importance of those events can be lost to others if care is not taken to arrange them in a way that is comprehensible and yet still in keeping with the intentions of the original creator. Also the medium of presentation is another factor that determines the arrangement of a story. If I am writing a story for the printed word then I must take into account the fact that it will be read by one person who has the ability to review a sentence if they are confused. Plays are seen once; thus they require narrative action and the clear delineation of character.

Once we had made the changes to the story we sent it back to the research committee for their reflection and comment, we presented the spoken story to each of the participants in the project. When the story was read back

to the participants they were asked whether they felt that the work was an authentic capturing of the sessions and whether it captured the way of being that had been shared. To a person they were thrilled with the distillation that had occurred with the play. To ensure the story kept a connection to the way of being from which it was created the participants in the project taught the actors how to embody their story for the stage.

In a conventional theatre process, actors will work with the scripts they are given and build their own visions of the characters out of the information contained in the text. For our presentation we took a different approach to embodying the voices of the story. Each of the participants identified their voices in the script and then taught the actors how to realize those moments. This was achieved by the actor imitating the physical nature of the participant, their vocal rhythms, and any other physical mannerism. The actor would then become the participant and give voice to their parts of the story. The participant would then coach them in meaning, importance, and background to what had been expressed. The exchange between the actor and the participant became, for me, a remarkable part of the project. The actors were nervous that they would offend the participants in the characterizations but the participants would watch with amazement as their way of being took shape in front of them. The act of embodied self-reflection that occurred at those moments was electric. In that moment the participants were seeing themselves; not a mirror that reflects the outer nature but a glimpse of themselves being. E.F. Schumacher (2004) captures the significance of this moment in when he describes of the four basic fields of knowledge that each of us must struggle to understand: the inner me, the outer me, the inner you and the outer you. Schumacher explains how we each have a great deal of knowledge about our inner selves, but very little knowledge of our outer selves – our way of being as we engage in the world. In those moments of recognition between actor and participant they were experiencing how

their being expressed in the world. The look of fascination and honour on the face of the participants was deeply moving. We had not only sourced their infinite story but given presence to their being.

Sharing the Story

The crowning moment in the process was when the story was presented at the Social Justice Encounter for an audience of 200. The presentation took place in the Reeve Theatre of the University of Calgary which also added to the level of presentational knowing in the project. This was not a lecture hall where we were trying to fit in a performance but a space that was designed to present theatre. We created a basic set of a series of chairs as well as setting a mood through the lighting that was available in the theatre. When the lights went down and the presentation began the audience sat drinking in the experiences of being that were presented. Audiences in the theatre often listens at the "empathic" level that Scharmer describes, and hear deeply what it may have only partially considered before. Friedrick Schiller (1935) captures this effect beautifully: "Sight is always more powerful to a man than description; hence the stage acts more powerfully than morality or law" (p. 340). For the participants from the ExCel Home in the audience their story was no longer an "unheard silence" but a shared experience.

Toward the Infinite Game

The presentation at the Social Justice Encounter was the final moment for our project. And it was a fitting place to end our work of collecting and expressing the experiences of our participants. Because for a story to begin its journey to myth it must be told so that it can live in another and be re-told. To have done this inquiry work, connected with the way of being in the participants, sifted through material, crafted the story, engaged in the process of embodiment and then had no space in which to share the story would be a grave failure. In the end, the ability to collect story is only as powerful as our ability to give it public expression. Because in giving public

expression to the "unheard silence" of people we are adding voices that question the "amplified" story. And this is a key action of the work. The infinite game of story is the attempt to release into our world the multitude of stories that represent alternative ways of being. We can do that by helping people recover connection to their authentic selves and support them in giving expression to what they discover. In the end it is not about the story created but about the creation of story. To be an infinite game it must be played "for the purpose of continuing play" (Carse, 1985, p. 3), so we must be encouraging more and more people to create and allow the space for people to listen.

Lessons Learned
Exhibit 7.4

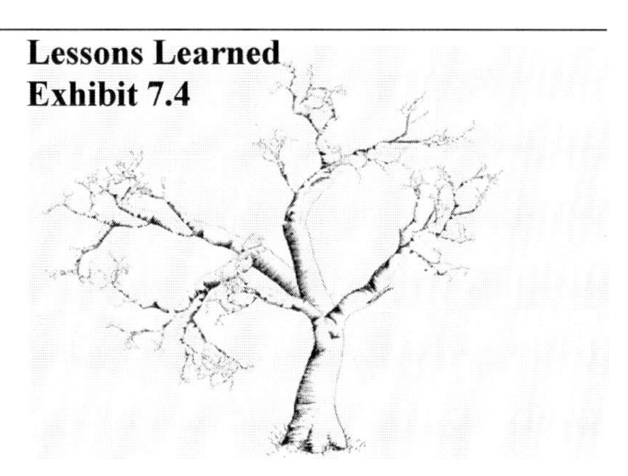

**Experience is brought into enlightening possibilities through its presentation.

** Direct experience provides the foundation for human learning.

Your Reflections…

....

....

....

....

....

....

....

....

....

....

PAR translates knowledge into action

It is now time for each player to listen to one another tell a story about our Faculty of Social Work course experience, or an experience in your own unique reality. After all, "if we cannot tell a story about what happened to us, nothing happened to us" (Carse, 1986). I do hope you are unwilling to accept that nothing has happened to you, especially while journeying through *Breaking Free*. Let's get on with our lifelong learning journey, unbound and free to roam where we will while engaging in our social justice work.

On courage. It takes courage to roam freely, both within the self and without. It takes courage to tell our stories. Sometimes it takes courage to listen to our stories. It takes courage of have hope. After a lifetime of struggle, exile, and transformation, Paulo Freire (1994) advised,

> Hope as an ontological need demands an anchoring in practice. As an ontological need, hope needs practice in order to become historical concreteness. That is why there is no hope in sheer hopefulness. The hoped-for is not attained by dint of raw hoping. Just to hope is to hope in vain. (p. 9)

Acting on our hope is a form of knowledge in itself – reflective knowledge according to Peter Park (2001). Drawing from Greek philosophers and Aboriginal statesmanship, Jonathan Lear taught us that it takes courage to be radically hopeful. Aristotle advises that a courageous person will always act in a way that avoids the excess of foolhardy recklessness and the defect of cowardliness (Lear, 2006, p. 17). This person will "find the appropriate way to behave courageously" (*ibid.*). Lear concludes by calling courage the capacity for living *well* with the risks that inevitably attend the human experience. He tells us, "To be human is necessarily to be a vulnerable risk-taker; to be a courageous human is to be good at it" (p. 123). Lear drew his lessons from a Greek philosopher and an Aboriginal Chief, and through their synthesis, he produced powerful imagery. Perhaps more useful to the practice of social justice work in indigenous places, we might draw upon our students' experience within their own realities.

Stasha Huntingford (2009) combined her experience as a street youth during her teenage years with Lear's lessons in her master's thesis in Social Work, documenting her work with the

Youth Recovery Coalition. She organized her findings by borrowing Lear's interpretation of Aristotle's five virtues:

1. A courageous person has a proper orientation towards what is shameful and what is fearful.
2. Courage aims towards what is fine.
3. A courageous person must grasp the situation he or she is in and, through experience, exercise good judgment.
4. Courage paradigmatically involves the risk of serious loss and of enduring certain pains.
5. Bold acts that derive merely from optimism are not themselves courageous. (Lear, 2006)

Exhibit 7.6: Radical Hope in Youth Recovery Coalition (Huntingford 2009). Quotes directly from participants in the study appear in **bold.**

1. A courageous person has a proper orientation towards what is shameful and what is fearful.

We work and live in a context where it is not always clear what is shameful. For example, a fourteen-year-old street youth who is on the run from Child Welfare and does not have a SIN number has about four general options for making money to survive. They can sell drugs, steal things, panhandle, or prostitute. In a survival culture like this, we see these "choices" in the context of what we had to do to survive. In "mainstream" society these survival techniques are viewed as shameful, and we are judged for these actions without our context of limited options being taken into account. As individuals, we feel shame about what we had to do to survive. As a community, we work on consciousness-raising. We do this in order to remind ourselves of how our options were limited, how we can transfer our strength into opening up what our options are, and to maintain an awareness of what factors are in our control and what are not. We still strive to make ethical decisions within our context of limited options. We also do consciousness-raising with mainstream culture in order to try and build understanding of the different contexts in which we all live.

A young person had a moral issue with selling crack due to selling crack to a thirteen-year-old girl who reminded him of his niece. He stopped selling crack and started prostitution because it only hurts him and so fit better with his moral code. Everyone should take some time to think about what "choice" they would make between panhandling, prostituting, drug dealing, or stealing to survive. And you know you can't answer that question unless you have actually had to choose. I know myself better because I had to choose.

This is why we view drug abuse as a symptom of larger problems such as poverty, trauma, and limited options for fulfilling basic needs. When we present to the youth about crystal meth, we use case studies of ourselves and others to show how at the beginning we started using drugs to solve other problems in our lives. For example, using meth to stay awake at night because you have no shelter, and the graffiti that we have that says "speed is cheaper than food." We view drug use in the same way that we view other survival strategies. We do not judge it shameful in the context of survival. We are united as a community because we understand the context of survival, and we help remind each other about the factors outside of our control.

I think people on the margins have the most potential to break free from this society but also paradoxically the least resources to do so. They also tend to face the worst consequences for doing so. Middle class kids with supportive families can often rebel for a while with few consequences. Kids with little support (and often criminal records) frequently get crushed.

When we move from the street youth community to the rent paying world, it is like moving to a different country, with different expressions of values, where there are some differences in context with what is viewed shameful. For myself it was a very lonely and isolating experience moving from what I felt was a communal culture where we were bonded by surviving together to a individualistic culture where the message was "every [hu]man for themselves." I felt that my actions that kept me alive on the street were judged shameful by the rent paying community. This lead me to feel more isolated and rejected by my new community.

The street youth and Youth Recovery Coalition (YRC) have coined a term for this feeling and role. We call it being a "veggie burger with bacon;" it is also known as being a social network entrepreneur. You experience it when you have traits of two "opposing" groups, and so you would think that you had the potential to be a bridge between these two groups, but sometimes they both end up hating you. This comes from the "with us or against us" mentality. Examples we have experienced are being bisexual, Métis, having hidden disabilities, and being a former street youth/current social worker. We consider our experience with this to be strength, especially in terms of the diversity of our networks and our ability to empathize with different groups.

The "veggie burger with bacon" role is a very powerful role and a very lonely one. Our experience has been that both communities mistrust you because of dualistic thinking. We think this comes from fear. We also think that radical hope and courage help you overcome fear.

2. Courage aims towards what is fine.

We work towards what is fine without being able to define what that might be. We follow the dream knowing that it aligns with our values.

"Without leaps of imagination, or dreaming, we lose the excitement of possibilities. Dreaming, after all, is a form of planning."- Gloria Steinem

We created the Medicine Wheel of Crystal Meth Healing to guide us on our journey with the dream. We created it together, as a group, in order to develop our shared moral code and agreed upon guidelines for conduct and healing. The path to the dream concentrates on how we can heal. We look at this need for healing not only in ourselves as individuals but communally, as a community of people whose biggest task is to strive first to be safe enough to heal, then to engage in the life-long process of healing, and to use our experience to help others heal. We depend on the collective to define what is "fine" and to hold us accountable to these values on our journey.

The YRC anchored me and gave me purpose. Becoming part of a larger struggle saved my life. I learned that I could heal, and I learned about the *process* of healing. The Medicine Wheel of Crystal Meth Healing is a foundation for me.

The YRC's holistic approach to drug treatment includes a six part medicine wheel. Our Medicine Wheel of Crystal Meth Healing encompasses what we believe humans need in order to achieve balance in our lives.

PHYSICAL

You can feel yourself healing and growing stronger.
You feel comfortable with your own body, and you have control over how it is used.
Because you are proud of who you are, you walk with your head up and your back straight.
You understand that your body needs balanced nutrition and exercise to stay strong.
You find fun ways to strive for physical balance.

MENTAL

You have identified your own super-powers, and you use these to change the world.
You know that your brain needs sleep in order to do the amazing things that you do.
You challenge yourself to learn new things.
You seek out other humans who can teach you things.

EMOTIONAL

You understand that emotions must be expressed and understood if you don't want to carry them around forever.
You don't say to yourself, "I shouldn't feel this way."

You try to have empathy for how others feel and to recognize how your actions make them feel.

SPIRITUAL

You spend time with yourself, other humans, and the natural world.
You respect yourself, other humans, and the natural world.
You feel like you belong to something bigger than yourself (like our community and our cause and the universe).
You are a small, insignificant, and very special part of the universe.
Your life and experiences are valuable and can help you teach other people, and you can learn from them yourself.

SOCIAL

You seek out a community of people that supports the same healthy goals that you have for yourself.
You have healthy boundaries in your relationships with other humans (this means that you do not accept abuse in your life).
You support the people around you and celebrate their goal achievements with them.

VOLITION

You understand that the risk of making choices and taking responsibility for the results is less scary than having no control over what happens to you.
You make choices and stand by them.
You weigh out the negative and positive consequences of decisions (taking into account the decision's effect on yourself, other people, and the natural world).
Your decisions all fit with your personal moral code.
You take the time to be proud of yourself and celebrate when you achieve personal goals.

We examined how shared vision motivates us and helps us work together. We examined how shared vision moves over the boundaries between personal and professional relationships.

I found that in the cases where I had an existing friendship with another member of the YRC things went smoothly in the context of the YRC. We knew each other's temperaments, mindsets, and so on, and wanting to maintain the friendship was a priority. I also think that having the YRC as our number one priority collectively made it easy to make things work, to smooth out disagreements. With Stasha I feel like the YRC is something she and I are both very passionate about, so our friendship really developed as we put our collective energies and hopes into the YRC.

It makes my personal relationships stronger to share the vision.

Are they doing it for Stasha or for themselves? Sometimes I get worried that people participate in YRC because I am asking them to, rather than because they believe in the cause. I don't know if it makes a difference, but I think it affects the culture of the agency and my personal relationships.

I feel sometimes that other members don't buy in to the shared vision. Like when I heard third hand that another member was talking about their dream of some out of town place to heal, not *our* dream, not talking about what we do now to achieve this. I don't know if they believe that what we do now builds towards this vision.

We are a youth driven organization because we believe that the youth can define what they need in order to heal. We feel that we are accountable first and foremost to the street youth community.

The YRC model is based on peer mentoring, both in how we provide services to the youth and how our staff team works together. This means that we value what we have learned from our life experience and that we hire people with this life experience. The staff supports each other by holding each other accountable to the values of YRC. We debrief situations that happen at work and discuss how we can do better. We also discuss issues with the youth to ensure that we are accountable to the community in the way we are delivering services.

Youth guiding the programs. We strive to be responsive to changing needs and to consult with youth about what programs are most needed. We assume that youth know best what they need.

The manifesto of the YRC includes the belief that in promoting ideas about justice and genuine cooperation to the youth, we serve means rooting our organizational structure in these same ideals. Leading with this tenet means that we are accountable to the street youth community foremost, then to our board and funders.

The communities of youth that we serve determine what services we will provide, keeping our services culturally appropriate and timely. The youth steer our programming decisions while the board finalizes policy and ensures that the budget is followed. The staff, being both active board members as well as employees, is also armed with practical experience with poverty and trauma. This practical experience ensures that the direct implementation of services by the staff is respectful and responsive to the needs of the youth.

3. A courageous person must grasp the situation he or she is in and, through experience, exercise good judgment.

We value learning from experience and being flexible because we experience changing contexts. We need to rely on our internal moral code because we sometimes receive conflicting messages from different communities and people about the definition of what is shameful. As Lear (2006) says in Radical Hope, "A courageous person must know how to act well in all sorts of circumstances," and this requires imagination, creativity, and flexibility to adapt to unknown contexts (p. 83). We draw strength from the resiliency of the street youth population and their experience with living in changing contexts.

Hope also springs from the obvious resilience of the youth who the coalition comes into contact with, those who helped out with the quilts, those who sit on the board, and those who sat in on coalition presentations.

Stef and I always talk about how we keep hope in our poverty because the kids have it worse and they keep trying. I often tell the kids that we are good at getting back up; I just wish we didn't have to so often. I think hope is about trying again despite the fact that you keep getting beaten down.

The resiliency of the youth helps me remember to try again, to take a chance.

Pride in having won. When you had to fight for something you don't take it for granted.

I feel hope because these kids are so resilient and interesting.

I saw so many young people drifting in and out of this daytime youth drop in centre.

Impression: Children wearing old, cynical expressions.

Impression: "Happy-to-see-you" expressions on some of the youth's faces that were not comfortable wearing happy expressions.

The Medicine Wheel of Crystal Meth Healing concentrates on developing your own super powers or capacities. Radical hope reflects this perspective with Lear (2006) telling the story given to Plenty Coups as a young man when the spirits tell him "We can give you nothing. You already possess everything necessary to become great." Plenty Coups responds by saying "I saw and understood that whatever I accomplish must be by my own effort, that I must myself do the things I wished to do" (p. 125).

Becoming involved with the YRC gave me hope when I didn't have any. Over the long term I came to believe in my own *power* and abilities (superpowers!). This led me to find myself and *keep* myself. Through my work with the YRC, I decided I want to be an art therapist. I am currently working on a Bachelor of Human Ecology, something I feel I wouldn't have done if I hadn't been involved with YRC.

The staff relations are collective because we are drawing from similar experiences giving us common goals and beliefs about structure. We reject hierarchal organization because we believe that it is unjust and doesn't serve the needs of the street youth community (or our own). We are always striving (and encouraging one another) to become our own "authorities" on various subjects because we believe that each human has their own superpowers that can be most effectively contributed to our communities. The organizational structure of the YRC is built upon inclusion; we believe in ability, not disability; in celebrating differences, not abnormalizing them.

We recognize the importance of being flexible as it relates to resiliency. We strive to build the organization to be flexible enough to meet changing needs, and we nurture flexibility in ourselves in our responses to the world.

Because YRC mainly works outside the system and its hierarchical power structures, I feel that Stasha and I (and anyone else involved with YRC) will actually be able to help youth. Yesterday YRC bought some prescriptions for a girl who didn't have any money and would have to wait until Tuesday to get another agency to fill them for her. If we worked for a larger youth-serving agency, we would never have been able to support her in this way—right when she needed it. Things like this give me hope in my ability to *really* support and empower (not save or control) youth.

4. Courage paradigmatically involves the risk of serious loss and of enduring certain pains.

We take risks without knowing specifically what we are taking a risk *for*. That is to say: "the commitment is only to the bare possibility that, from this disaster, something good will emerge…Why or how this will be is left open" (Lear, 2006, p.97).

The most common risks we take are the risks of trusting each other, of being vulnerable, honest, and open with each other. Safety, love, and security are viewed as risks by us for many reasons. First, we are not used to that context, and some of our coping mechanisms don't make sense and actually hurt us. This new context requires a period of adaptation and processing of unknowns. Second, it is a risk because if we have love and security, then we have something to lose. This is a process of fear, where we don't want to have something because it might be taken away, and this would crush our hope and ability to try again. Third, love means then you are accountable for your actions because the community is watching. A lot of us have experienced periods of very lonely time where we couldn't think of anyone who cared whether we lived or died, let alone someone who cared about the morality of our actions. Becoming used to being held accountable and belonging to a community requires a fear-filled period of adjustment as well.

We recognize as a community that we have to take these risks in order to pursue the dream. That is why you have to earn integrity with the street youth community, through your actions, by following through on what you say you will do. We try to share the risk as a community and create safe places to experience love and security together.

It was hard for me to see the results of our efforts. The evidence is things that didn't happen and people that didn't die. You can't tell if the youth would have been the same or better without having formed a relationship with you. We are trying to help the youth believe in themselves and have hope; this is why it is so hard when we can't feel hope ourselves. One great success that gave me hope was when one of the youth let us have a community kitchen birthday party for her. The hardest thing for them to do is accept love. Nothing scares us more than being safe. Because when you are safe your entire trauma flies up to meet you. Because if someone loves you, you are vulnerable, and they can hurt you more. I have known this girl since she was fourteen; I know how hard she has fought through years of every adult abusing her and being in care and never having stable housing and living in violent environments and being exploited and hurt. The fact that she let us love her made me well up with hope. It only took seven years of building trust and being consistent in her life! When I think about giving up, I think of how much she needs

the goat farm and how long the goals we are trying to accomplish take to achieve.

The worst mistakes I have made have been about trust. These are the mistakes you cannot take back. As I said the most important thing you have in the street youth community is your reputation, which is why the most insulting thing you can do is to insult someone's integrity. I knew that I had to take a break from youth work because of this mistake. After the DI I had lost my trust in myself and other people. My co-worker at another agency I worked for had given a youth a backpack before he had done the chore that he was doing to earn the backpack. I made some comment very publicly about how she shouldn't have given him the backpack before he did the chore. I basically called him un-trust worthy in front of his community. It actually pains me to write about this incident because I couldn't fix the relationship with this youth, and there was *no reason* for me to disrespect him in this way.

Experience as inclusion or exclusion. When we were starting YRC and building trust with the youth, we began with me telling my story about doing meth and getting off meth. We did this because it is not fair to ask youth to share their most vulnerable story, if you haven't shared first. There is a trend of funders asking non-profits for stories from clients that represent their most vulnerable moments. It takes courage to share, but it opens up a safe place for other people to discuss their stories. It helps us create inclusion when we start off by sharing.

5. Bold acts that derive merely from optimism are not themselves courageous.

We don't take risks because we assume that everything will work out, we take risks because we believe that taking these risks leads us to the "right way to be." That is we take risks to stand up for our values, for what we believe is right. We emphasize Volition on the Medicine Wheel of Crystal Meth Healing because we believe Volition makes us free to control some things in our own lives. As we state in the Medicine Wheel: **You understand that the risk of**

making choices and taking responsibility for the results is less scary than having no control over what happens to you.

Lear (2006) defines wistful hope as hope that avoids reality, in contrast to radical hope which is about embracing reality and choosing how you will act in response to this reality. Wistful hope is the belief "that the world will be magically transformed into conformity with how one would like it to be—without having to take any realistic practical steps to bring it about" (Lear, 2006, p. 150). We believe in taking action towards achieving our dream because we have radical hope. We believe in empowering people (including ourselves) to make choices in their own lives, rather than taking no action and "hoping for the best." We believe that doing nothing is also a choice.

My hope involves action and changing actions. I don't have so much faith in things working out; I have the most trouble when we have done all the action and now have to *wait*. It makes me feel helpless, whether we are waiting on a funding proposal or to wait through the night when a youth is feeling suicidal.

YRC helped me to begin thinking of the long term benefits over short term pain (usually poverty). It helps me learn to wait and have faith that I have done all I can.

When I am talking to my friends about taking chances, I ask them if they know how to be poor. If you know how to be poor, you can do anything. YRC helped me realize that other people have dependents or can't be poor, so I can't expect them to take the same chances that I do. Knowing how to be poor and being willing to be poor has allowed me to be ethical. It means I can quit jobs when I don't feel the agency is behaving ethically.

I told my co-worker because it's not my place to decide what information she can handle, and it helps to share the burden of this info and then move to action mode. Ok, that sucks; now what should we do? How can we adapt? I think that is the main reason YRC gives me hope. The cycle of reflection and action helps me feel better because I know we are learning and going forward and

adapting. It turns negative experiences into positive learning, which is the basis of our programs and our staff.

We discuss the idea of "freeman's prison" frequently in our work and our lives. The term "freeman's prison" is used by the street youth community to describe an adult homeless shelter in Calgary. The bigger concept that it is used to describe are situations where you feel trapped, but you are the only one with the key to let yourself out; situations where you have to decide to choose the exit door, and you have to have the courage to take the risks associated with this exit. Examples of this include recovery from drug addiction and leaving the streets. It is freeman's prison when you have the opportunity to get out but you are held back by your fear of the unknown or your fear of the healing process. Safety, love and security are the unknown goods that we work towards.

With issues like drug addiction and living on the street, we always are careful not to blame individuals for forces beyond their control, but rather to search for opportunities where people can make a choice. People or agencies can shower you with opportunities to get out, but if you don't have the radical hope to believe in your own ability to navigate the unknown you will not have the courage to take these opportunities. It is important to note that we understand how oppressive forces such as marginalization and abuse wear away at our radical hope and our belief in our own superpowers. We try to heal this through our peer modeling and our creation of safe places where people can feel that they belong. Our community works to showcase and reward people's superpowers and courage in order to help people identify and believe in their own superpowers and courage.

I believe it encapsulates what YRC is about. We believe in bringing a safe and supportive environment with us wherever we go.

Although oftentimes we were sharing food it was usually the contact that people valued.

I think that providing an outlet for people to use their voices is very powerful and necessary in healing. Our projects have

always been designed with this in mind. We always try to make it clear that we are interested in people's voices and healing, not in using their voices to push our own agenda—I think that this makes us trustworthy and encourages sharing.

YRC's visibility and credibility in the community is largely due to consistency in all of these areas. (18-30)

** Direct experience provides the foundation for human learning.

** Knowledge-making is a democratic collective relationship of equals.

** Disciplined, thoughtful hope.

Lessons Learned
Exhibit 7.6

Your Reflections...

....

....

....

....

....

Although conditions on the streets of Calgary are different than Athens twenty-five hundred years ago, the wisdom of the great Athenian philosopher has practical application to our on-going search for social justice and understanding.

Can we identify courageous acts in our routine individual and collective social justice work? Does it take courage to practice liberatory education? What might this courage look like? Answers lie in our stories, in the richness of our knowledge and experience, and in our willingness to risk the consequences of acting upon our knowing. We know more than we have been taught to think we know. Change is the one certainty we face. Canadian political scientist Thomas Homer-Dixon (2006) advises us

> ...to adopt an attitude toward the world, ourselves within it, and our future that's grounded in the knowledge that constant change and surprise are now inevitable. The new attitude—which involves having a *prospective mind*—aggressively engages with this new world of uncertainty and risk. A prospective mind recognizes how little we understand, and how we control even less. (p. 29)

Basing my view on the richness housed within this guide, I would argue that our liberatory education tradition recognizes how much we actually understand when we listen deeply to one another. As we come to appreciate our understanding through our collective resiliency, we have no need to control, but rather we have a need to share our strength.

I have one additional offering to this collective learning journey. I have resisted organising the PAR circles into a model; all models are inherently faulty. Nevertheless, the urge to see them all on one page found me casting about for a helpful guide. I am borrowing one from a development team working in Indonesia (Zainuddin & Sweeting, 1989). In addition to the usual cycle of planning, analysing and evaluating, the Indonesian model brought Islam and its values into the process of rural development (See Fig. 1).

Figure 1. *Indonesian PAR Model (Zainuddin & Sweeting, 1989).*

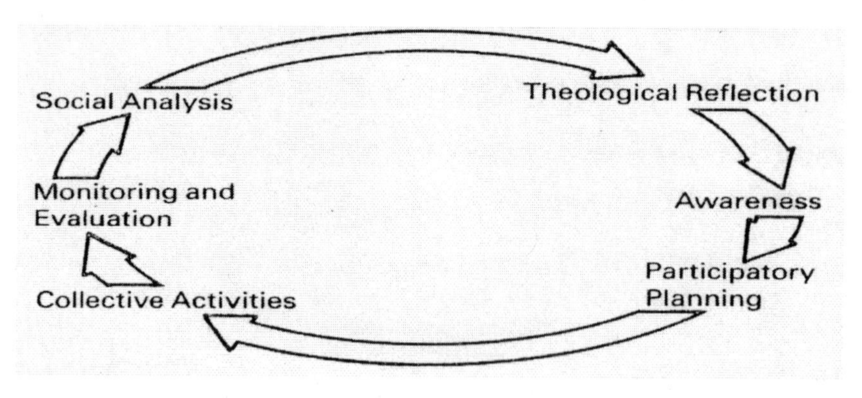

This clear introduction of spirituality into a development model is in keeping with my growing understanding of PAR as a transcendental phenomenon. With that model in mind, the twelve circles could place themselves as follows (See Fig. 2). A model begins to emerge. If we view the Indonesian model as a spiral rather than a circle—and its open design suggests an additional dimension—the organic and evolving nature of PAR is preserved. At some point, perhaps where "Theological Reflection" and "Awareness" occur, the circle becomes a spiral in the sense that what has come around from the start of the process has been transcended. For design purposes, the flow of learning moves into a higher level of understanding with the possibility of new knowledge emerging. The PAR lessons, especially those relating to hopefully seeking coherence while our spiritual selves are resonating as we come to understand our personal and collective selves, may arrange themselves at a similar point. Each reader of *Breaking Free* is free to place the circles into your own reality—to use your own magnet to arrange the particles—your own hand.

Figure 2. *The Circles of PAR.*

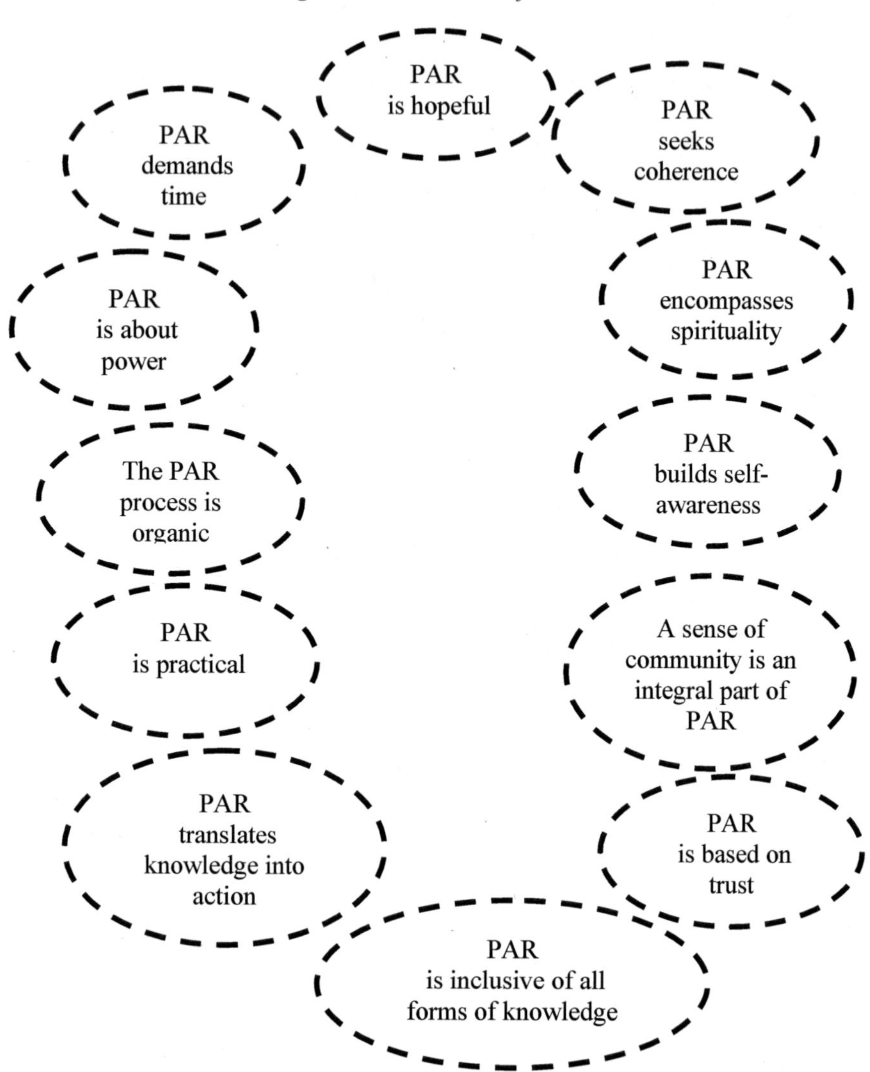

What actually happens during theological reflection where we might imagine concentrating on bringing everything together into a holistic view in a manner similar to Leroy Littlebear's vision of spirituality? Is new knowledge—foam in the Ganma sense—created? Yet, I am puzzled whether new knowledge could/should, always/sometimes appear during/after people share their learnings. If I detect no foam, is the occasion something other than PAR?

Could my "detection mechanism" be faulty? On the other hand, does knowledge have to be created new or rather simply reconfigured? Bateson (1994) is helpful here:

> Discovering the connections and regularities within knowledge you already have is another kind of homecoming, a recognition that feels like a glorious game or a profound validation...If teachers were to approach their classes with an appreciation of how much their pupils already knew, helping to bring the structure of that informal knowledge into consciousness, students would have the feeling of being on familiar ground, already knowing much about how to know, how knowledge is organized and integrated. This might be one way for schooling to assume the flavour of learning as homecoming: learning to learn, knowing what you know, cognition recognized, knowledge acknowledged. (pp. 205-6)

Validating the knowledge all learners have is, put simply, just good adult education. It may be that knowledge acknowledged more accurately reflects the relationship between knowledge and PAR, especially in the sense of respecting people's knowledge. Coming to recognize our own knowledge while valuing the knowledge of others in mutually respectful dialogue, coming to share openly while openly sharing others: this is PAR. This is what the Youth Recovery Coalition discovered. One form of knowledge is shared with other forms, enriching rather than displacing. In this spirit, Bateson writes,

> If we can find ways of responding as individuals to multiple patterns of meaning, enriching rather than displacing those traditional to any one group, this can make a momentous difference to the well-being of individuals and the fate of the earth. What would it be like to have not only colour vision but culture vision, the ability to see the multiple worlds of others? (p. 53)

PAR is accepting of the multiple worlds of others and is inclusive of all forms of knowledge.

Breaking Free is not merely a book, not merely a story, not merely an idea; it is a practical act. PAR helps us focus on the immediate, reachable, and desirable things we can do to transform and transcend the human condition bound by manic capitalism and injustice. All of us can find ways of acting in our own particular reality. *Breaking Free* is not merely a practical act; is a political act. The stories show that people are not as passive as some theories suggest. Their actions are local, human-scale, and unspectacular. In order for uncertain voices to gain confidence in themselves, they need to hear how like-minded souls are functioning. Silent resistance must be transformed into stories of resistance, and these stories must be presented in accessible and inviting ways. *Breaking Free* is not merely a political act; it is an act of love. PAR is providing a legitimate way to love, to feel close to the wonderful people in the stories, to participate but remain within the safety of a system, to celebrate community in circles of learning.

Learners within the Faculty of Social Work willingly share their wisdom, and we need to attend to them lest we miss the courage being discovered and wielded at the grassroots during these fearful days. I can do no better than share the following words written by BSW learner Tyler MacPherson in 2009 for my Popular Education course.

> As we place much emphasis and identification in people of “higher” status (our social construction of something which does not exist) we begin to gauge our worth accordingly upon standards set by others. We lose identification with ourselves, authenticity and realness evades us in order to create personas for the appeasement of “highers.”
>
> Insecurity and inferiority complexes abound as others become our superiors and we invent our own self-destruction. Insecurity becomes such a powerful force that often leads people to attempt to dominate and fight for the control over others in order to impress and prove ourselves to others. If we had proven our worth to ourselves and truly believed in ourselves (with all genuineness), would there be such importance placed upon proving ourselves to others?

Everyone wants to relate and be loved by others, and often such relations come with a compromise of our true selves. If we perceive of ourselves as perfect authentic people in the process of constant growth and change (always making mistakes), then we may have less concern for what others think of us. We need to learn to love ourselves in order to move forward and love others (in a true sense which does not compromise our authenticity). Love is the key to building and preservation. Love is the key to life progression. Love is missing from a world that sets its priorities on domination, control and destruction. We live in a world which ignores hope and searches instead for a false sense of status in the eyes of others; and as a result, a false sense in our own eyes, as our eyes have become a shadow following the eyes of others and have consequently lost their true vision.

"The Traveller Sets Out Again"

I borrow the title of this last page of *Breaking Free* from the Portuguese poet Jose Saramago, 1998 Nobel Prize laureate for literature. Saramago ends his book *Journey to Portugal* (2000) with these highlighted words following "The Traveller Sets Out Again",

> **But that is not true. The journey is never over. Only travellers come to an end. But even then they can prolong their voyage in their memories, in recollections, in stories...The end of one journey is simply the start of another. You have to see what you missed the first time, see again what you already saw, see in springtime what you saw in summer, in daylight what you saw at night, see the sun shining where you saw the rain falling, see the crops growing, the fruit ripen, the stone which has moved, the shadow that was not there before. You have to go back to the footsteps already taken, to go over them again or add fresh ones alongside them. You have to start the journey anew. Always. The traveller sets out once more. (p. 443)**

THE END

Another traveller, James Carse (1996), ends *Finite and Infinite Games* saying "Infinite players are not serous actors in any stories, but the joyful poets of a story that continues to originate what they cannot finish" (p. 176).

My finite game ends on this page but my infinite game continues. I join Saramago in setting out once more heartened by his brilliant imagery. I invite you the reader to set out again in pursuit of liberatory education and a PAR lifestyle.

THE END

Bibliography and Works Cited

Alary, Jacques (1990) (Ed.). *Community care & participatory research*. Montréal: Nu-Age Editions. Translation by Susan Usher of the book *Solidarités*.

Al-Krenawi, Alean & Graham, John (2009). *Helping professional practice with indigenous peoples*. Lanham, Maryland: University Press of America.

Barrie, Doreen (2006). *The other Alberta: Decoding a political enigma*. Regina: Canadian Plains Research Centre.

Bastien, Betty (2004). *Blackfoot ways of knowing*. Calgary: University of Calgary Press.

Bateson, Mary (1994). *Peripheral visions*. New York: HarperCollins.

Bateson, Mary (2000). *Full circles, overlapping lives*. New York: Random House.

Beatty, Ramona, Bedford, Judy, Both, Peter, Eld, Jennifer, Goitom, Mary, Heinrichs, Lilli, Moran-Bonilla, Laura, Massoud, Mona, Ngo, Hieu Van, Pyrch, Timothy, Rogerson, Marianne, Sitter, Kathleen, Speaker, Casey Eagle & Unrau, Mike (2008). Recording action research in a classroom: Singing with chickadees. *Educational Action Research*, 16(3), 335-44.

Belich, James (2009). *Replenishing the earth: The settler revolution and the rise of the Anglo-World, 1783-1939*. Oxford: Oxford University Press.

Bookchin, Murray (1989). *Remaking society*. Montreal: Black Rose.

Bratton, John, Mills, Jean, Pyrch, Timothy & Sawchuk, Peter (2003). *Workplace learning: A critical introduction*. Toronto: Garamond.

Brookfield, Stephen & Holst, John (2011). *Radicalizing learning: Adult education for a just world.* San Francisco: Jossey-Bass.

Brown, Robert (2005). *Re-connecting social justice and social work practice: A testimonio.* (Master's thesis, University of Calgary, Canada).

Carr, E.H. (1961). *What is history?* London: Penguin.

Carroll, James (2011). *Jerusalem, Jerusalem: How the ancient city ignited our modern world.* Boston: Houghton Mifflin Harcourt.

Carse, James (1986). *Finite & infinite games: A vision of life as play & possibility*. New York: Ballantine.

Catano, G., Restrepo, G., Bonilla, E., Sandoval, R.P. & Vizcaino, M. (1987). *Ciencia y compromiso - En torno a la obra de Orlando Fals Borda.* Bogotá: Asociación Colombiana de Sociologia

Chambers, David (1984). *Putting nature in order*. Geelong, Australia: Deakin University Press.

Chambers, Robert (1997). *Whose reality* counts? *Putting the first last*. London: Intermediate Technologies.

Coady, Moses (1939). *Masters of their own destiny*. New York: Harper & Bros.

Colorado, Apela (1988). Bridging native and western science. *Convergence*, 21(2, 3), 59-72.

Dossey, Larry (2004). Immortality. *Resurgence*, (224), 28-32.

Dunlap, Louise (2007). *Undoing the silence: Six tools for social change writing*. Oakland: New Village Press.

Elliott, Charles (1999). *Locating the energy for change: An introduction to appreciative inquiry*. Winnipeg: International Institute for Sustainable Development

Elton, G. R. (Ed.) (1962). *The Tudor constitution: Documents and commentary*. Cambridge: Cambridge University Press.

Esteva, Gustavo & Prakash, Madhur (1998). *Grassroots post-modernism*. London: Zed.

Fals Borda, Orlando (1979-86). *Historia doble de la Costa.* Bogotá: Carlos Valencia Editores, 4 volúmenes.
Vol. I : Mompox y Loba, 1979.
Vol. II : El presidente Nieto, 1981.
Vol. III : Resistencia en el San Jorge, 1984.
Vol. IV : Retorno a la tierra, 1986.

Fals Borda, Orlando (1988). *Knowledge and people's power.* New Delhi: Indian Social Institute.

Fals Borda, Orlando (1998). *People's participation: Challenges ahead.* Bogotá: Instituto Colombiano de Investigaciones Cientificas.

Fals Borda, Orlando (2001). Participatory (action) research in social theory: Origins and challenges. In Peter Reason and Hilary Bradbury (Eds.), *Handbook of action research* (pp. 27-37). Thousand Oaks, CA: Sage Publications, Ltd.

Fals Borda, Orlando & Mora-Osejo (2003). Context and Diffusion of Knowledge: A critique of Eurocentrism, *Action Research,* 1/1, 29-37.

Fals Borda, Orlando & Rahman, Anisur (Eds.) (1991). *Action and knowledge: Breaking the monopoly with participatory action-research.* New York: Apex Press.

Finger, Matthias & Acún, Jose Manuel (2001). *Adult education at the crossroads: Learning our way out.* London: Zed.

Fisher, William & Ponniah, Thomas (Eds.) (2003). *Another world is possible.* London: Zed.

Galbraith, John (1954). *The Great Crash: 1929.* New York: Mariner Books.

Foley, Griff (2001). *Strategic learning.* Sydney: Centre for Popular Education.

Fordham, Paul (1984). Universities and non-formal education: What kind of contribution? In Robert Höghielm (Ed.), *Rekindling Commitment in Adult Education* (pp.19-29). Stockholm: Stockholm Institute of Education.

Freire, Paulo (1970). *Pedagogy of the oppressed.* New York: Seabury Press.

Freire, Paulo (1994). *Pedagogy of hope*. New York: Continuum.

Gherardi, Silvia (2003). Knowing as desiring. Mythic knowledge and the knowledge journey in communities of practitioners. *Journal of Workplace Learning, 15*(7/8), 352 - 358.

Gould, Stephen Jay (2003). *The hedgehog, the fox, and the magister's pox*. New York: Harmony Books.

Greider, William (1997). *One world, ready or not: The manic logic of global capitalism.* New York: Simon & Schuster.

Griffin, Virginia (2001). Holistic learning/teaching in adult education: Would you play a one-string guitar? In T. Barer-Stein & M. Kompf (Eds.), *The Craft of Teaching Adults. Third Edition.* Toronto: Irwin Publishing, Ltd.

Hall, Budd (1981). Participatory research, popular knowledge and power: A personal reflection. *Convergence*, *14*(3), 6-19.

Hart, Joseph (1927). *Adult Education.* New York: Thomas Crowell.

Heron, John (1992). *Feeling and Personhood.* London: Sage Publications, Ltd.

Heron, John (1998). *Sacred science: Person-centred inquiry into the spiritual and the subtle*. Ross-on-Wye, England: PCCS Books.

Hill, Christopher (1972). *The world turned upside down.* London: Penguin Books.

Hobsbawm, Eric (1985). History from below – Some reflections. In Frederick Krantz (Ed.), *History from Below: Studies in Popular Protest and Popular Ideology in Honour of George Rudé* (pp. 63-73). Montréal: Concordia University.

Homer-Dixon, Thomas (2006). *The upside of down: Catastrophe, creativity, and the renewal of civilization.* Toronto: Knopf.

Hope, Anne. & Timmel, Sally (1984). *Training for transformation: A handbook for community workers*: Books 1-3. Gweru, Zimbabwe: Mambo Press.

Hudson, J. W. (1851). *The history of adult education.* London: Longman, Hurst, Rees, Orme, Brown & Green.

Huntingford, Stasha (2009). *Radical hope in Youth Recovery Coalition.* (Master's thesis, University of Calgary, Canada).

Illich, Ivan (1970). *Deschooling society.* New York: Harper & Row.

Kawalilak, Colleen (2006). Reclaiming space and dialogue in adult education, *International Electronic Journal for Leadership and Learning*, 10.

Kilpatrick, William (1929). Statement, *World Conference on Adult Education, Cambridge, 1929.* London: World Association for Adult Education (1930).

Klein, Naomi (2007). *The shock doctrine: The rise of disaster capitalism.* Toronto: Knopf Canada.

Kumar, Satish S. (2008). Dance of diversity, *Resurgence,* (250), 2.

Kvale, Steinan (1995). Themes of postmodernity. In W. Anderson (Ed.), *The Truth about the Truth* (pp.18-25). New York: Tarcher Putnam.

Lear, Jonathan (2006). *Radical hope: Ethics in the face of cultural devastation.* Cambridge: Harvard University Press.

Lindeman, Eduard (1926). *The meaning of adult education.* New York: New Republic.

Livingstone, David (1999). *The education-jobs gap.* Toronto: Garamond.

MacIntyre, Alasdair (1984). *After virtue.* Notre Dame, Indiana: University of Notre Dame Press.

Canadian Association for Adult Education (1943). Food for thought. *Manifesto of the Canadian Association for Adult Education,* 3. Toronto: Author.

Marika, Raymattja, Ngurruwutthun, Dagawa D. & White, Leon (1992). Always together, Yaka Gäna: Participatory research at Yirrkala. *Convergence,* 25(1), 23-29.

Marino, dian (1997). *Wild garden.* Toronto: Between the Lines.

Martin, Ian (2009). Whither adult education in the learning paradigm: Some personal reflections. *Rhizome*, 3. Retrieved from http://www.rizoma-freireano.org

Max-Neef, Manfred (1991). *Human scale development*. New York: Apex.

Max-Neef, Manfred (1998). Economy, humanism and neoliberalism. In Orlando Fals Borda (Compiled), *People's Participation: Challenges Ahead* (pp. 63-79). Bogotá: Instituto Colombiano de Investigciones Científicas.

Mayo, Peter (2004). *Liberating praxis: Paulo Freire's legacy for radical education and politics*. Rotterdam: Sense Publishers.

Monbiot, George (2003). Why we conform. *Resurgence*, (221), 16-17.

Nazemroaya, Mahdi (2011, February 5). Revolution: Is 1848 repeating itself in the Arab world? *Global Research E-Newsletter.* Retrieved from http://www.globalresearch.ca/index.php?context=va&aid=23096. Accessed on 24 November 2011.

Newman, Michael (1999). *Maeler's regard.* Sydney: Stewart Victor.

North America Alliance for Popular and Adult Education (1994). *Resistance and Transformation.* Toronto: NAAPAE.

Notes from Nowhere (Ed.) (2003). *We are everywhere: The irresistible rise of global anti-capitalism.* London: Verso.

Obama, Barack (2006). *The audacity of hope*. New York: Crown.

Pagels, Elaine (1979). *The gnostic gospels*. New York: Vintage Books.

Palmer, Parker (1993). *To know as we are known.* San Francisco: Harper.

Park, Peter, Brydon-Miller, Mary, Hall, Budd & Jackson, Ted (1993). *Voices of change: Participatory research in the United States and Canada*. Toronto: OISE Press.

Plumptre, Adelaide (1937). Never Too Old To Learn, *Adult Learning*, 1.

Pyrch, Timothy (1983). *An examination of the concept of community development as discerned through selected literature in the adult education movement in Canada and the United States, 1919-1960*. Vancouver: University of British Columbia.

Pyrch, Timothy (1996). The PAR challenge re-issued in Colombia. *Convergence, 29*(3), 5-15.

Pyrch, Timothy (2002, May). In B. Hall (Conference Chair). *Responding to '911:' Coolie Verner's call to action in the 1950s.* Paper presented at the 21st Annual Conference, Canadian Association for the Study of Adult Education, University of Toronto. Retrieved from http://www.casae-aceea.ca/sites/casae/archives/cnf2002/2002_Papers/pyrch2002w.pdf. Accessed on 24 November 2011.

Pyrch, Timothy (2007). Participatory action research and the culture of fear: Resistance, community, hope and courage. *Action Research, 5*(2), 199-216.

Pyrch, Timothy, Morris, Paul, & Rusted, Brian (Producers) (1990). *Investigating reality in order to change it* [VHS]. Translated into Spanish.

Pyrch, Timothy & Castillo, Mariá. (2001). The sights and sounds of indigenous knowledge. In Peter Reason & Hilary Bradbury (Eds.), *Handbook of Action Research: Participative Inquiry and Practice* (pp. 79-85). London: Sage Publishing, Ltd.

Rahnema, Majid (1990). Participatory action research: The "last temptation of saint" development. *Alternative: Global, Local, Political, 15*(2), 199-226.

Rawnsley, Andrew (2008, November 1). Barack Obama's impressive road to the White House. *The Observer*, Retrieved from www.guardian.co.uk/commentisfree/2008/nov/02/us-elections-2008-barack-obama. Accessed on 24 November 2011.

Rifkin, Jeremy (2009). *The empathic civilization.* New York: Tarcher/Penguin.

Rusted, Brian (1992). *Knowledge from the north* [VHS].

Sandel, Michael (2009). *Justice: What's the right thing to do?* New York: Farrar, Straus & Giroux.

Saramago, Jose (2000). *Journey to Portugal.* New York: Harcourt. Translated from Portuguese and with notes by Amanda Hopkinson & Nick Caistor. Published in Portuguese in 1990.

Saul, John Ralston (2008). *A fair country: Telling truths about Canada.* Toronto: Penguin.

Scharmer, Otto (2007). *Theory U: Leading from the future as it emerges.* Cambridge: Berret-Koehler Publishers.

Schumacher. E. F. (1997). *A guide for the perplexed.* New York: Harper & Row.

Scott, James (1998). *Seeing like a state.* New Haven: Yale University Press.

Scott, James (1990). *Domination and the arts of resistance.* New Haven: Yale University Press.

Seeley, Chris & Reason, Peter (2008). Expressions of energy: An epistemology of presentational knowing. In Pranee Liamputtong & Jean Rumbold (Eds.), *Knowing Differently: Arts-based and Collaborative Research Methods* (pp. 25-46). New York: Nova Science Publishers, Inc.

Sennett, Richard (1998). *The corrosion of character.* New York: Norton.

Shields, Katrina (1991). *In the tiger's mouth: An empowerment guide for social action.* Newtown, Australia: Millennium.

Shiva, Vandana (2002). Paradigm shift: Earth democracy. *Resurgence*, (214), 30-32.

Skolimowski, Hedryk (1994). *The participatory mind.* London: Penguin.

Smith, Susan, Willms, Dennis & Johnson, Nancy (Eds.). (1997). *Nurtured by knowledge: Learning to do participatory action research.* Ottawa: IDRC Books.

Soron, Dennis & Laxer, Gordon (2006). *Not for sale: decommodifying public life*, 15-37. Peterborough, Ontario: Broadview.

Spretnak, Charlene C. (2000). Sacred cosmos. *Resurgence*, (201), 34-5.

Spring, Joel (1975). *A primer of libertarian education.* Montreal: Black Rose.

Steele, Tom (2007). *Knowledge is power.* Bern, Switzerland: Peter Lang.

Terkel, Studs (1972). *Working.* New York: Avon Books.

Terkel, Studs (2003). *Hope dies last: Keeping the faith in troubled times.* New York: The New Press.

Thompson, Jane (2007). *More words in edgeways: Rediscovering adult education.* Leicester, England: National Institute of Adult Continuing Education.

Tisdell, Elizabeth (1993). Feminism and adult learning: Power, pedagogy and praxis. In Sharon Merriam (Ed.), *An Update on Adult Learning Theory* (pp. 91-103). San Francisco: Jossey-Bass.

Toulmin, Stephen (1995). Forward. In Robert Goodman & Walter Fisher (Eds.), *Rethinking Knowledge: Reflections across the disciplines* (pp. ix-xv). Albany, SUNY.

Toulmin, Stephen (1996). Introduction. In Stephen Toulmin & Bjorn Gustavsen (Eds.), *Beyond Theory: Changing Organizations Through Participation* (pp. 1-4). Amsterdam: John Benjamins.

Unrau, Michael (2008). *Physical actions in the performing Arts: A physical and social inquiry into awareness.* (Master's thesis, University of Calgary, Canada.)

Von Kotze, Astrid (2002). Producing knowledge for living, *Studies in Continuing Education*, 24(2), 233-46.

Waldegrave, Charles (2003). Just therapy. In Charles Waldegrave, Kiwi Tamasese, Flora Tukaka & Wanhi. Cambell (Eds.), *Just*

Therapy – A Journey (pp. 3-61). Adelaide, Australia: Dulwich Centre Publications.

Walsh, Christine, Rutherford, Gayle & Sears, Alexandra (2010). Fostering inclusivity through teaching and learning action research. *Action Research, 8*(2), 191-209.

Watson, Helen & Chambers, David (1989). *Singing the land, signing the land.* Geelong, Australia: Deakin University Press.

Watson-Verran, Helen (1992). *Garma maths.* Yirrkala, Australia: Yirrkala Literature Production Centre.

Welton, Michael (1987). *Knowledge for the people* (pp. 1-19). Toronto: University of Toronto Press.

Welton, Michael (1987a). "On the eve of a great mass movement:" Reflections on the origins of the CAAE. In Frank Cassidy &Ron Faris (Eds.), *Choosing Our Future: Adult Education and Public Policy in Canada* (pp. 12-35). Toronto: OISE Press.

White, Leon (1991). *Aboriginal secondary education: From Yolngu aspiration to thwarted realisation.* (Master's thesis, Deakin University, Australia).

Whyte, William Foote (1991) (Ed.). *Participatory action research.* Newbury Park: Sage Publications, Ltd.

Willis, Peter (2008). The work of portrayal: Expressive approaches to educational research. In Pranee Liamputtong & Jean Rumbold (Eds.), *Knowing Differently: Arts-based and Collaborative Research Methods* New York: Nova Science Publishers, Inc.

Woodcock, George (1992). *The monk and his message: Undermining the myth of history.* Vancouver: Douglas & McIntyre.

Zapf, Kim (1997). Voice and social work education: Learning to teach from my own story. *Canadian Social Work Review, 14*(1), 83-97.

Zapf, Kim (1997a). Profound connections between person and place: Exploring location, spirituality, and social work. In

John Coates, John Graham & Barbara Swartzentruber (Eds.) with Brian Ouellette (Contributor), *Spirituality and Social Work* (pp. 229-42). Toronto: Canadian Scholars' Press.

Zapf, Kim (2009). Rural regions. In A. Gitterman & R. Salmon (Eds.), Encyclopedia of Social Work with Groups (pp. 272-275). New York: Routledge.

Zapf, Kim, Jerome, Les, & Williams, Margaret (2011). Team teaching in social work: Sharing power with bachelor of social work students. *Journal of Teaching in Social Work, 31*(1), 38-52.

* 8 1 4 9 2 8 5 *